*Becoming St. Louis*

# Becoming St. Louis

## *Family, Faith, and the Politics of Citizenship, 1820–1920*

SHARON HARTMAN STROM

UNIVERSITY OF ILLINOIS PRESS
Urbana, Chicago, and Springfield

1 2 3 4 5 C P 5 4 3 2 1
∞ This book is printed on acid-free paper.

This book will be made open access within three years of publication thanks to Path to Open, a program developed in partnership between JSTOR, the American Council of Learned Societies (ACLS), University of Michigan Press, and The University of North Carolina Press to bring about equitable access and impact for the entire scholarly community, including authors, researchers, libraries, and university presses around the world. Learn more at https://about.jstor.org/path-to-open/

Cataloging data available from the Library of Congress

ISBN 978-0-252-04674-2 (hardcover)
ISBN 978-0-252-08884-1 (paperback)
ISBN 978-0-252-04827-2 (ebook)

*For my colleagues in the Providence Women's History Collective Barbara, Gail, Judy, Kate, Mari Jo, Sue, Sonya, and Tina*

*and in memory of Susan Porter Benson (1943–2005)*

*and Natalie Boymel Kampen (1944–2012)*

# Contents

# Acknowledgments

Generous archivists have assisted me with their time and helpful suggestions: Molly Kodner and Lauren Sallwasser at the Missouri Historical Society, Zachary Palitzsch at the University of Missouri at St. Louis, Trent Sindelar at the St. Louis Public Library, and Sonja Rooney at the Washington University at St. Louis. My editor, Alison Syring, who saw promise in an early proposal, has nurtured this manuscript with kindness and insightful reading. The Huntington Library in San Marino, California, has provided me with a steady and fruitful research environment over more than twenty years. Patient readers guided this project from the beginning. I thank Daniel Horowitz, Malcolm Rohrbaugh, Carol Rigolot, Sherry L. Smith, Michael Edelstein, and Randall Miller. Frederick Stirton Weaver saw this project through many iterations. Our travel together to ferret out the resources we need for both of our scholarly endeavors has sustained us for decades with intellectual stimulation and playful excursions too numerous to detail.

# Introduction

## *Family, Faith, and the Politics of Citizenship in St. Louis, 1820–1920*

By 1861, with civil war on the horizon, Missourians Minerva Grimsley Blow and Elizabeth Hobbs Keckley were living different lives and facing different futures based on the color of their skin. Former slave Elizabeth Keckley used payments from her dressmaking skills to purchase the freedom of herself and her only child George in St. Louis in 1855. She left Missouri for Washington, DC, where she took jobs as a seamstress to wives of prominent politicians Stephen A. Douglas, Abraham Lincoln, and Jefferson Davis. Varina Davis implored her to go south with her family, as the Davises headed for the new headquarters of the Confederate States of America. But Keckley, who was about to lose her son at the Battle of Wilson Creek in Missouri, "preferred to cast my lot among the people of the North."[1]

Minerva Blow, whose husband, Henry Taylor Blow, was a Missouri representative in the US Congress, lived in Carondelet, a fashionable suburban neighborhood on high bluffs overlooking the Mississippi River. Minerva also did a lot of sewing, but she did so as a proper wife whose family did not require her paid labor. As the crisis of the Union deepened, her husband insisted on flying the flag of the United States of America from the rooftop of their house. With her husband away in DC, Minerva was left to negotiate the family's standing in the community, reporting to her daughter Susan Blow, "Friends are divided in every sentiment, and . . . relations are estranged."[2]

The domestic ideal Minerva Blow lived in her happy marriage in white St. Louis was unavailable to most African American families, whether free or enslaved, before and after Emancipation. As historians of the lives of Black women underscore, the "working wife" was more the norm than the exception in their communities at midcentury. Elizabeth Keckley faced terrible conditions as an enslaved woman in Virginia, and hard work was a constant in her life. Her white master was her biological father, and George Hobbs, the man she considered to be her "real" father, was sold to Tennessee, her mother was threatened with backbreaking domestic labor, and Elizabeth was sent to a slave-breaker to make her obedient. Dispatched to another relative in North Carolina, she was raped and became a mother. After winning her high-priced freedom, Elizabeth married, but when her husband "insist[ed] on dissipation," she "informed him . . . that we must separate."[3] On her own for the rest of her life, Elizabeth Keckley would write a memoir in 1868 describing "my life as a slave" and "four years in the White House," one of the first histories of slavery and the Civil War published in the United States. Her remarkable independence and self-respect would be reproduced over several generations of Black women in St. Louis, culminating in the life of Julia Davis, a beloved teacher at Simmons School in the Black community known as the 'Ville, formerly the village of Elleardsville. Davis made it her life mission to document and promote Black history.

Minerva lived most of her life in St. Louis, focused on the moral and physical nurturing of six children. She used her considerable writing talents in letters to her husband and children, testifying to the leisure time and privacy she had for using her pen. That time and privacy were made possible for many white women by servants and Black peoples' labor, the kind that Elizabeth, her mother, and her father provided in slavery and in freedom. African American and white families—their different constructions, their different gender roles but their mutual importance in the character building and training in citizenship of the next generation—make up the first layer of the narrative of *Becoming St. Louis: Family, Faith, and the Politics of Citizenship, 1820–1920.*

A second layer takes up the Protestant churches and the civic organizations these two women and the men in their lives helped to create. Protestant faiths changed the character of St. Louis at mid-nineteenth century. I argue that Protestantism in St. Louis, initially dominated by white migrants from the northeast and the upper south but seized upon almost immediately by free Blacks and enslaved people of color in churches of their own, was not only the engine that challenged Catholic control of St. Louis but one that sparked a vigorous antislavery movement nurturing hopes for emancipation.

The evolution of the politics of citizenship in Missouri, in constant contention in St. Louis and often commented on by federal courts and national figures in Washington, DC, is the third layer of this narrative. The family of hired-out slaves Harriet Robinson Scott and Elthelread (Dred) Scott is the most famous example of how the ongoing trade of the enslaved and the kidnapping of the free created anxiety and fear in the Black community and how that anxiety resulted in the most infamous US Supreme Court decision of the nineteenth century, a case that necessitated defining citizenship in the United States. The Scotts petitioned for their freedom in St. Louis in 1847, partly because they feared their daughters might be kidnapped and sold downriver. They argued that having lived in the US Northwest Territories, where there was no slavery, and then being brought to slave-holding Missouri, they were being held as slaves illegally.

The Scotts' legal challenges were sent to the federal level by the Missouri state courts and adjudicated by a split US Supreme Court in 1857. The Dred Scott decision set the tone for most future discussions of Black citizenship in St. Louis and much of the nation. In the most extreme assent to the decision, Chief Justice Roger B. Taney argued that persons of African descent could not be considered citizens of the United States. Once the American Civil War began, this extreme point of view would become untenable politically, even as a vociferous minority, often headed by the Francis Preston Blair family of Silver Spring, Maryland, would continue to use it as a rhetorical weapon.

The city of St. Louis in the nineteenth century was a central piece of the American landscape claiming to be the "gateway to the West." French male trappers and explorers established the first trading posts on the Missouri and the Mississippi, followed by Yankee traders who built the first commercial establishments that imported goods from the East and brought their families with them as well. Situated at the confluence of the mighty Missouri, Mississippi, and Illinois Rivers, St. Louis had grandiose plans for its future in the American economy and body politic. St. Louis was a hub for goods shipped in all directions, a last stop on the way to the Western plains and for wagon trains to California and during the Mexican War and Civil War a military staging arena. As David P. Thelen says, "Rivers gave Missourians the choice of ways to live. . . . Those who dreamed of wealth . . . settled near . . . navigable rivers that provided access to large markets."[4] But St. Louis was also on the eastern edge of a thinly populated state made up of small towns and farms and managed by landowners, some of them employing enslaved Black labor. The Yankees used their profits to build factories and retail establishments and to speculate in purchases of real estate that became more valuable over time. With river transportation linking the city to destinations all over the United States, the importance of St. Louis to the nation's economy and its political well-being seemed self-apparent to its entrepreneurial families.

These Northeasterners brought their mostly Protestant churches with them, along with a civic-minded consciousness that paved the way for educational and benevolent institutions in a growing metropolis facing the

Mississippi waterfront. Religious commitment was a driver of their social reform movements, their families sites of character building and commitment to community building and civic growth. African American Protestants and Catholics with similar values were able to make progress, despite the physical, psychological, and economic oppression of slavery. A steadily growing free Black population in St. Louis often spearheaded this progress. As Eric Foner concludes in *Reconstruction*: "The freedmen's political and civil equality proved transitory, but the autonomous black family and a network of religious and social institutions survived Reconstruction. Nor could the seeds of educational progress planted then be entirely uprooted," and "the doors of economic opportunity that had opened could never be completely closed."[5]

Slavery, notions of racial difference, and ideas as to what constituted citizenship were entwined in Missouri's birth as a state in 1821 to, some might say, the present. The Missouri Compromise of 1820 brought free-state Maine into the Union and allowed for the slaveholding statehood of the territory of Missouri, putting off for the time being the grave questions of what to do about the balance of power in the US Senate and what future expansion might portend. The architect of the compromise, Henry Clay of Kentucky, grew the Union but laid the groundwork for another forty years of bitter debate over the spread of slavery into a nation expanding westward.

The Compromise of 1850 welcomed California into the Union as a free state, balancing the admission of Texas in 1845, but at the insistence of Southern lawmakers came along with a draconian Fugitive Slave Law that put urban Black citizens, including in St. Louis, in grave danger. The Kansas-Nebraska Act of 1854, another national compromise imposed on the middle of the expanding country, brought tragic results on Missouri's western state border and highlighted the growing polarization of the nation's views on slavery.

At midcentury St. Louis was a cosmopolitan outlier more akin to Chicago or Cincinnati than the rest of Missouri and the slaveholding South. German and Irish immigrants were pouring into St. Louis and forever changing its French and native-born character—both Black and white—into a more diverse population with competing interests in religion and politics. While German freethinkers throughout Missouri influenced the intellectual and antislavery communities at midcentury and helped to found the Republican Party, the largely urban Irish would use their voting power to influence the politics of the Democratic Party after the Civil War.

The importance of St. Louis and its strategic position meant that securing it as a Union military stronghold was a major priority of the new Lincoln administration in 1861, even as battles around the nation's capital in the

East consumed most of the newspaper headlines. Prominent citizens from Missouri played critical roles in Washington, DC, politics and the Lincoln administration. With its important connections to the federal government and politics in Washington, DC, anchored by Missourians Edward Bates, Montgomery Blair, Frank Blair Jr., Jessie Benton Fremont, William Greenleaf Eliot, and Henry Taylor Blow, St. Louis was a site of far-reaching experiments that changed the nation as a whole: the tightly organized and modern medical practices of the Western Sanitary Commission, the early drafting and arming of Black soldiers, and heated discussions of how to effect what was, by 1863, the inevitable emancipation of the enslaved.

A border state that stayed in the Union during the Civil War, Missouri did not undergo federal Reconstruction but had to devise its own future in the face of the Thirteenth, Fourteenth, and Fifteenth Amendments to the US Constitution that ended slavery, established birthright citizenship, and granted the vote to Black men.[6] White Republicans in St. Louis continued to be more progressive on the question of race than the rest of Missouri, which had largely been on the side of maintaining slavery and in sympathy with the Confederacy, echoed during the Civil War on the western side of the state by bushwhacking gangs and violence against newly freed people of color. The exclusion of alleged pro-Confederate voters in Missouri by a loyalty-test oath ended in 1875. The Northeasterners who, along with leaders from the upper South, had ensured Republican Party dominance from 1865 to 1875 and even considered women's rights, could not maintain their positions of power in state government. Conservative Democrat Party control resumed with a new state constitution two years before the Hayes-Tilden political compromise of 1877 and the end of the federal presence in other parts of the South. As Missouri chronicler Louis Gerteis describes, "the metropolitan ambitions of St. Louis never meshed smoothly with the political culture of Missouri."[7] St. Louis was a cosmopolitan urban center in a mostly rural slaveholding state, so whatever its forward-thinking elites thought did not mirror the state's white population as a whole and met with strong resistance in the Missouri state legislature.

Although Progressive-era coalitions of Blacks and whites sometimes cooperated to fight racial discrimination, by World War I Jim Crow practices were widespread in St. Louis and the state of Missouri, epitomized by the East St. Louis, Illinois, race riot of 1917. At this same moment the city of St. Louis was losing its dominance as the most important city in the center of the United States. Drawing on its vast hinterland to build a modern city infrastructure and to produce and process goods and ship them by rail, Chicago had become the new "gateway to the west." "Then came the railroads," writes geographer and historian William Cronon, in his *Nature's Metropolis*, "and Chicago's sudden rise . . . is a case study in the ways capital can rearrange geography."[8]

What Cronon does not discuss is how the social history of families and the racial divide in nineteenth-century America influenced the outcome of this new metropolis. Walter Johnson's *Broken Heart of America* situates St. Louis not as much as the center of a new economy but as a metaphor for a nation plagued by systematic violence directed at both Native Americans and African Americans, with most of Johnson's focus on the twentieth century. Thelen's *Paths of Resistance* is an admirable attempt to take the narrative beyond the usual political framing, underscoring the engine of industrialization after the Civil War as it bumped up against white Missourians' resistance to change. *Becoming St. Louis* challenges Thelen's assumption that "in the old order, family, work, leisure, friends, community, natural surroundings, and worship had interwoven to form an integrated fabric."[9] The inherent assumption in Thelen's work, as in many others, is that slavery was a manageable piece of the past buried in a consensus to keep things as they were. It omits Black resistance to the established order and the emotional turmoil some whites endured as the result of owning other human beings. There was in fact a continuous struggle to upend—and to defend—slavery, a prelude to the vigorous struggle for freedom that emerged in Missouri once the Civil War began. Diane Mutti Burke's *On Slavery's Border: Missouri's Small-Slaveholding Households, 1815–1865* assumes, as do I, that the city and county of St. Louis should be viewed as a different economic and political entity than the rest of the state.

Teasing out how the Fourteenth and Fifteenth Amendments would be applied in Missouri rested on the vigor of Black civil rights organizations and the sympathies of antislavery whites. But most whites did not really see Black Americans as political and religious equals. The power of racial privilege and economic superiority allowed some to envision incremental progress for African Americans but ended up preserving old institutions dressed up in new clothes. No matter how fervently they believed in preserving the Union, ending slavery, and trying to help their Black neighbors move ahead, assumptions based on racial difference—both explicitly stated and unconsciously assumed—were barriers to Black equality most whites could not overcome. Subordination and segregation were the outcomes of this built-in raison d'être. The decline of St. Louis by the early twentieth century seems to have returned the state of Missouri to its original character as a border state with some of the characteristics of liberal democracy but mostly one with conservative values and an assumption that the whites should hold positions of power.

As the citizens of St. Louis and the state of Missouri entered the twentieth century and contemplated the past, they evaluated the conditions of slavery, the Civil War, and Reconstruction. White narratives of the Civil War and Reconstruction framed Missouri as a state where slavery had been benign and best forgotten to boost what the elites still believed to be the promise of the "gateway city" to the West. Black communities in St. Louis, Jefferson City, and Kansas City, joined by allies in Illinois, Ohio, and Washington, DC, created an alternative narrative, remembering the travesties of slavery, the contribution of Black Union troops to Civil War victory, and the history of their churches and Masonic orders as sites of protest and progress. The rewriting of Black history in St. Louis and in Missouri is an ongoing piece of the civil rights movement that insists on not forgetting and at the same time remembering what the past entailed.

# 1 Slavery and Freedom at the Bend of the Mississippi

Slavery, Catholicism, and a complicated class structure made up the fabric of life in early white settlements near the Missouri and Mississippi Rivers. Spanish and French explorers and traders confiscated the lands and river routes of Indigenous peoples and sometimes took Native American women as mistresses or wives, relationships that often began with sexual assault or enslavement of Indigenous women. Over time these relationships provided familial warmth but also enabled the commercial penetration of Native American tribes. A first import of five hundred enslaved peoples from Santo Domingo in 1720 were commandeered to work in lead mines in "Illinois Country." Trading posts and forts at St. Charles, on the Missouri River just northwest of St. Louis, and St. Louis on the Mississippi grew into cities by the late eighteenth century. The Chouteau brothers Auguste and Pierre later recognized numerous children born of their sexual liaisons with Osage women. By the time Missouri became another slave state in the United States in 1821, the oldest families of St. Louis were a racial mix of European whites, Indigenous peoples, and Africans.[1]

The Osage were the largest tribal group in Illinois Country at the time the Europeans arrived. The Osage moved west in the mid-seventeenth century from the old Northwest and changed their traditional way of life as they acquired horses, allowing for more efficient hunting but undermining the status of women gatherers. Indigenous groups throughout "New France" practiced slavery as they captured enemies in battle. The Osage welcomed chances to trade enslaved persons and furs for guns and other manufactured goods with the French and the Spanish, but whites brought disease and death as well. Smallpox and other infectious diseases, St. Louis founder Auguste

Chouteau believed, killed as much as half of the Osage and Otoe populations. Military offensives decimated resident Mississippi River tribes like the Natchez as armed groups moved upriver from New Orleans. The deaths of so many men who fought white invaders resulted in unbalanced gender ratios in Native American societies.[2]

Preserving Native American cultural identity in Missouri became more difficult over time. The Osage allied with British troops in the French and Indian War of 1754 to 1763, aroused animosity among white settlers, and paid with their lives in battle. In 1808 the Osage agreed to a treaty robbing them of their ancestral lands of about two and a half million acres in Missouri and Arkansas, and most of the tribe was forcibly moved to lands in Kansas and Oklahoma territories. The relentless westward movement of whites, launched in American culture by the travels of Meriwether Lewis and William Clark and the popular stories of Native American killers like Daniel Boone and Davy Crockett, decimated their homes and villages in Missouri and across the southeastern United States. The Indian Removal Act of 1830 set in motion a chain of forced migrations during the second presidential administration of President Andrew Jackson, beginning with the removal of the Missouri Illini and the Osage and culminating in the Trail of Tears, the forced migration to "Indian Territory" of the "Five Civilized Tribes" from the southeastern United States. The Cherokee traveled across southern Missouri between 1836 and 1840, and although it is likely some individuals peeled off into mixed-race communities along the way, in today's St. Louis there is no significant number of persons who identify as Native American. Some individuals identify culturally as Black Indians, an identity that reflects the larger demographic presence of Africans than Native Americans as time went on, and as Indigenous peoples were run off, were decimated, or were absorbed by white and African American communities, some mixed-race individuals retained a sense of "being Indian."[3]

The Spanish governors of the Louisiana Territory ordered an end to the practice of enslaving Indigenous peoples in the late eighteenth century, but enforcing the edict was difficult and spotty, so some governing whites continued to blur the lines between Native American women, who were supposed to be free, and African men, who were largely enslaved, and confused the status of these families' offspring. The cultural memory of tribal ways and identity was probably cultivated by the Native American women who reared their mixed-race children with enslaved Black men. Native American women were still enmeshed in their homelands, while Black men had been forcibly removed from their cultural anchors.[4]

Roman Catholic religious and political guidelines were supposed to prevent treating enslaved peoples with harsh discipline and excessive physical punishment, but recent research shows that Catholics were just as likely to separate enslaved family members and to abuse the enslaved with physical beatings as whites of other faiths. Catholic orders of nuns and Jesuits exchanged enslaved individuals, broke up families, and used enslaved labor to build the Catholic institutions that gave St. Louis a cosmopolitan feeling: St. Louis College, the Sacred Heart Academy, a Sisters of Charity hospital, parochial schools for children, and in time grand cathedrals. Some enslaved families were practicing Catholics and formed kinships based on their religious identity, received the sacraments, and had the sanctity of church marriages.[5]

Marie-Jean Scypion is a vibrant example of the self-worth inspired by these kinships. Marie's Natchez mother, Mariette, was coupled with an African slave in the mid-eighteenth century and through exchanges between white family members ended up in Chouteau households. Marie, who died in 1802, taught her three daughters that because she was free under Spanish edict, they were, by birthright, free as well. Marie's three daughters filed lawsuits for freedom between 1825 and 1830, lawsuits whose outcome would determine not only their fate but also the future of their twelve children and three grandchildren. In 1834 the Missouri Supreme Court ruled that because matriarch Marie was an Indigenous woman, her descendants could not be enslaved.[6] Some migrants from the upper south who arrived in St. Louis in the 1830s and 1840s were blended Black and Indigenous families like the Scypions. The Griffin Brander family descendants knew, because of handed-down family lore, that Griffin's wife, the family matriarch, was the daughter of a Native American in the region of Petersburg, Virginia. Legends of Native American ancestry were a source of pride commonplace in nineteenth-century "Black" families.

The Chouteaus laid out an initial grid of streets in St. Louis in 1764, accumulated great wealth from the fur trade, and welcomed Jesuit priests, Christian brothers, and Catholic orders of nuns to the new city to build churches and schools with Indigenous and enslaved Black labor. French nuns provided much of the administrative, teaching, and nursing labor for Catholic institutions, and by 1852 three thousand children were taught in thirteen Catholic schools. Irish-born Bishop Peter Kendrick made a large donation to the Sisters of Charity Hospital in 1841 with the caveat that it should be "free to all, regardless of creed or color."[7] The hospital would later be a lifeline in medical care during the Civil War.

The Sisters of St. Joseph arrived in 1836 and settled on bluffs overlooking the Mississippi River in rural Carondelet, where they opened the first school for the deaf in Missouri in 1839 and, as Carondelet had no public school, educated the town's girls as well. In 1845 the St. Joseph sisters opened a school for nearly one hundred free Black children in downtown St. Louis, and enslaved children could receive the sacraments after school and on weekends. "We felt at home and were happy," one pupil said, "because the time and attention of the Sisters was all our own, and there was no one to tease us."[8] But this idyll was short-lived. Neighbors who objected to an integrated school took to the streets in protest, and the mayor ordered the school closed. Governing whites of Missouri and St. Louis knew education was a dangerous tool in the hands of the enslaved and free people of color. Education would be a terrain of contestation as more Black people won their freedom, established their own institutions, and saw education as a critical factor in the advancement of their race.

At mid-nineteenth century, despite the constant paranoia and demonization of Black people in St. Louis and the state of Missouri at large, enslaved peoples made up only about 3.5 percent and free Black people less than 2 percent of the St. Louis population, a total proportion of Black persons to whites that never changed very much. These proportions meant that even as the city grew, Black residents would always be at a disadvantage politically because they were vastly outnumbered by both immigrants and the white native-born. While some of the enslaved labored in their masters' households, farms, or mines, others were hired out as domestic servants, coopers, carpenters, and laundresses in St. Louis, with some sent on the thriving steamboats that carried goods and people along the Missouri and the Mississippi and the rivers that connected to them. The free mixed-race Catholic Clamorgans, some of them descended from sons and daughters of the Chouteaus, dominated barbershops and steam baths in St. Louis and on Mississippi steamboats and were the most privileged class of people of color in Missouri.

The power and religious influence of the old French and Catholic families of St. Louis like the Chouteaus, the LeCledes, and the Clamorgans were challenged by the arrival of Protestants from the Northeast and free Black migrants from the upper South as early as the 1820s. While Catholics had a strict hierarchy of clergy governed by male cardinals, bishops, and priests, the Protestants did not believe that parishioners needed the assistance of the clergy to communicate with God, even as they sought dynamic and inspiring preachers. Protestants were inspired by the Second Great Awakening from about 1780 to 1820 to spread the Gospel to new converts and save their souls and believed that lay and self-nominated clergy could serve as messengers of the Almighty. This new element in American religion opened the way in

St. Louis, as elsewhere in the United States, for congregation-led denominations that disapproved of long-accepted practices like theatergoing, gambling, prostitution, and alcohol consumption. The sin of holding others in slavery would be the most contentious of these Protestant dicta, but many Protestant congregants continued to defend the ownership of slaves and slavery as a practice sanctioned by the Bible and traditional institutions.

The Catholic hierarchy in the United States accepted slavery as legitimate social and economic practice. Catholic orders engaged in buying and selling the enslaved, legacies that have emerged as controversies in the recent past at Georgetown University—and at St. Louis University. In their forays into the New World, Spanish and French Catholics sought to convert Indigenous peoples to save their souls and in the process make them a more docile labor force but did not proselytize to others in the way that Protestants did. Catholics sanctioned parish churches that benefitted Black worshippers but also enforced doctrinal practices that did not allow much for parishioner dissent. As more radical Protestants like Frederick Douglass, William Lloyd Garrison, Wendell Phillips, Frances Watkins Harper, and the Grimké sisters Angelina and Sarah emphasized "immediatism, a rejection of gradual emancipation over an unknown period of time, " in the 1830s and 1840s, slavery would be seen by some Protestants as a grievous sin that should be abolished as soon as possible, with no monetary recompense for slaveholders. Congregations could band together to find more radical ministers or to endorse social and political platforms that suited their preferences. Periodic revivals created a sense of community and purpose that could turn religious fervor into political reform.

Even before Missouri statehood, Presbyterian, Methodist, and Baptist missionaries organized revivalist camp meetings and itinerant preaching on horseback to reach remote settlements and Indigenous tribes. The Protestants were popular among African Americans, both free and enslaved. Led by Timothy Flint, Presbyterians arrived in 1816 in St. Charles to convert Indigenous peoples and, like the Methodists, had little luck in doing so. Presbyterians built their first church in St. Louis in 1819 and by 1828 had ten churches on either side of the Missouri River.[9] Two Baptist missionaries opened a Sabbath school for free and enslaved Black people in St. Louis in 1818.[10]

Early St. Louis law mandated that Black people worship under the supervision of whites, a restriction nearly impossible to enforce. Determined to hear their own preachers of color, Black Baptists and Methodists began worshipping separately from white parishioners in congregations they named African Baptist and African Methodist Episcopal (AME), respectively.[11] White Protestant churches had not foreseen that formerly enslaved Black worshippers, such as Jordan Winston Early and Ralph Harrison, would escape the supervision of white ministers and establish their own congregations, inspired by the revivalist fervor and perfectionist tendencies of the Second Great Awakening and its approval of self-ordained preachers. Beneath the cloak of saving souls, Black Protestant churches became the civic and religious engines of the communities of people of color in St. Louis. Priscilla Baltimore, a nurse who purchased her husband's and her own freedom, made her home a meeting place for one of the first of these churches, rowing a minister back and forth from Illinois across the Mississippi to escape arrest.

White Methodists, heirs of their founders, the Wesley brothers in Britain, had resolved in 1780, "Slavery is contradictory to the laws of God, man and nature . . . and contrary to the dictates of conscience and pure religion."[12] In 1822 Methodists in St. Louis welcomed ninety-five white and thirty-two "colored" congregants. Black Methodists began worshipping on their own as early as 1830, although their meeting place was owned by white Methodists who also, technically, governed the African Methodist congregation in the Methodist state and national hierarchy. White Methodists in St. Louis, with many Southern slaveholding migrants to Missouri now worshipping in their churches, revisited their early position on the sinfulness of slavery. In 1844 a discussion of the wrongs of slaveholding Methodists, like Bishop James O. Andrew of Georgia, resulted in a national Plan of Separation, dividing Methodists into Northern churches that condemned slavery and Southern churches that welcomed their slaveholding brethren. All four Missouri delegates to the 1844 national Methodist conference voted against the expulsion of Andrew and for the Southern conference. As a result, one of the main founders of white Methodism in St. Louis, James Jamieson, left Missouri for Illinois.

In 1846 the African Methodist Episcopal (AME) congregation in St. Louis took the bold step of aligning itself with the Northern Methodist conference and argued that its members should continue to use the Green Street church building that had been supported by their attendance and donations. The white Fourth Street Methodists refused to grant this demand, forcing the Black congregation to move to an inferior building on Gully Street. The AME filed a lawsuit to regain its property at the same time as the Dred Scott case was going through the Missouri courts. The Missouri State Supreme Court ruled against the AME in 1854.[13] By 1852, however, the AME had built a new church on Seventh Street and was no longer connected to the Southern Methodist convention.

As Black churches were gaining strength, native-born Protestant migrants from the Northeast and the upper South were coming to Missouri and its riverfront city to make their political and economic fortune. "Yankee peddlers" from the Northeast arrived with goods to trade and sell but also brought Calvinist and evangelical faiths that challenged the hegemony of Catholicism and its top-down modes of governance. Presbyterian and Congregationalist worshippers in the Northeast were close allies in "disestablishing" churches in their towns and believed that the particulars of religious doctrine should be determined by congregants themselves. The Congregationalists of New England were founded on this principle, but the better-organized Presbyterians, facilitated by a plan of union with Congregationalists that was arranged in New York, dominated the early Protestant landscape in St. Louis. With a shortage of local Presbyterian and Congregationalist ministers in St. Louis and the upper South, New England pastors were often invited to head these new congregations that proliferated after the War of 1812. By 1821 the First Presbyterian Church, with its pastor from New England, Samuel Giddings, added a notable new family to its roster, the Kerrs.[14]

Matthew Kerr, son of Scots-Irish immigrants to Pittsburgh, Pennsylvania, and his wife from Philadelphia, Hannah Skinner Kerr, were Presbyterians. Matthew is said to be the first English-speaking merchant in St. Louis when he established a trading post in 1809.[15] He served in the War of 1812, was a commissioner of the Bank of Missouri and a prominent member of the Whig Party, and was invited to be a pall bearer at the funeral of Henry Clay in 1841. By the time of Missouri statehood he and Hannah were at the heart of the retail and real estate economy and Presbyterian religious affairs. They provided $200 for the First Presbyterian Church, opened in 1825 at a final cost of $9,000, and gave land to the city for nonsectarian schools, parks, and an orphan asylum. Hannah was one of sixteen Presbyterian women who founded the St. Louis Association of Ladies for the Relief of Orphan Children in 1834 and was its first director. The orphanage accepted two Jewish children and took in Catholic children but would not place Protestant orphans in Catholic homes. One scholar concludes that Saint Louis churchwomen like Hannah "played an extraordinary . . . role in expanding the reach of benevolence" by promoting Sunday Schools, a Bible Society, and temperance commitments. They convinced their husbands to donate property for churches and civic improvements.[16]

The Kerrs and other Pennsylvanians built the first two-story brick houses in St. Louis and planned a central grid a few blocks from the courthouse with streets named after those in Philadelphia: Locust, Chestnut, Poplar, and Pine. The Kerr family lived at the corner of Fifth and Franklin in a fashionable home with front and back parlors and three bedrooms, a stable, horses, and carriages, their house full of books and magazines and decorated with portraits of the family's favorite ministers.[17] The Kerrs employed white domestic servants and were masters of a small number of enslaved people. William S. Potts of New Jersey, the minister of their new and more progressive-minded church, the Second Presbyterian, converted newly arrived Maine schoolteacher and future antislavery martyr Elijah Lovejoy in a three-day prayer meeting in 1831. By the 1840s Presbyterians were dividing into pro- and antislavery factions, with the "New Light" Presbyterians following their consciences into the condemnation of slavery, closely aligning them with New England antislavery believers.

Faced with a glut of lawyers, ministers, and other professionals in the Northeast, young men with elite training were arriving in St. Louis to ply their trades. The Kerrs' three daughters attracted eligible suitors from Massachusetts with the same religious affiliations and political ideals. Pardon Dexter Tiffany from Worcester married Hannah Kerr, Samuel Knox of Blandford wed Mary Kerr, and Elizabeth Kerr became the wife of Irwin Z. Smith of West Granville. Graduates of Harvard Law School, Knox and Tiffany were students of Simon Greenleaf and Joseph Story, both famous legal scholars and Story a future US Supreme Court Justice, who wrote Tiffany a glowing statement of recommendation.[18] Samuel Knox grew up listening to the ringing fire and brimstone oratory of Calvinist ministers. Once established in Missouri, Knox was said to be an "eloquent speaker," who "engaged in many . . . hotly contested and protracted lawsuits with marked success. Many times . . . he has moved jurors to tears," and "his chaste diction, modeled largely on King James's version of the Bible, delighted and instructed . . . the courts."[19]

Roswell Field of Newfane, Vermont, arrived in St. Louis in 1839. Son of a prosperous farmer in Newfane, he attended Middlebury College, a Congregationalist stronghold with a cluster of abolitionists, and opened a law practice in his hometown but had few clients. Vermont's "young doctors, lawyers, preachers and teachers" were "on the march" to the West, a march joined by many other New Englanders.[20] Devout Presbyterian Charles Daniel Drake from Cincinnati, Ohio, described the scene for ambitious young lawyers when he arrived in St. Louis in 1835:

> It was, as I supposed, the best field in the United States for a young lawyer, so far as quick success in getting practice was concerned. Almost the whole of the business operations of the city was compressed into a space about half a mile in length and a quarter of a mile in width; so that an active and enterprising young fellow had no difficulty in making himself known . . . in a comparatively short time. . . . Oftentimes the speeches before juries would attract numbers of passers-by; and so a single trial might make a young lawyer known to many.[21]

Reuben Knox, a graduate of Columbia Medical School and an uncle of Samuel Knox, joined his nephew in St. Louis in 1840 and was soon a mainstay of the Second Presbyterian congregation. He and his wife, Eliza, a North Carolina widow, who owned more than a few enslaved people, hoped to emancipate them in a responsible way that would provide for their future welfare. In his attempts to recruit a new minister, northeastern Congregationalist Truman Post, Reuben Knox wrote that the Presbyterian congregation had "an unusual proportion of young men of energy and enterprise . . . already prominent, not only in mercantile circles but in the ranks of law and medicine." Post demurred at first, declaring that he was "unwilling to lay my bones in a slave state, or commit my family to its destinies," and he "regarded holding human beings as property as a violation of the first principles of the Christian religion." There were some slaveholders in the church, Knox argued. But they were in the minority, and even they were opposed to the institution and longed "to see the curse removed."[22] Post did come to St. Louis and would encourage the growing antislavery sentiments of his congregation.

The First Congregational Church of St. Louis, soon renamed the Church of the Messiah, was organized in 1835 by two young men in their twenties, Wayman Crow and William Greenleaf Eliot Jr. Crow, an accomplished bookkeeper, who arrived from Kentucky with human property and a large fortune that made him one of the richest businessmen in St. Louis. Eliot was a graduate of Harvard Divinity School and a professed Unitarian but one who had avoided the radicalism of Ralph Waldo Emerson's transcendentalist views. Future famous sculptor Harriet Hosmer, who stayed at the Crow home while she studied anatomy at McDowell Medical College in 1849, wrote letters home describing the harmonious family life of the Crows, made comfortable with Black servitude.

Eliot came to St. Louis via Louisville, where he visited his dear friend and fellow Harvard Divinity School graduate John Freeman Clarke. Eliot and Clarke learned German and studied German philosophy, which would later garner them credibility with 1848 free-thinker refugees. They were committed to "the West," believing that serving as cultural evangelists in new communities would bring both civilization and liberal Protestantism to the frontier. They saw cities like Louisville, Kentucky, and St. Louis as places where "worn garments of the former generations are laid aside."[23]

Eliot was a slim blond with large, brown eyes and an aristocratic bearing and soon became a popular preacher and successful promotor of civic causes in St. Louis. He had powerful family connections in the East. His father, William Greenleaf Eliot Sr., was a New Bedford merchant and shipowner bankrupted by the War of 1812 embargo. Eliot Sr. moved his young family to

Washington, DC, at the behest of his brother-in-law William Cranch, a US Circuit Court justice, part of the extended family of John and Abigail Adams.

Eliot Jr. saw the early years of nonpartisan political cooperation in the "era of good feelings" firsthand when he was a student at Colombian College in Washington, DC, and attended Universalist church meetings, said to have congregants John Quincy Adams, John C. Calhoun, and the architect Charles Bullfinch. Universalism was a free thinker's religion, dissenting from the established churches of the early Republic and promoting freedom of religion, the importance of scientific inquiry, and the Bill of Rights. Eliot's friendship with Kentuckian Crow was a confirmation of Eliot's view that building consensus across sectional divides was essential in a border state like Missouri. Eliot saw his church as a religious and political force that would transcend sectionalism and sectarianism and be an engine of a great city's development, with himself as a ministerial and organizational pioneer. He would need the backing of the elites of St. Louis, whether they were slaveholders or not. Eliot often had grandiose visions for the improvement of the waterfront city that he could make a reality with Crow's and other businessmen's funding.

Virginians, Black and white, were the largest block of migrants coming to St. Louis from the slaveholding South. Presbyterian Edward Bates, another veteran of the War of 1812, was the State of Missouri's first attorney general and a drafter of its constitution. Bates and his sister Sarah hailed from a large, and dying, plantation in Goochland, Virginia, and in 1814 came to St. Louis with some of their human property. Bates invested with his law partner, Rufus Easton, in 1817 in a ferry across the Mississippi to Alton, Illinois, a town that became a symbol of freedom just across the river. Bates and Kerr were among the wealthiest of the Protestant newcomers to St. Louis. An 1821 taxpayer roll listed Pierre Chouteau as worth $13,025, his brother Auguste $9,105, Bates $1,000, and Matthew Kerr $3,600. Kerr's retail establishment, Kerr, Bell, and Company, was assessed at $20,000.[24]

Virginians Peter and Elizabeth Blow, impoverished parents of seven surviving children, arrived in St. Louis with their young enslaved man Dred Scott in 1830 and opened a boardinghouse. Scott was one of the few assets widower Peter Blow could sell to avoid bankruptcy before he died. The Blow sons and daughters, by all accounts both enterprising and charming, were left to live by their wits. Charlotte Blow married Joseph Charles Jr., son of the prominent St. Louis and Irish-born newspaper editor, and Martha wed Charles Daniel Drake, graduate of the US Naval Academy at Annapolis and recently from Cincinnati, Ohio. Henry Taylor Blow studied law at Jesuit St. Louis College and married Minerva Grimsley, who attended a Sacred Heart convent school and was the daughter of a wealthy St. Louis saddle manufacturer. Henry's younger brother Taylor Blow had been the playmate of Dred Scott, one of the family's enslaved, and would be his advocate when Dred sued for his freedom. Despite their Catholic educations, the adult Blows were ardent Presbyterians except for Taylor, who converted to Catholicism in his dissolute middle age.

Members of the extended Blow family would become a major influence in St. Louis society and Missouri state politics. Henry Taylor Blow joined his brother-in-law Joseph Charles in manufacturing castor oil, linseed oil, and white lead, a product in growing demand for glass and paint manufacture. The brothers-in-law had considerable interests in lead mining in Missouri and Illinois, and their Collier White Lead and Oil Works at Tenth and Clark Streets became one of the largest white lead–producing companies in the United States—and a major polluter of St. Louis's major water supply, Lake Chouteau. Blow, Drake, Knox, and Field would take their Congregationalist and Presbyterian views into a new political party, the Republicans, seeing slavery as a kind of national sin.

Many of the first arrivals of free Black people to Missouri were from Virginia, the slave state that after Maryland had the largest antebellum population of free Black persons, forty-seven thousand in 1830. The works of Black-history scholars Carter G. Woodson and Luther Porter Jackson explain how some persons of color could afford to leave Virginia. Draymen, barbers, boatmen, carpenters, coopers, stonemasons, and laundresses all had marketable skills and might own real estate and extensive personal property. Jackson argued that slavery was no longer profitable in Virginia by the turn of the nineteenth century and that some of the enslaved, especially hired-out people, were able to bargain for their freedom and think about migrating with their tools and trades to another state.[25]

The Brander extended family showed up in Woodson's and Jackson's detailed census research and analysis of tax rolls and wills. Born in 1814 in Petersburg, Griffin Brander was the son of William Brander and Lucy Scott, a woman Griffin's descendants believed was from a local Native American tribe, perhaps the Chickahominy. Woodson found thirteen free "Negro" Branders in Petersburg in the 1830 census. Jackson's more detailed analysis uncovered Shadrack Brander, a cooper who owned more than $1,000 in property and left an estate valued at $533. His possessions included cooper's tools, a sideboard, writing desk, a wagon with its gear, two plows, two cows, and three horses, "a gray, a sorrell, and a roan."[26]

Griffin Brander may have inherited some of Shadrack's or other Branders' property and learned skills from the Virginia Branders in the riding and use of draft horses. Griffin is described in his "free man" pass, issued by the

Commonwealth of Virginia in 1840, as a "dark brown" man about five feet six inches tall, with "a large mole on the right side of his mouth, and a scar on his left arm." A tobacco twister in Petersburg, Virginia, he purchased property from a white man, Ashton Johnston. Johnston left Petersburg for St. Louis in the early 1840s and was soon a prosperous merchant. Brander decided on Missouri as well. He transferred his real estate property in Virginia to his brother Henry and went to St. Louis, a trip made safely with his free pass, endorsed with an addendum by Johnston: "the within named Griffin Brander is a colored man of good character, and we recommend him as such."[27]

Griffin may have gone to Missouri because his wife, Catherine, and their two daughters, Lucy and Mary Ann, were taken by their owners to Callaway County, Missouri, where the three were sold to James and Matilda Gill. Griffin bought Catherine and Lucy from the Gills for $600 in 1851 and later returned for Mary Ann in a perilous journey, described by his descendants in oral remembrance, keeping his free pass close and hiding himself and his daughter from slave catchers. He filed emancipation papers for Catherine, Lucy, and Mary Ann in 1856, witnessed by Johnston. Griffin worked as a porter, a laborer, and a servant; he was also a tobacconist and a teamster and, as he earned more capital, invested in his own business, hauling coal and oats in St. Louis to and from the waterfront and across the Mississippi River to Illinois. He first appeared as a drayman on Cass Avenue in the *St. Louis City Directory* in 1854. Brander established himself before a new Draconian state law in 1847 outlawed the migration of any "free negro or mulatto" into Missouri. The law was difficult to enforce, but it guaranteed that all free Black men and women in St. Louis would face hurdles in obtaining and paying for licenses now required to remain in the state and practice their trades. Griffin Brander postponed registering his status until 1856.

Griffin and Catherine Brander's family history reveals how perilous and tenuous life was for even the most prosperous Black families in Missouri. Separations of slave families were a constant fear. Slaveholders sold enslaved people to other whites, moved elsewhere, or when they died left wills and estates that divided up Black families. Family members were mere pieces of property in these arrangements, and routine sales of persons on the auction block were front of mind for all Black people. Slave catchers were a persistent threat, especially after the passage of the Fugitive Slave Act of 1850. Brander kept his free pass, the sales agreements with the Gills, his marriage license, and receipts for his license fees in his personal possessions until the day he died in 1888. Tattered and torn, folded into a neat square that could be carried in a pocket or a wallet, his free pass was testament to his greatest fears, his greatest triumphs, and his hard-won identity.

The Branders and the Dred Scott family were African Baptists, an affiliation made possible by the Baptist missionaries who came through Missouri before statehood. John Berry Meachum led the First African Baptist Church in St. Louis. Born into slavery in Virginia, he was taken by his master to North Carolina and then Kentucky. With savings from his work in a saltpeter mine and his skills as a carpenter, he purchased his freedom and that of his parents, siblings, wife, and children. Ordained a minister in 1825, he was by 1827 teaching Black people to read in the basement of the first African American church west of the Mississippi.

African American churches articulated notions of Black identity that encouraged self-help and political resistance. Meachum underscored the possibilities of freedom and the history of Black America in his *Address to All the Colored Citizens of the United States*, published in 1846. Based on its derivation from the Niger River in Africa, he spurned the term "negro" as one of opprobrium and preferred "citizens of color," stressing the first arrival of Black people in America to "about 1620."[28] Meachum dated the beginning of the mixed-race new country, like recent historians of the 1619 Project, with the arrival of enslaved persons at Jamestown, Virginia. "Citizens of color," Meachum argued, had long been of North American descent and should be called Afro-Americans.

Meachum argued that since the population of the American continent was made up of immigrants, including unwilling ones, and if recent Irish and German migrants could find greater opportunities in St. Louis, so could Afro-Americans. Underscoring ideas that presaged those of Booker T. Washington, Meachum urged Black men and women to purchase their freedom, buy land and property, educate their children, build houses, and receive training in the carpentry, coopering, and construction trades. Vocational education and thoughtful methods of farming would be the keys to unlocking the door to prosperity and self-respect. Meachum and his wife, Mary, used this model to their own benefit and that of "the race." They purchased some twenty "colored friends" and hired them in businesses they ran, then were repaid by their adoptees, and saw them launch themselves in St. Louis and elsewhere. (Not all these transactions were happy ones; the Meachums were sued by some of their "beneficiaries" for their freedom.)

At the Second African Baptist Church, Richard John Anderson, usually called John, was a remarkable orator and beloved pastor who preached to a mixed congregation of enslaved and free people. Anderson was born in Illinois in 1818 as his mother, Chloe, was en route to St. Louis with her Virginian owner, Sarah Bates. Sarah freed Chloe and her son John in 1830.[29] John was said to have learned to read and write in what Black people referred to as the "curbside" method, "using a blue back spelling book" so that "friendly white boys and girls on their way to and from school . . . would teach him and answer his questions." Hired as a newsboy at the *St. Louis Missouri Republican*, he learned to set type.[30]

Working at Lovejoy's controversial newspaper in Alton, Illinois, Anderson saw rioters murder the editor and destroy the press in 1837. Anderson married a free Black woman in Illinois and was ordained to preach at the Alton Union Baptist Church. But he returned to St. Louis as a "whitewasher," one of the artisanal trades open to Black men and, in a challenge to Meachum, began the city's Second African Baptist Church in 1846, meeting in a hall near the St. Louis fire station but moving to a dedicated sanctuary on Eighth and Green Streets in 1852. White Baptist minister Galusha Anderson estimated John Anderson's congregation at a thousand persons, half enslaved and half free, by the 1850s. Historians believe that Galusha Anderson put Harriet Robinson Scott, Dred Scott's wife, in touch with the Scotts' first lawyer in St. Louis, Francis Murdoch. As district attorney of Alton, Illinois, Murdoch tried to bring the murderers of Lovejoy to justice and then aided a handful of St. Louis enslaved people in their suits for freedom before leaving abruptly for California in 1849.[31]

White Baptist minister Galusha Anderson described John Anderson, somewhat romantically, as "a large man of commanding presence, a descendent of an African chief. He was very black . . . his forehead high and broad. . . . His manner was quiet, suggesting reserved power; his thought was orderly and clear. He had great power over an audience. . . . While he sometimes burned with indignation, he never lost control of himself. He was a man of rare balance of mind."[32] Black Baptist church lore depicted him as a veritable legend, a hero who gave members of his community funds to escape to a free state or Canada and bought several of them about to be sold from the auction block and made them church deacons. Anderson would die in 1863, poisoned by a tincture prescription—perhaps for a toothache—that did not seem to create suspicion of murder. His funeral was said to be the largest ever held in St. Louis up to that point, except for that of Missouri US Senator Thomas Hart Benton.

John Thomas of Nashville, Tennessee, is an improbable, but real, rags-to-riches story of another free Black migrant to St. Louis. Born in 1827, Thomas was the son of hard-working laundress Sally Thomas and though never acknowledged as such of a white father, John Catron, a future Tennessee Supreme Court justice. Sally used her earnings to negotiate a promise of her son's emancipation and sent him to New Orleans at age twelve, where he was apprenticed to a barber and returned home to open his own shop in Nashville. Arriving in St. Louis in 1857 after travels to Nicaragua and Kansas-Nebraska

Territory, John was employed on a Mississippi steamboat and then worked at Henry Clamorgan's barber shop, where he met and pursued Antoinette Rutgers, another Clamorgan descendant. More interested in cock fights and fiddling contests than Black church services, he converted to Catholicism and would marry Antoinette in the St. Louis Cathedral. He and his wife were wealthy real estate developers in St. Louis and lived a lavish lifestyle.[33]

John Thomas landed on his feet in St. Louis and lived an exceptional life as a free Black man. Dred Scott, who became a national celebrity when he lost his suit for freedom in 1857, highlights the tentative hold on stability many Black enslaved families had as their owners moved or died and descendants managed wills that separated family members. As a hired-out worker, Scott escaped the worst aspects of slavery for many years. Peter Blow sold Scott to army surgeon John Emerson in 1833 to settle a debt. Emerson took Scott to Fort Armstrong in Illinois and then to Fort Snelling in the Wisconsin Territory (in what is now Minnesota), where Dred married Harriet Robinson in 1836 or 1837. US Indian agent Major Lawrence Talliferro, a Presbyterian, married Harriet and Scott in an official and religious ceremony that was unusual for the enslaved at the time.[34] Their two infant sons died but two daughters, Eliza and Lizzie, survived. The Scotts were sent back to St. Louis in 1838, where they were, for all practical purposes, on their own.

The Scotts lived on an alleyway street in the center of St. Louis. Dred was a cleaner and porter at white hotels and offices, and Harriet worked at a grocery and was a laundress at home. Dressmaking and laundry work were preferred by Black women to domestic service in white households because they were somewhat independent of white control and could care for their families as they worked at home. The Scotts were always mindful to protect their two daughters from roaming slave catchers eager to sell able-bodied young people downriver. Parents of "valuable" young people like the daughters of the Scotts and of the Branders wanted to purchase their freedom or file emancipation suits as quickly as possible.

As the short-staple-cotton plantation industry widened in Alabama, Mississippi, Louisiana, and Texas in the 1840s and 1850s, prices for able-bodied adults increased, and a crackdown on emancipations and the movements of free Blacks accelerated in St. Louis. So many of the enslaved were coming through the St. Louis market that sales were moved from the auction houses to the steps of the courthouse, where lewd men could ogle nearly naked Black women. The Fugitive Slave Act of 1850 gave free rein to slave catchers who might or might not recognize the freedom of their human snares.

The centrality of St. Louis to the river trade and its border-state importance atop the slaveholding South made its slave markets among the busiest in the United States. Historian Frederick Bancroft argues that "as elsewhere in the border slave States, it was soon learned that it was more profitable to sell slaves [to the far South] than to keep them for their ordinary labor." Bancroft found thirty slave traders in the 1851 *St. Louis City Directory* who used auction-block markets in the center of town. They served as grim reminders for Black people of what might happen to them if found in the wrong places.[35]

Enslaved Black people were freeing themselves with a variety of strategies. Escape routes, like crossing the Mississippi or the Missouri or via rivers like the Illinois, Cumberland, and Ohio and via canals to the Great Lakes were discussed in the Black community, as were rumors of enslaved persons who had won and lost cases in the courts and the lawyers who represented them. Their "familiarity with the law's power and its limits," describes Kelley Kennington, "speaks to the ubiquity of legal information in the slave community and the complex processes that took place beyond the confines of freedom suit courtrooms."[36]

The enslaved continued to escape through the porous exits of St. Louis. Ads posted in the *Missouri Republican* for valued runaways in 1849 hint at how much they had emotional ties to and were acknowledged as individuals by their owners. Thirty-eight-year-old Martin was "spare built . . . and a pretty smart boy." Seventeen-year-old Theresa was "well grown and very good looking." Martha was "a bright mulatto" who "is quick spoken and intelligent." Her companion Caroline ran away wearing new shoes, a muslin dress, and a "buff colored bonnet" and carrying two other dresses. Scholar Tiya Miles details the haunting importance of the items like the ones Caroline took with her in a portrayal of a nine-year-old South Carolina girl named Ashley who was separated, permanently, from her mother with "all that she carried": a tattered dress, three handfuls of pecans, and a braid of her mother's hair in a flour sack converted into carryall bag with a strap.[37]

Cases of escaping slavery through flight, purchasing freedom with hired-out wages, or by suing in the courts in the 1840s and 1850s were common enough but not the general rule. Many slaveholders clung to their property as prices for enslaved people rose. Federal marshals seized fugitives, and professional slave catchers returned runaways to their owners. A thriving market in the business transfers of human bodies continued to tear families apart. William Wells Brown's narrative, relied upon by Frederick Bancroft, a founder of the genre of American history, included an account of a slave trader's transport by land and riverboat of human property purchased along the way from farms in Missouri's interior in the 1840s. The shackled group was headed for sale in St. Louis and markets farther south. At St. Charles a woman with a four-week-old infant was added to the group. The baby was fussy and offended the driver. He "took the child by one arm, as you would a cat by the leg," walked into a nearby house and offered the baby to its owner. "The mother's frantic appeals were not only in vain but caused her to be chained with the gang."[38] She would have had painful breasts without her nursing infant on her chest, and she would be vulnerable to rape. She had to grieve the loss of her child while walking in chains.

Galusha Anderson describes one of these heartbreaking losses in his autobiography. One of his congregants was hard up for cash in 1860 and decided to sell an enslaved mother to a New Orleans trader but wanted to keep her young daughter as a servant. Mother and daughter attended services at John Anderson's Second African Baptist Church. Galusha argued with the slaveholder in vain, but in the end neither pastor could save the mother from being sent downriver:

> The day came when, with a hundred or more consigned to the same pitiless fate, she boarded the steamer at the levee to be carried to her doom. Her little slave daughter was there to give her the last tearful kiss and embrace. Her faithful pastor stood by filled with sorrow and deep down in his soul hot with righteous wrath. The steamer moved out from the levee, the anguished mother and the pastor waved to each other their red bandanas, and slowly the vessel with its freight of sorrow disappeared down the river.[39]

Black men and women in the South during "slavery times" in the nineteenth century did not leave behind anything like the rich trove of letters, diaries, sermons, and personal accounts that white middle- and upper-class people did. That fact means we have disparate kinds of texts available for analyzing the lives of the enslaved, their masters, and antislavery whites. As enslaved people were freed or emancipated themselves, they created a genre of narratives and novels that recounted their lives in slavery. The first slave narratives were written by escaped slaves, such as Douglass, Brown, and Harriet Jacobs, and later amplified by the Works Projects Administration interviews in 1938. They are often histrionic, romantic, "looking back," and "summing up." They are products of memory, not day-to-day life accounts. But they are indispensable because they are often all that we have of the voices of the enslaved.

Elizabeth Keckley, Lucy A. Delaney, and William Wells Brown were Missourians who wrote narratives after their emancipations. Their accounts are personal remembrances of family life, the cruelties of family separation through wills and inheritance, sexual assaults, the cruelties of physical and psychological abuse, and tactics used to contest legal standing or to escape to freedom.

Delaney's family story, *From the Darkness Cometh the Light*, illustrates the dangers of quixotic wills and kidnapping. Matriarch Polly Crockett Berry claimed to have been born a free person in Illinois, then captured as a child, and sold into slavery in Missouri. She married an enslaved man in St. Louis and had two daughters, Nancy and Lucy. Deaths of their several owners, personal transfers among family members, and wills separated the three women, who had often talked about ways to escape when the time was right. Mother Polly urged daughter Nancy to fade into Canada when Nancy accompanied her mistress on a honeymoon to Niagara Falls. Polly was captured in Chicago by slave catchers in 1839. But back home in St. Louis she filed suit arguing that she should be emancipated on the grounds that she had been born free in Illinois. Edward Bates took up her case in 1843, with Bates arguing that Polly had been kidnapped as a free person in Illinois.[40]

Lucy was meanwhile enduring beatings at the hands of another mistress, who was angry that Lucy had done the laundry in unfiltered, muddy water from the Mississippi. Put up for sale, Lucy ran away on the eve of the transaction. Arrested and returned to St. Louis, she was thrown in jail for more than seventeen months as she waited to hear if she could attach her case to her mother's and that as the daughter of a free mother, she, too, should be free. Lawyer Murdoch took Lucy's initial case, but the successful arguments for mother and daughter were made in court by Bates. Himself a slaveholder, he believed in upholding the law and the finer points of right and wrong in the abuse of the enslaved. His argument, recalled by Lucy in her narrative, combines both moral outrage and legal precedent:

> Gentlemen of the jury, I am a slave-holder myself, but, thanks to the Almighty God, I am above the base principle of holding any a slave that has as good right to her freedom as this girl has been proven to have; she was free before she was born; her mother was free, but kidnapped in her youth, and sacrificed to the greed of negro traders, and no free woman can give birth to a slave child, as it is in direct violation of the laws of God and man.[41]

Keckley lost a family member to the slave trade and was then herself "traded." Born enslaved in Virginia in 1818, Elizabeth grew up believing George Hobbs was her father but learned later she was the biological child of her master. Hobbs was taken away from Virginia to "the West" (Shelbyville, Tennessee) when she was a young girl: "My father cried out against the cruel separation . . . his wild straining of my mother to his bosom . . . the fearful anguish of broken hearts."[42] Hobbs was literate, saved money to purchase his freedom, and wrote to his wife and daughter when he could but died before he could return.

With the decline of plantation agriculture in Virginia, Elizabeth's owners fell on hard times. She was assigned laborious household tasks but, following her mother's example, became an expert dressmaker. Beaten viciously by members of the Burwell family for her continued intransigence and turned over to a "slave breaker," at the age of eighteen she was sent to the household of a Presbyterian minister in North Carolina, where Protestant rectitude did not fend off sexual assault: "The savage efforts to subdue my pride were not the only things that brought me suffering and deep mortification . . . and for four years a white man . . . had base designs upon me. . . . and I—I—became a mother." She named her son, George, after the man she viewed as her true father.[43]

Elizabeth next went to live with a Burwell daughter and her new husband, Hugh Garland, who, coincidently, would be defendant John Sanford's lawyer in the Dred Scott case in St. Louis. Her new owners, now nearly impoverished, moved to St. Louis and took her, her mother, and Elizabeth's son, George, with them. The new owners threatened to put her aged mother out to domestic service, but Keckley could not bear the thought of her mother "working for strangers." Elizabeth pleaded with Garland to leave her mother at home and allow Elizabeth to launch a dressmaking business. She gave most of her earnings to him and recalled that "with my needle I kept bread in the mouths of seventeen persons for two years and five months." She was now one of the most renowned dressmakers in St. Louis, and some of her white patrons contributed to the cost of her emancipation. She negotiated a price of $1,200 and purchased George's freedom and her own in 1855. George was now sixteen, she was thirty-seven, and it is estimated that in late twentieth-century dollars, she paid more than $33,000 for her new standing. She had married a man named Keckley but left him behind due to his "dissipation" and raised her son on her own.[44] She settled in Washington, DC, where she made wrappers, dresses, and gowns for the wives of prominent politicians.

The mighty Mississippi took Black people away from their loved ones but also offered avenues of self-improvement—and escape. Reverend Meachum frowned on the adventurous life of steamboat workers, "for boatmen are apt to be rude" and to wander away from home and family.[45] But steamboat occupations for enslaved persons, hired-out Black people, and free men and women "of color" were critical to the progress of Black workers and their families. An 1850 survey of St. Louis found that almost a third of the city's free Black men worked on riverboats.[46] Women might be domestic workers, men could be "roustabouts" (those who laded and unladed goods), barbers, firemen, and waiters but never pilots, an occupation that Missourian, and white man, Mark Twain landed with ease. Traveling the Mississippi and its connecting rivers, the Missouri, the Ohio, the Illinois, and the Cumberland, widened Black workers' worldview and might even offer a path to liberation.

Brown and Moses Dickson both took advantage of this widening world on the Mississippi. Brown was born in Kentucky, brought to St. Louis as a young man, and hired out to work on steamboats on the Missouri and Ohio. In 1834 he left a boat that docked in Cincinnati and escaped to freedom. Brown worked as a boatman on Lake Erie when he settled in Buffalo, New York, helping several dozens of enslaved persons to escape into Detroit or across the lake to Canada.[47]

Born free, Dickson of Cincinnati trained as a barber and took a job on a steamboat in 1840. In three years of river travel as a teenager, he saw much of the South and horrors of slavery firsthand. Recruiting Black men he encountered in his travels as a barber, Dickson formed a secret fraternal organization in 1846, "the Knights of Liberty," intending to someday incite a slave insurrection and overthrow bondage in the United States. Brown was said to be one of its members. Dickson married widow Mary Peters, a butcher-shop owner in Galena, Illinois. The couple married in 1848, settled in St. Louis, and became members of the AME Church. Conductors on the Underground Railroad, they took enslaved persons in secret from St. Louis across the Mississippi to Illinois. Both Dickson and Brown were actively contriving to send Black people to freedom and end the institution by whatever means necessary. Despite Meachum's misgivings about steamboat men, they were inspired to act against injustice as boatmen in the wider world while religious leaders like Meachum and Anderson worked on the same cause at home.

White minister Galusha Anderson was one of many Northeasterners who came to St. Louis in the 1840s and 1850s. Like Anderson they were often professionals—lawyers, doctors, and clergymen—who brought a moral ethos with them that emphasized Enlightenment values and the personal sense of responsibility inherent in the Second Great Awakening. They sought economic opportunity and at the same time, coming from states that had abandoned slavery, were affronted by what they viewed as moral failings in the slave state of Missouri. They would have ambivalent feelings about remaining in St. Louis, and they kept their ties to home bases in the Northeast close at hand. They would play critical roles in the development of a new politics in the 1840s and 1850s and the crises of 1849 that roiled the city of St. Louis and put into stark relief these migrants' sometimes seemingly conflicting ambitions: pursuing moral reform—and using new opportunities to amass wealth and political influence.

# 2 Domesticity, Immigration, and the Crises of 1849

The white Protestant churches that created opportunities for separate Black worship in St. Louis in the early nineteenth century continued to grow in numbers of congregants and ran across a spectrum of antislavery views. Presbyterians, Congregationalists, Methodists, and Unitarians, many of them Northeastern migrants, were at the core of a new white consciousness in St. Louis that condemned slavery. They would soon be joined by German freethinkers and antislavery Lutherans.

As white Protestants gained more wealth in an exploding city, they shared some of that wealth with churches and civic organizations. They emancipated their own enslaved persons or represented men and women seeking freedom in the courts. The intersection of their lawyering and Protestant piety bolstered claims to freedom and by 1856 the fostering of a new antislavery political party. But Black and white antislavery efforts did not come together in a coordinated way. This bifurcation of efforts undermined what might have been not only the goal of ending slavery but of granting civil rights to Black men and women. Many white Protestants disliked slavery but assumed their own racial superiority and rarely formed lasting relationships of equality with people of color.

A deadly cholera epidemic, a riverfront fire, and the discovery of gold in California disrupted and tested the faith and fortitude of St. Louis in 1849 and 1850. In recovery the city was modernized, fortunes were lost and made, and dynasties built on real estate and investment ventures—both in St. Louis and in California—put Protestants at the top of a prosperous class hierarchy that would take control of Missouri state politics during the Civil War. That class hierarchy was made more complicated by the arrival of thousands of immigrants searching for employment and housing in a rapidly changing city landscape.

St. Louis grew by six thousand inhabitants between 1820 and 1830 and by 1845 to thirty-five thousand. The potato famine in Ireland sparked a huge migration of Irish families to urban sites all over the United States between 1845 and 1852, and a political crackdown on freethinkers and a crushing of the Revolution of 1848 across the states of the German Confederation led to in an even-larger migration of Germans to Missouri. Between 1849 and 1854, more than forty thousand Forty-Eighters arrived in St. Louis, along with fiercely conservative Lutherans who would create the Lutheran Church Synod in Missouri. By midcentury St. Louis had nearly seventy-eight thousand residents of whom 43 percent were German or Irish. Most Irish people settled in crowded city wards in inadequate housing and faced near destitution upon arrival. But they found employment as domestic servants and as laborers in the city's new industries and the building of a civic infrastructure that made St. Louis so up and coming a city before the Civil War.

Germans often settled in the rural suburbs of St. Louis or in center city wards, with the neighborhood around Hyde Park soon dubbed Bremen, annexed to the city of St. Louis in 1855. A new Nativist Party, the Know Nothings, demonized the recent immigrants, especially the Irish.[1] But it was easy for both German and Irish men to become naturalized citizens and voters. The Know Nothings fizzled, the Whigs sputtered, and the Republicans emerged in 1856. Both Democrats and Republicans would compete for the immigrant vote.

Irish immigrants were largely Catholics and eased themselves into the French network of institutions and schools already functioning throughout St. Louis. The Mullanphy family, early Irish migrants to St. Louis from Baltimore, Maryland, and Frankfort, Kentucky, were successful merchants. Patriarch John Mullanphy was the benefactor of the Mullanphy Hospital, established in 1827, that was open to all, including the indigent, and managed by the Sisters of Charity. Son Bryan Mullanphy, who capitalized on the migration's explosion in real estate, was elected mayor of St. Louis in 1847 and when he died in 1851 left nearly half a million dollars for immigrant relief. St. Patrick's Church at Sixth and Biddle Streets and St. Lawrence O'Toole Church at Fourteenth and O'Fallon Streets provided church services for a rapidly growing working-class population spreading to the northwest of downtown St. Louis. Like attempts to educate Black children, Irish migration lit a flame of resentment with assaults on Catholic institutions and businesses. In 1849 a Nativist mob "systematically destroyed the furniture and interiors of O'Brien's, Murphy's Boarding House . . . and Terence Brady's Coffee House at Fifth and Morgan."[2]

Three midwestern cities and their rural farmlands were the destinations of many German immigrants in the mid-nineteenth century: St. Louis, Milwaukee, and Cincinnati, but St. Louis attracted the largest number. Why did so many Germans settle in Missouri? Word had spread in the German states and provinces about opportunities in the Midwest to acquire inexpensive farm land, practice freedom of religion, maintain the German language and culture, and become naturalized citizens. As repression of free-thinking German university students increased in the 1820s, Gottfried Duden published *Report on a Journey to the Western States of North America*, encouraging immigration to Missouri. Duden argued that four thousand to six thousand thaler "is more than abundant to provide for a happy life for an entire family on the banks of the Missouri . . . [where] the immigrant can buy two adult slaves . . . and establish himself in such a manner that he can live more happily . . . than if he possessed six times that amount in Germany." The travelogue was widely read in Germany, especially by those who later led the unsuccessful uprisings of 1848.[3]

Earlier German immigrants created communities that welcomed the larger migration of the 1840s. Hessian Friedrich Munech, a Lutheran minister, witnessed the tragic crushing of freethinkers and Marxists and advocated leaving political turmoil behind for the American Midwest, leading a group of immigrants in the 1830s to Warren County, just west of St. Charles. The town of Hermann on the Missouri River was founded by the German Settlement Society of Philadelphia to attract their countrymen and women and build a community in America to protect German culture. As one German newspaper describes it, the town would be "a welcome refuge and new home for thousands . . . who would gladly leave their fatherland if only they would not have to miss . . . the beautiful familiar German folkways."[4] German immigrants established farms in the outer suburbs of St. Louis and in Gasconade and Osage Counties, and some owned enslaved people. Arnold Krekel arrived in the United States in 1832, studied the law, established a German-language newspaper, and acquired property in St. Charles County. In a letter to his family in Germany, he explains why he owned human property: "Slaves were something that 'one has to buy because one cannot work a farm alone.'"[5]

The Germans often arrived with more education and capital and faced less hostility from native-born residents than the Irish. Catholic Germans found a home in the Catholic institutions of St. Louis, and German Lutherans began building churches and a parochial school system. The "freethinkers," some of whom were Marxists and socialists, were armed with the philosophies of religious dissent, prodemocracy, and equal rights. They found allies in the Protestant and intellectual communities of middle- and upper-class St. Louis, and as early as the 1850s, St. Louis became a center of a German-influenced nexus of thought.

As young men, William Greenleaf Eliot and his friends John Freeman Clarke and Harm Jan Huidekoper studied the German language and German philosophy at Harvard Divinity School and as Unitarian ministers were opposed to absolutist thought. Their questions about traditional Protestant doctrines of faith intersected easily with those of the German rationalists. The son of a Lutheran minister, freethinker and German exile Eduard Muehl describes "free thinking" as "the 'Light of Reason' . . . uncovering the innate truths of a natural religion long obscured by dogma and superstition." "Rationalists," Muehl claimed, "stressed moral behavior, open discussion of religion issues, and . . . spontaneous participation of pastor and congregation in the church service."[6] Most Unitarians and Congregationalists agreed with these principles and practices.

Unitarian Eliot was especially influenced by Johan Fichte, who in the early nineteenth century in Berlin called for the total reform of German schooling and a new philosophy of education. Fichte wanted students of all social classes to have academic and artisanal training in a nonsecular environment that would prepare them for careers and make them good citizens as well. Eliot implemented these ideas as soon as he came to St. Louis. He saw his role in civic life as important as his job as a minister and is credited with establishing the city's first public school system in St. Louis, supported by a property tax he proposed and that was put into law in 1849. He was joined in these efforts by Connecticut-born William Torrey Harris, who arrived in St. Louis in 1857, taught for decades, and as the superintendent of schools helped St. Louis achieve its reputation as one of the best public school systems in the United States.

Harris helped build what was known as the St. Louis Movement, started by his friend Henry C. Brokmeyer, a German immigrant who settled in Warren, Missouri, before coming to St. Louis in 1858 to promote the ideas of philosophers Emmanuel Kant and Georg Hegel. He gained an attentive audience of students eager to read his translations of the philosophers' works. Brokmeyer and Harris founded the St. Louis Philosophical Society, and in 1867 Torrey began a new *Journal of Speculative Philosophy.* As he was building his new Washington University, Eliot was eager to hire Harvard-trained James Kendall Hosmer as a professor of German and English literature.

Members of the Henry Taylor Blow family had a deep personal relationship with another European immigrant family, the Taussigs. William Taussig completed a classical course at the University of Prague and studied medicine and chemistry in New York. Arriving in St. Louis in 1848, he was employed by Henry Blow at his Collier White Lead Company, helped doctor the sick during the cholera epidemic, and became a favorite of the whole Blow family. The Taussigs followed the Blows to the delightful suburb of Carondelet, where Taussig had a large medical practice and became the town's mayor in 1852. He oversaw the building of the Eads Bridge in 1873, a marvel of steel design and the first substantial crossing of the Mississippi to Illinois. Taussig was an informal guide for the Blow children into the most modern educational practices, focusing on philosophy and literature, and they encountered the ideas of William T. Harris in more public settings. Susan, the oldest child of the Blows, was a formidable young scholar and later said of Harris's lecture on Hegel that "the open secret was revealed and I knew that I stood upon the delectable mountains and discerned from afar the shining pinnacles of the Eternal City. . . . I was a novice admitted to a school fellowship."[7]

The native-born population of St. Louis struggled to make their way alongside new immigrants in the rapidly changing terrain of the "gateway city." As the Kerr daughters married lawyers from New England, the Eliots, the Drakes, the Blairs, and the Blows also married and became parents at midcentury. They found quite wonderful economic prospects in the burgeoning city of St. Louis, despite—but also because of—the expansion of the city required by its growing immigrant population. They increased their fortunes as they bought railroad bonds and real estate, collected rents, and maneuvered endless currency and banking crises, even as devoted churchgoers they were building congregations and discussing the morality of owning human beings. Like many in the prosperous white middle classes before the Civil War, they kept diaries, wrote letters, and published essays and letters to the editor, literary practices that Black Protestant congregants in St. Louis, mostly without literacy and leisure time, were rarely able to accomplish: John Berry Meachum's 1846 *Address to All the Colored Citizens of the United States* is a rare exception.

The writings by members of white families paint a nuanced portrait of gender roles, religious faith, death and disease, the consumption of goods, and the accumulation of property. Their economic and religious commitments required a carefully managed division of labor. Husbands were gone for weeks at a time in the state capital of Jefferson City serving in the state legislature and in distant cities buying bonds, real estate, and bank and railroad shares. Local banks went under or produced currency not easily exchanged. Eastern banks were more reliable, requiring trips to New York, Boston, or Philadelphia. Wives were left at home to keep the fabric of domestic and civic life intact, often assisting their husbands in important financial undertakings. Proper entertainment for white Protestant families took place in church. Services, prayer groups, and sewing circles were especially important to married women, who had few other ways of learning new ideas, forming friendships outside their extended families, and contributing to civic institutions. Most of them had been well educated in private female academies in the East. The "bonds of womanhood" these formal and informal gatherings created, scholar Nancy Cott argues, created a new consciousness of the parallels between Black people's enslavement and the oppression of women in the family and in the public sphere. Their "learning to stand and speak" would enable them to enter the public sphere and advocate for their own rights in the 1850s and 1860s.[8]

When Henry Blow was in New York buying carpets, dishes, and furniture in 1842, Minerva described the revival meetings at the Presbyterian Church that lasted most of the week. "I enjoy them very much; and attend the early morning prayer-meeting from which I hope to be much benefited. . . . Never have I listened to such searching powerful sermons as Mr. P[ost] preaches—he was portraying the importances [*sic*]of Eternity and the responsibilities of Christians with regard to the impenitent around them."[9] And when Pardon Dexter Tiffany left abruptly for California in early 1850, Hannah Tiffany was stuck at home with a newborn and a difficult schoolboy and what she described as "a servant problem." She said of an evening service she and her sisters Mary and Elizabeth attended, guided by Truman Post, "The sermon was most excellent & interesting. Subject Our Duties as American Christians. . . . I can remember most of it, it was so impressive, and striking."[10]

Motherhood and housework often interrupted these mothers' chances to read and reflect. In a letter to a friend from school days, Mary Kerr Knox bemoaned the loss of her youth: "I have much time for reflection while I sit sewing—and my mind travels back to those old school days . . . and mingle with the fancies of my brain. . . . [But] of course I have no business to say anything of the kind. Matter of fact, matron as I am . . . here comes little Hannah . . . 'our dinner, Mamma, our dinner.'"[11] While little Hannah's grandmother Hannah Kerr struggled to keep mess and disorder at bay, she preferred her time reading or being at church or in a sewing circle that supported a Presbyterian missionary in China to "the awful job of house cleaning." Pardon Dexter Tiffany, one of her future sons-in-law reported that he paid a visit one day and found Hannah "reading the life and writings of Benjamin Franklin all day, though everything was out of order in her house."[12]

These women all faced the terrors and joys of pregnancy and childbirth. Mary Kerr was nineteen when she married Samuel Knox and gave birth to six children between 1847 and 1860. Her mother and sisters often mention how weak she was from these close-together pregnancies. Hannah Tiffany struggled with an unwanted pregnancy ("I was not much pleased"). She rocked the fussy baby, "a squaller," in the evening by putting a foot on the cradle and rocking her own chair, catching up on mending and sewing while soothing her child. But when the colic passed and Lizzy was six months old, Hannah was "delighted" with her cheerful, cooing daughter. Her son had overcome his difficulties in school and made her proud.[13]

Abigail Adams Cranch married William Greenleaf Eliot in June 1837 and by April 1838 was expecting her first child. In one of only a handful of surviving letters, she wrote to her mother Mary Cranch that while she was "the greatest sight" and shouldn't be seen in public, she took a walk every day. "I know I shall have every comfort and every attention," she assured Mary, "a good doctor and nurse, and I mean to be very brave and smart." Her fears of childbirth but relative ease with her job of reproducing the next generation comes through in an 1875 letter to one of her daughters-in-law, who was disappointed not to have had a boy: "My darling child. Safely through! Oh how grateful I am! I know you are both happy enough it makes very little difference after it comes, which sex—*always* welcome!"[14]

Abby was pregnant and nursing, miscarrying on occasion, for much of her adult life. She bore fourteen children, her last baby in 1862, when she was forty-five (she would outlive her husband by twenty-one years). William kept a detailed journal of his parishioner visits, his ideas for sermons and lectures, and copies of letters to donors, politicians, and other parsons but rarely made entries about members of his family. The few times he did so have great import. In Eliot's view, he and his wife were a harmonious team, and in his will drafted on July 13, 1849, he left his entire estate to Abby. But when Abby lost a premature baby in April 1852 and was confined upstairs for five weeks, Eliot complained that this rest cure "added to my duties."[15]

As did so many of their parishioners, the Eliots lost children in unexpected deaths to sudden and fatal fevers, drownings in the Mississippi, typhoid, dysentery, or pneumonia. William died at two in 1841, but a harder blow was the death of their oldest child, Mary Rhodes Eliot, in January 1855 at the age of seventeen. Abby would not leave the house for weeks, and on February 28, William wrote in his journal that it was the "last day of winter, and of the winter of greatest discontent. A heavy heart." More heartbreak followed:

Margaret died at nine in 1858, and little Abby at seven while skating on thin ice at a local pond in 1862. Seven years later, Eliot recorded that on January 1, 1869, Frank, "our darling baby: two years and twelve days old" had died of a two-day "membranous croup."[16]

Cholera was epidemic in big cities in the United States by 1848 and arrived in St. Louis in December. White elites believed German immigrants brought in the disease, but whoever the first carriers were, the poor sanitary conditions of St. Louis allowed it to spread rapidly, and 1,250 people died in June alone. Although the city government formed a provisional committee to take special measures for quarantining patients on Arsenal Island and provide new hospital spaces, the disease was unstoppable because city leaders and physicians were just coming to understand that the cause of cholera was the contamination of drinking water with human feces. Most of the victims were immigrants, and a third of all victims were children younger than six. The St. Louis Protestant Orphan Asylum took in children whose parents died of cholera and then suffered an outbreak of the disease in 1850 that killed twenty-one children. No records were made of enslaved and free Blacks who died, but anecdotal evidence suggests they were chief among the victims. In the middle of the epidemic, another calamity: a fire that began on the steamboat *White Cloud* swept over the waterfront, destroying fifteen city blocks of central St. Louis east of Third Street between Walnut and Locust Streets and numerous riverboats.[17]

Hannah Tiffany describes these events and the hardship they caused in letters to her husband Pardon Dexter after he left for California in the spring of 1849 on what the extended family nervously described as a rest cure. "Sickness is so prevalent among the laboring classes," she relates, "that those who are alive & well will not work for any price."[18] By June Hannah wrote that "cholera is everywhere. . . . What have I to tell but of disease & death. . . . Dysentery prevails among the better classes. Business is at a standstill." Doctors were in constant demand, and Reuben Knox, uncle of Samuel Knox, exposed himself to cholera victims in quarantine on Rock Island and came down with fever. Hannah was worried that Dex, her young son, who was terrified that his father might be killed by so-called Indians in California, would catch the disease: "I do not let him out of my sight for indeed I am all anxiety & watchfulness." Pardon wrote infrequently, if at all. In Hannah's view, doses of brandy, the continued support of her parents, and the always helpful "Mr. [Samuel] Knox," along with constant prayer and faith in God's will, helped her keep her sanity.[19]

Hannah, left with the family's business affairs to deal with as best she could, reports frequent visits from lawyers and property managers. A shrewd evaluator of real estate, she thought the recent fire and the scourge of cholera would help to remake St. Louis: "People are actively engaged in rebuilding and contemplate great improvements in widening the streets & levees and constructing sewers & fire-proof buildings and some say it is the luckiest fire that ever happened for the prosperity and well doing of the city."[20]

The steady drip of deaths in his own family and at the bedsides and funerals of his parishioners had already taken their toll on William Greenleaf Eliot by 1849, when the disasters of "fire, pestilence and death," as he describes them, nearly destroyed the city of St. Louis. He was often depressed, had an upset stomach and signs of a vague "neuralgia," and suffered a temporary paralysis of his right hand. He sometimes took opium and laudanum.

William's parishioners at the Church of the Messiah were white and reasonably well-off, mostly living in single-family homes with decent plumbing. Many of his flock came down with cholera anyway, especially the elderly, small children, and women weakened by pregnancy or childbirth. The epidemic provoked a deeper crisis in William's health and his spiritual grounding. He was often called to sit with the dying and their families, and in several heartbreaking episodes, patients who seemed to rally died a few hours later. These were intimate encounters, ones in which he bent close for bedside confessions, but he did not come down with cholera, probably because he went home to drink his tea made with uncontaminated, boiled water. On August 8, though deaths were beginning to fall, he laments, "When will it end? I do now so long for freedom from care and anxiety that I am almost sick at heart."[21] He kept careful track of the counts of deaths and burials at the city's cemeteries. These showed, not surprisingly, that Protestants, who were more likely to be middle and upper class, were less likely to die than less well-off Catholics or the foreign born. Some Catholic families were upper class, even the most prosperous and oldest "aristocracy" of St. Louis, but most were working class and, like recent immigrants, living in poorer, crowded neighborhoods, with inadequate sanitation.

The city of St. Louis responded to the crisis with one good measure: mandating new cemeteries be built outside city limits. Except for the Methodist Wesleyan and limited spaces in Catholic burial grounds, these cemeteries were closed to Black people. Older cemetery records provide some information on African Americans who died. Estimates are that at least one-third and as many as one-half of the Methodists in St. Louis were Black. The Wesleyan Methodist Cemetery had a segregated section for "colored persons," and twenty-four hundred—a huge proportion of people of color—were buried there between 1847 and 1868, giving an idea of how serious the incidence of cholera and other causes of death were in the Black community.[22] The Roman

Catholic Calvary Cemetery allowed slaveholders to bury their enslaved dead in family plots. "Dick," "a colored servant," was interred there in 1849 by his employer and owner, John Withnell, who provided the blocks of stone to build the St. Louis Cathedral. The cathedral's belfry was completed with the help of a Black laborer, William Johnson, who dared climb up to place the final stone at the top. He, too, is buried in Calvary.[23]

In the middle of the cholera epidemic, the California Gold Rush further disrupted family life in St. Louis. Prominent Presbyterian minister Artemus Bullard lectured on the dangers of going to California "on account of the hardships—the temptations and the great danger of irreligious influences on each and all."[24] But the beckoning call of gold and prime real estate enticed even the most pious Presbyterians. Hannah Tiffany reported, "Many would like to go west, even Mr. Knox, but Mary would oppose it." Dred and Harriet Scott's lawyer Francis Murdoch left abruptly in 1849, leaving them temporarily without legal representation in their lawsuits for freedom.[25]

In early 1850 Reuben Knox set off by wagon train with his two oldest sons and two enslaved carpenters and their families, whom he hoped to free in Sacramento. A letter home to his wife in June 1850 sent "Love from all—black and white to all—All well." On their way through Fort Kearney to Fort Laramie the trail to the West was littered with buffalo hides and graves of those who died after bouts of vomiting and diarrhea. Knox sent his wagon train on and stopped to attend the stricken. Cholera, it turned out, could be anywhere in 1850. At Fort Laramie he met Kit Carson and in San Francisco found Pardon Dexter Tiffany, busy buying city lots, "entirely restored in mind and body. . . . He says if cousin Samuel [Knox] was here now he could . . . [be] realizing a fortune in speculation."[26] But there were also fatal dangers in the West. Having survived cholera and the Gold Rush trail to San Francisco and then freeing his enslaved cotravelers, Reuben practiced medicine and bought a large land grant, the Novato Ranch, north of Sausalito, but died in 1851 in a capsized sloop while crossing San Francisco Bay.

St. Louis was bulging at the seams, despite the California Gold Rush exodus and deaths from cholera. Old-line, native-born families were seeing their neighborhoods become more crowded and disease ridden, even before cholera arrived. The once-fashionable neighborhood of the central city that was home to the Kerrs, the Bateses, and most lawyers' offices, was plagued by raw sewage, bad drinking water, and yellow fever. The influx of seemingly rowdy immigrants unsettled the Northeasterners. Over the Fourth of July 1847 weekend, Grandmother Hannah Kerr wrote to her eldest daughter there was a "a day of great riot ushered in by the firing of cannon beatings of drums & I never did witness such a Sabbath before & hope we may never again . . . but . . . we are well & as happy as we are capable of being in this wilderness world."[27] By 1856, when both Kerr parents died, their once-fashionable house at Fourth and Franklin Streets was practically worthless. Son-in-law Dexter Tiffany was outraged when Samuel Knox rented it to Germans, who converted it into a theater and beer garden. The *Missouri Republican* opined that the inner city was "inundated" with "beer gardens, Swiss cheese, and sausage shops."[28]

A shift to more expansive and healthy neighborhoods in the suburbs had begun. Rents and land prices skyrocketed, and parcels ten miles from the city center that sold for $7 an acre twenty years earlier were $150 an acre by 1853. An observer, mixing commerce with a flight of fancy, said that the "gigantic expansion in values . . . was truly romantic."[29] Frank Blair sold his house in the center of town and moved two miles away to a ten-acre lot with a large house in Carondelet. The Henry Taylor Blows and Roswell Fields had property there as well. "I find it very delightful," Blair comments, "to spend the evenings in the country after the bustle & heat of business is over."[30]

Frank Blair and brother Montgomery arrived in St. Louis in 1842. The Blair brothers' father, Francis Preston Blair, was invested, psychologically and economically, in plantation slavery in Silver Spring, Maryland, but had raised his sons for professional careers and economic ventures in the West. Frank Blair attended the fledgling Transylvania University in Kentucky and joined Montgomery's law practice in St. Louis, while their older brother James became a high-ranking naval officer, assigned to the Pacific fleet.

The Blair family was obsessed with real estate. In 1851 correspondence with his brother James, who was on the Pacific Coast and purchasing lots in what would become downtown San Francisco, Frank suggested that if James loaned him the funds, he could invest them in St. Louis and together make them a tidy sum. Frank and a partner had purchased "a large lot in a business part of town, upon which we intend to build stores with the money we borrow from you." Even though his legal practice was booming, Frank was not enthused about the law, using his practice instead to discover clients who "have good title to land who are themselves not aware of it" and would therefore be "willing to sell for very little."[31]

Frank's newest scheme never materialized. James, recently retired from the US Navy, began a steamboat business on the Sacramento River in California in 1852, hoping to form a partnership with George Aspinwall, one of the richest transportation magnates in the Far West. In a tragedy that rocked the Blair family and was eerily like the fate of Reuben Knox, James drowned when his steamboat was upended in the Sacramento River in early 1854.

Montgomery went west to settle James's affairs, as Frank believed him to be "the better lawyer." Montgomery reported from San Francisco that James's estate totaled more than $58,000, enough to maintain his widow and children indefinitely.[32]

Whites were not the only ones to make money in real estate. Barber Bob Wilkinson, an African American, took his wife with him when he left for the West in 1850, opened a saloon, and returned to St. Louis with a substantial fortune he invested in property. Accomplished barber and free man James Thomas went to Kansas-Nebraska Territory, where he purchased lots and shares in towns in both Kansas and Iowa and then retreated to St. Louis in 1857 after being harassed by "pro-slavery ruffians." Thomas visited Chicago but agreed with St. Louisans who "dismissed Chicago as a place owned entirely by or heavily mortgaged to capitalist New York." He predicted that Chicago "could never surpass St. Louis in growth or even equal it." With his connections to the Catholic, mixed-race Clamorgans, Thomas opened a brokerage firm, leveraged his properties, and financed new endeavors on the assumption that St. Louis could only continue to prosper. He lived in a prominent house on Seventh Street and built and sold some of the first apartment buildings in St. Louis, trading rent for the labor of skilled workmen. By the census of 1870 he was the most well-to-do Black man in Missouri.[33]

The bet the New England lawyers made on making it big in St. Louis paid off. While not necessarily a precise accounting of their actual wealth, the US Census of 1850 lists Samuel Knox and Pardon Dexter Tiffany with real estate and personal property worth $100,000 each. By 1860 Tiffany's shaky St. Louis fortunes were in order. He had purchased land to the west of the St. Louis township in the 1840s that was now worth $150,000. He retained some of the acreage he hoped to sell to the city government for a public park and sold the rest to make a profit. "This is almost as good as California," he claims, "as I have not had to do a single thing to it."[34]

More of Pardon's real estate deals followed, but during the Panic of 1857 he describes "a war on the currency . . . begun here in earnest," with regional banks paying less than par on competing banknotes. He had trouble selling his railroad bonds, and with the arrival of the Panic of 1857, property and stockholders in St. Louis were in danger of losing everything. The prestigious banking firm of Bacon and Page went under, leaving many of its Northeastern clients in St. Louis in cascading bankruptcies. "The difficulty" in St. Louis, Pardon wrote to his wife, "is that the country is full of Illinois & Wisconsin Bank notes called currency which no man can use and which cannot be converted into specie at any price—so that in reality there is no money here." By 1858 he was on firmer footing, reporting that his tenants in St. Louis were paying their rents, and his yearly income was increasing.[35]

The Northeastern families who moved to St. Louis at midcentury maintained their connections in the East and felt ambivalent about living in the West. Summer weather in the East was healthier, the culture more familiar, and the region where they had extended family. They often returned to their Eastern homes and families. By the late 1840s the journey from St. Louis to Massachusetts could be completed in four or five days, thanks to a blossoming transportation system of steamboats, canals, railroad spurs, and stage coaches, although we can only imagine how difficult these journeys were for mothers transporting small children, boxes, and baggage. When he returned from California in 1852 Pardon dispatched his wife, Hannah, and their children to a magnificent home in Worcester, Massachusetts. He stayed in St. Louis to manage investments but unable to overcome what appears to have been chronic manic depression committed suicide in 1861.

The Eliots had close family in Quincy, Massachusetts, and Washington, DC. William Greenleaf Eliot's brother Thomas Dawes Eliot was a Massachusetts state senator and a delegate to the Free Soil convention in Worcester in 1855. The two brothers conferred on evolving Whig politics as they flirted with the Republicans. William was often invited to speak in the East, and after a trip to Europe, and in Boston in 1847, he seriously considered abandoning his church in St. Louis. But he went back to the West, seeing first his friend Wayman Crow and wrote, "Now that I am here, in this thriving city . . . I am content."[36]

As William Greenleaf Eliot settled in for good, the recently arrived lawyers were making their way in a chaotic and burgeoning St. Louis. Edward Bates, another Presbyterian, arrived in St. Louis with enslaved persons, emancipated them all between 1850 and 1860. Samuel Knox, Daniel Drake, Pardon Dexter Tiffany, and Roswell Field had offices within walking distance of the fine new Planter's House Hotel, the Court House—and the enslaved holding pens, one of them just across from the Second Presbyterian Church. St. Louis lawyers took up lawsuits for both Black plaintiffs and white defendants in the courts. Edward Bates represented six plaintiffs in the 1820s, and Francis Murdoch took twenty-two cases for enslaved persons' freedoms, including that of Harriet and Dred Scott, before leaving for California in 1849. Pardon Dexter Tiffany represented eleven slaveholder defendants trying to retain their property, and Samuel Knox and Roswell Field each took a small number of cases for both defendants and plaintiffs. Tiffany represented slaveowners seeking to prevent the liberation of their "property," while Francis Murdoch and Field mainly represented Black plaintiffs seeking freedom.[37]

The auction blocks and traders of the enslaved were becoming more odious to many whites in St. Louis. For a variety of motives—costs of maintaining the enslaved in an urban environment, sympathy with individuals they owned, antislavery sentiments, or their own growing distaste with the institution of slavery—some whites began freeing their human property through arrangements made in the courts. Some were allowing individual Black people to purchase their own freedom, as John Berry Meachum and Elizabeth Hobbs Keckley had done.

The artificial divide between the tasteful world of white Protestants and the horror of the public auction block was underscored by Galusha Anderson, who arrived in St. Louis in 1858 from New York State to pastor the Second Baptist Church and befriended fellow Baptist John Anderson of the Second African Baptist Church. Galusha Anderson wrote that his church was half a city square away from Lynch's Slave Pen, where runaways were held along with candidates for sale on the auction block. He was appalled by the proslavery Protestants in St. Louis, and the indifference of most nonslaveholders to the tragedies of "the peculiar institution." When Galusha hosted a visit from Eastern ministers in 1859, he took them first to the Eliot and Crow Mercantile Library to see fine works of art. "'Now,' I said, 'since we are always impressed by contrasts, let us go from tasteful rooms, books and art to Lynch's slave pen,'" and then on to a slave auction at Fifth and Myrtle Streets, where "the traffic in children seemed to be especially brisk and profitable."[38] Recently arrived immigrant Heinrich Boernstein dwelt on the same scenery: "German-Americans watched with horror as human beings such as themselves . . . were displayed for sale in the open air like cattle." They were especially offended when mothers were separated from their children, "never to see one another again in their life-times." According to Boernstein, the Germans' "disinclination to slavery grew into a grim hatred of this accursed institution and its friends and defenders."[39]

Hannah Skinner Kerr, despite her family's success in St. Louis, had long-lasting doubts about living in a slave state, doubts that reflected her Philadelphia heritage and Presbyterian antislavery piety. As she attempted to create a haven of Eastern gentility and moral refinement, she bemoaned life in Missouri: "The evils of these slave states are more and more apparent to my mind every day, they unfit men and women too, for usefulness in life."[40] The Kerrs began emancipating people they owned in the mid-1820s and by the time of the Kerrs' deaths in 1857 had released them all.

Thomas Hart Benton and his wife, Elizabeth, perhaps for attachments to particular individuals, emancipated Sarah in 1835 and forty-year-old Ralph Harrison in July 1843. Harrison was by then a leader of the AME Church in St. Louis. Thomas Benton described him as "a sober, honest, industrious and capable man."[41] In 1859 Sarah Bates, sister of Edward, on her deathbed at the age of eighty-six, "by one single deed, set free all her remaining slaves," thirty-two in number, "very good-looking," and worth about $20,000. "She has long wished to accomplish this," said her brother. "Her late severe sickness, and the thought of leaving her slaves to be held as property and to serve strangers after her death seemed to give her great distress. She talked of it painfully, sleeping and waking."[42]

Unitarian William Greenleaf Eliot considered slavery distasteful but decided early on not to preach abolitionism from the pulpit. He argued the slaveholders of the upper South, especially in the Commonwealth of Virginia, were tired of slavery and that prodding them with demonstrations and admonitions was counterproductive. In 1835 he condemned abolitionism as an expression of Massachusetts intolerance and mob rule: "I would make any degree of effort, to induce emancipators to be still. Their zeal is without knowledge; they know nothing of the true difficulties of the case, or they would not speak and act as they do." In 1836 he justified the lynching of a Black man in St. Louis because "the victim was 'obnoxious' and 'insolent' . . . probably a murderer and connected with abolitionists."[43] His stance in the 1840s was to propose gradual emancipation and colonization of the freed to Liberia or Central America. Most moderate antislavery white people in the United States held the same views, including Abraham Lincoln in next-door Illinois. Like most antislavery Germans, Eliot did not believe once slavery was ended that Black people should become citizens "all at once," rather, through education and training they would "grow into" citizenship.[44]

Eliot thought he was personally doing what he could to ameliorate slavery. As enslaved women, Lucy Delaney and Elizabeth Keckley had common enough experiences of beatings and sexual assault. Conscientious whites in St. Louis like Eliot knew about these kinds of incidents but felt powerless to prevent them except through moral persuasion. In the winter of 1840 he tried to stop the brutal beating of a "young mulatto woman tied up [at a] joist by her thumbs . . . stripped from her shoulders to her hips." She had refused to submit "to the wishes of her master." Eliot reported the crime, it was brought before a judge, and Eliot testified as a witness, but the verdict was "not guilty."[45] He tried to convince members of his congregation to emancipate their enslaved, and some did so. He noted in 1853 that his friend

Wayman Crow was going to free three house servants and hire them on as wage workers, but the St. Louis Circuit Court records do not list any Crow emancipations.[46]

Families like the Kerrs, the Eliots, the Crows, the Blairs, the Knoxes, and the Blows employed household servants and laborers to ease the toil of domestic life, and some owned or had owned Black people. The closest relationships between Black and white people before the Civil War did not take place in public but in the privacy of the home, where intimacy, rage, and sexual desire complicated household lives. Knotty questions of race crept into whites' homes even as they were purifying their moral positions on slavery.

Prosperous white families hoping to avoid the emotional complexities of race, and perhaps because they preferred to associate with whites, were moving away from the hiring of Black servants. In her late-in-age memoir of the Eliot family's first days in St. Louis, Abigail recalled, dismissively, "There were only colored servants and they were generally ignorant, but good natured." In an editorial he sent to the *Missouri Republican* in 1848, William argued that slavery was dying a natural death in St. Louis and that the employment of hired-out enslaved servants was both uneconomical and bad practice: "You may hire out a prime house servant (male) for one hundred and fifty dollars; a woman, very seldom, for more than seventy-five dollars per annum. This sounds well. But . . . servants hired out in this way soon become worthless and discontented. For this reason . . . a preference is given more every year, to white servants, even at a higher wage. In fact, our citizens are more than half from free States, and not knowing how to manage blacks, never employ them."[47]

In St. Louis Irish and German servants were the obvious alternative to Black household help. The Germans were often Protestants, and the women known for their housekeeping skills. Anthony Trollope, the British writer of novels and travelogues, who swept through St. Louis in late 1861, observes, "Slaves are not generally employed in St. Louis for domestic service, as is done almost universally in the towns of Kentucky. This work is chiefly in the hands of Irish and Germans."[48] The shortage of labor in general during the Civil War led to a dearth of servants for hire that created headaches for white housewives dealing with sick children, meals to cook, and dirty laundry to wash. In February 1864, Minerva Blow wrote to daughter Susan that she had at last found two servants to hire, even though the cook was deaf. One of the women had been recommended by Mrs. Taussig, and per the recommendations of her friend, Minerva "decided to employ Germans altogether."[49]

Although any number of rationalizations were made, the growing "distaste" for hiring Black people as servants in St. Louis was plain, whether employers hailed from free or slave states, made clear in the US Censuses of 1850 and 1860. By 1860 Henry and Minerva Blow had five children. He had made a considerable fortune as a "miner, smelter and manufacturer," and his family lived in fashionable Carondelet, their real estate valued at $200,000, their personal property another $200,000. But in both 1850 and 1860, the family's live-in servants were either Irish or French. Edward Bates had been gradually freeing his enslaved people for some time and in 1850 had four Irish servants in his large household of parents, adult children, and grandchildren. Martha Blow and her husband, Daniel Drake, whose real estate was valued at $30,000, had four children and three live-in Irish servants named Anne or Anna. Samuel Knox, who was recorded in the Springfield, Massachusetts, census of 1850, had two live-in Irish teenage servants, as did William Greenleaf Eliot's household in St. Louis.

Frank Blair was aware that continuing to own enslaved people in Missouri, if he wished to make progress in the new Republican Party, would not be looked upon favorably. He manumitted some, but in the Slave Schedule of the Census of 1850, he still possessed three people. Montgomery Blair owned real estate valued at $120,000 and employed three Irish servants in his home in St. Louis. Holding court in his Silver Spring plantation in Maryland, near Washington, DC, patriarch Francis P. Blair showed up with twenty slaves on the "Slave Schedule of 1850" and fifteen in 1860.

These same censuses showed that some free Black families in St. Louis had made remarkable, if limited progress. By 1850 Reverend Meachum owned two brick buildings in St. Louis and a farm in Illinois, and with his real personal property he was the third wealthiest Black person in Missouri. Griffin Brander moved from Cass Street downtown to a home to the Northwest he purchased on Warren Avenue in the suburb of Clayton in 1859. A more rural setting allowed him to keep his draft animals and wagons at hand and provide a pleasant life for his two daughters. Their descendants recalled that the daughters had friendly relationships with some of the German families who lived nearby.

The census of 1860 showed ninety-four Black property owners in St. Louis with an average holding of $4,560, putting them ahead of their counterparts in Baltimore, Maryland; Richmond, Virginia; and Wilmington, North Carolina. Bob Wilkinson, who had invested his California fortune in St. Louis real estate, had $20,000 worth of property. But, ominously, notes scholar Loren Schweninger, "In the midst of new restrictive laws, the proportion of free black property owners in the most lucrative occupations declined."[50] The preference of white employers for white domestic servants, carpenters, coopers, and bricklayers created ever-greater obstacles for Black people to make economic progress in the future.

Some whites were moving toward radical antislavery positions in the public sphere. Samuel Knox's connections to abolitionists in Massachusetts informed his growing commitment to what was characterized by conservatives as "Black Republicanism" in St. Louis. The Knox family was commuting to western Massachusetts for the summers, where Samuel maintained his family's ancestral farm in Blandford. He was much attached to his former law partner (and brother-in-law) Reuben Atwater Chapman, a legal mentor and abolitionist compatriot who lived in nearby Wilbraham, just outside Springfield, where he practiced law. The Congregational Church minister in Wilbraham was rumored to shelter Black runaways in his root cellar. Springfield, a Black resident reported, had a vibrant community of color, many of whose members had taken "French leave" from their masters and helped other runaways make their way to Canada. Samuel Knox bought a home in Wilbraham and then a grand home in Springfield, hoping to convince Mary's parents to leave St. Louis and come East.[51]

These plans were not realized. The lives of the Kerrs, Knoxes, and Fields illustrate how slim a grip even the most prosperous families in the nineteenth century had on their health and prosperity, making the turn to religious faith a near necessity for an explanation of the inexplicable. New baby Matthew Knox died in the summer of 1856, and Mary Knox's parents, Matthew and Hannah Kerr, the next year. Mary was exhausted and "had a cough," and the grand house in Springfield suffered a disastrous fire in 1860. Mary's cough was prophetic: she died of consumption at her sister Hannah's home in Worcester, Massachusetts, in 1863. Knox sold the property in Springfield, Massachusetts, and boarded his three older children at private schools in New England, a fate Mary had hoped to avoid. Her sister Elizabeth, now married to lawyer Irwin Z. Smith and with a child of her own, took in the two youngest Knox children, but she died of pneumonia in St. Louis in 1868, and the children were raised to adulthood by relatives in Boston.

The family of Knox's colleague Roswell Field faced similar tragedies. Field married in 1848 and sent his wife and their new baby to Vermont in the summer of 1851. When his wife, Frances, died at age thirty in 1856 of complications from another difficult childbirth, and the new baby died as well, Roswell sent his other children to live with his sister in Amherst, Massachusetts. Samuel and Roswell continued to practice law in St. Louis after the deaths of their wives. Neither man remarried, and both boarded for some years in downtown hotels.

Harriet and Dred Scott were contemplating their future and a new beginning. They approached lawyers from New England to bring what they viewed as a valid case before the Missouri courts and, when that failed, on to the

Supreme Court of the United States. Martha Blow Drake and her brothers Henry Taylor Blow and Taylor Blow would, evidently, view Dred Scott sentimentally as a childhood companion and help Dred and Harriet Scott out of bondage. Francis Murdoch, Roswell Field, and Montgomery Blow would argue the legal cases in St. Louis and Washington, DC, to secure the Scott family's freedom, and Samuel Knox's abolitionist connections in Springfield, Massachusetts, would lead to the arrangements that would make the Scotts free forever.

# 3 Redefining Citizenship from the Dred Scott Case to the Emancipation Proclamation

The New England lawyers began their practices in St. Louis in the 1840s, and they sometimes took on cases with enslaved and free Blacks as plaintiffs. Harriet and Dred Scott made use of these lawyers' services as they took their cases, soon joined as one in the Dred Scott suit, through the Missouri courts. The case was decided by the US Supreme Court in the spring of 1857 and quickly became a signifier of sectional conflict in the nation at large.[1] It was one in a string of events that began with the Missouri Compromise of 1820, bringing Maine into the Union as a free state and a year later Missouri as a slave state, continuing the balance of power in the geography of the United States and its evenly divided Senate.

Missouri was now a border state, on the edge of Southern slavery and Northern freedom, just east of a vast territorial expanse yet to be conquered by white Americans, a boundary Abraham Lincoln describes in his annual message to Congress on December 1, 1862, as the "the line along which the culture of corn and cotton meets." The Compromise of 1850 brought California into the Union as a free state and seemingly balanced the statehood of Texas in 1846. But a punitive Fugitive Slave Law in the Compromise did little to mollify Southern slaveholders' fears that abolitionist extremism was on the rise in the North and would eventually assault their "peculiar institution." Missouri became a template of the power struggle between North and South over the politics of westward expansion. As a self-described "gateway to the west," the citizens of St. Louis and the political elites of Missouri were caught up in this midcentury crisis of the nation.

On Missouri's western border, where the institution of slavery was the strongest in the state, Kansas, not yet a state, was usually assumed to be an extension of Missouri. And by 1850 the territory of Kansas-Nebraska was now the home of many Indigenous Native American tribes and groups resettled from homes in the old Southwest after the passage of the Indian Removal Act in 1830. White squatters were pouring into the territory and illegally occupying land belonging to the Kickapoo, the Peoria, and the Potawatomi. Native American sovereignty in Kansas was destroyed when many of a series of treaties were soon broken. Few white Americans were concerned about the destruction of Native American personhood and culture, but antislavery factions in the East were alarmed when the legacy of the Northwest Ordinance of 1787 and the Missouri Compromise of 1820 were compromised by the Kansas-Nebraska Act of 1854. Presented by Illinois' US Senator Stephen A. Douglas, the act made "popular sovereignty" federal policy in territories of the United States. The old dividing line between slavery and freedom could be overturned, its slaveholding realm extended west, if the residents who moved to the territories decided to make their new homes slave states.

The politics of the State of Missouri were in rapid transition as the 1854 legislation went into effect. The Whigs and the Know Nothings were in decline, the Republicans were about to form a new political party, the ascendency of the Democrats was in question, and the Missouri Supreme Court was dominated by slavery sympathizers. The most important leaders of the Democrats were an old hand, Thomas Hart Benton, and a much younger newcomer, Frank Blair. With his hot temper, red hair, and his prominent family's reputation, Blair quickly gained notoriety in St. Louis in the 1840s. Benton came to St. Louis from North Carolina in 1815, established a newspaper, and was one of Missouri's inaugural US Senators. He was a close ally of Democrat Andrew Jackson, elected President of the United States in 1828, and of Jackson's close friend, Francis Preston Blair, father of Francis (Frank) Preston Blair Jr. An ardent believer in "Indian Removal" and the "Manifest Destiny" of the United States to spread westward, Benton argued that slavery was not an objectionable institution where it already existed (he and the Blairs both owned enslaved persons) but that the extension of slavery dampened the economic prospects of whites. This was an appealing point of view for a wide swath of American voters, including German immigrants in Missouri, now naturalized and eager to vote. Nearly twenty-five hundred Germans in Missouri were naturalized in 1854 and 1855.

Benton and Frank Blair, pitching their message of "free labor, free soil, free men," both courted Irish and German immigrants in St. Louis, and Blair was elected to serve in the Missouri legislature in 1854 while Benton was still in the US Senate. A dilemma for both men was that while Germans in Missouri were eager to move westward and in favor of a Homestead Act, a significant element of the Forty-Eighters was ardently antislavery. Benton and Blair also had to patch over the divide between Irish Catholics and the anticlericalism of many Protestant Germans and deal with the intense nativism and anti-Catholicism of many residents of Missouri, some of them milling around in the Know Nothing Party in destructive mobs.

These were floating political coalitions that could easily be disrupted, and in the wake of the Kansas-Nebraska Act of 1854, the Benton and Blair machine fell apart. As the *Anzeiger des Westens*, the first German-language newspaper in St. Louis, editorializes, the "immediate abolition of slavery" was "neither possible nor advisable. . . . No one disturbs you in the possession of slaves, but remain where you are with them." The question for most Germans, promoters of the Homestead Act and the settlement of Kansas and Nebraska by freeholding whites, "was who should own the new lands: white workingmen, mechanics, operatives and small farmers, or a few rich aristocratic owners of slaves."[2] Benton lost his Senate seat in 1851 and his seat in the House of Representatives in 1855, perhaps due to his vote for the Kansas-Nebraska Act. By 1856, when the Republicans emerged in the national election with John C. Fremont as their candidate for president, Benton's contradictory positions were no longer viable. But by switching his allegiance from the Democrats to the Republicans, Blair continued to thrive as a US congressman, where his chief goal was to promote the "colonization" of Black Americans outside the United States.

By 1854 the turmoil in Kansas reached drastic proportions. Some slaveholders in Missouri crossed the border to fight antislavery forces to protect what they saw as a buffer to prevent runaways from leaving Missouri. Missouri speculators bought cheap real estate in Kansas and Nebraska with the hope that it would accumulate in value once statehood arrived. Among them were African Americans James Thomas, who bought land in Kansas but left the state for St. Louis when he encountered "pro-slavery ruffians," and Griffin Brander, who bought three lots in Prairie City, Nebraska, for $15 and paid taxes on them until 1862. The Topeka Constitution of 1855 claimed Kansas as a free state, but the "Bleeding Kansas" wars continued for several years, seeming to predict what a real civil war in the United States might entail. Supported by both Samuel Knox and his brother-in-law Reuben Atwater Chapman, the New England Emigrant Aid Society sponsored "Free-Staters" moving west to Kansas and allegedly sent Sharps' rifles along with them. The most famous of these migrants was John Brown, who in response to a raid on the antislavery city of Lawrence, Kansas, laid siege to citizens of Pottawattamie Creek, killing five of them in what became known as the Pottawattamie massacre. William Greenleaf Eliot was harshly critical of the New Englanders' sending rifles to Kansas and noted in his diary that the Emigrant Aid Society "is but piece and parcel of the unwise, ill-tempered, unfraternal antislavery movement . . . that . . . has brought this country to the verge of civil war."[3]

Harriet and Dred Scott had the misfortune to launch and then lose their case in the federal courts in 1857, just as these kinds of no-holds-barred confrontations were taking place from the local to the national level. Discussions of popular sovereignty and the Dred Scott case in the Lincoln-Douglas debates of 1858 alerted the American public to what might await the nation if Douglas, a Democratic and popular sovereignty advocate, was elected to the US Senate by the Illinois legislature (as he was) or in 1860 if he was elected to the presidency (which he lost to Abraham Lincoln) in the popular vote and the electoral college. Dred Scott, the State of Missouri, and Kansas-Nebraska were now the focus of the nation's most prominent headlines. In his June 16, 1858, House Divided speech, Abraham Lincoln warned that slavery might be made lawful in every state if the Dred Scott decision was followed to its logical conclusion: "We shall *lie down* pleasantly dreaming that the people of *Missouri* are on the verge of making their state *free*; and we shall *awake* to the *reality*, instead, that the *Supreme* Court has made *Illinois* a *slave* State."[4] Lincoln's most important campaign oration, delivered at Cooper Union in New York City on February 27, 1860, underscored how serious a threat to the nation the decision was: "Wrong as we think slavery is, we can yet afford to let it alone where it is, . . . but can we, while our votes will prevent it, allow it to spread into National Territories, and to overrun us here in these Free States?"[5]

Dred Scott was a young enslaved man who in 1830 was transported with the Peter Blow family to St. Louis from Virginia via a failing Alabama farm. He was sold to army surgeon John Emerson to settle family debt in 1833, and Emerson took Dred to Fort Armstrong in the state of Illinois and then to Fort Snelling in a US territory that later became Minnesota. Dred met Harriet Robinson there, and they set up household in a modest, private dwelling unusually comfortable for enslaved families at the time. Emerson was transferred to Louisiana but in 1840 left his wife, Irene, and the Scotts in St. Louis, where Dred was "hired out," and Harriet managed the family at home while working as a laundress.

Irene inherited Dred when John died in 1843 and continued to hire Dred out in St. Louis. (White widows often counted on the wages of enslaved hired-out persons to supplement meager incomes.) Irene left Missouri when she married Calvin Chafee in 1850 and went to Massachusetts, putting her brother John F. A. Sanford (misspelled in the lawsuit as Sandford) in charge of the Scotts. Sanford, who had worked for the Chouteaus' American Fur Company, married Pierre Choteau's Emily, and after her death he remained closely allied with her family. This connection may partly explain his resistance to the Scotts' freedom as the powerful Chouteaus frowned on manumissions argued in the courts.[6]

With no success in purchasing their freedom from Irene Emerson, Dred and Harriet Scott filed their first cases for freedom together in 1846, on the beginning of a long procedure that would engage several lawyers. These early legal initiatives were funded by siblings of the Blow family, Taylor, Martha, and Henry. The Scotts attended the Second African Baptist Church, pastored by John Anderson, where they may have learned of Francis Murdoch, the lawyer who took their cases into the St. Louis courts in 1846, where the suits languished for a few years on a technicality. Murdoch left for California in 1849, and the cholera epidemic and the great fire of the same year in St. Louis suspended most legal activity. The Scotts' search for a new lawyer took them to the office of Roswell Field, where Dred may have worked as a porter.

The Scotts were not alone in thinking that having lived in the Northwest Territories they should no longer be enslaved. The proximity of Missouri to Illinois and Ohio meant that enslaved people could escape to freedom or, as had the Scotts, be deemed free if taken to the Northwest Territories by their masters. In addition to the rarely used and difficult tactic of proving abusive treatment, time spent in free states and territories had been grounds for emancipation from a master in Missouri and used in court with some success. Several enslaved women filed law suits in St. Louis beginning as early as the 1820s. Rachel, also from Fort Snelling, sued for her freedom in 1836 and won her case. The successful argument rested on the premise that the enslaved "became entitled to their freedom as a result of an extended stay on free-soil—even if they later returned to a jurisdiction where slavery was permitted. . . . Once free, always free."[7]

Roswell Field filed new briefs on behalf of both Harriett and Dred Scott, suing John Sanford for their freedom. Their depositions were taken in the office of Charles Daniel Drake, the husband of Martha Blow. As the case evolved, Harriet's case and those of their daughters were attached to Dred's, although legal scholars agree that Harriet had the greater expectation of a successful suit, and their older daughter, Eliza, an even stronger one, as she was born on a steamboat in the Mississippi River in free territory en route to St. Louis. When the decision denying the Scotts their freedom was rendered in the State Supreme Court of Missouri, Field asked Montgomery Blair, recently returned from settling his brother James's estate in California, to take it before the US Supreme Court.

In a January 7, 1855, letter to Montgomery Blair, Field explained how he strategized the case and how easily he grasped its consequences for the political questions of the 1850s. Field served papers on Sanford, who regularly lived in New York, when Sanford was in Missouri on business. Field's idea was to argue that "as a citizen of Missouri," Dred could sue Sanford as "a citizen of New York." Sanford and his attorney, Hugh Garland (the owner of Elizabeth Keckley and her son), appeared before the Missouri Supreme Court, anticipated US Supreme Court Chief Justice Roger B. Taney's later formulation, and claimed that Dred was not a citizen "*because* he was a negro of African descent."[8] Missouri Supreme Court Justice Robert B. Wells dismissed that theory, which for Field opened a door to a legal strategy that might hold up in the Supreme Court of the United States. Field laid out his premise:

> Supposing Dred had any capacity to sue in the United States Court, the proceeding is perfectly regular. If in fact . . . a black man may sue his master in the Federal court, the right of a *trial by jury* is still left to the slave in an action at common law which if brought in the Federal courts may be enforced in the judgement through the Union. And this jurisdiction, if it exists at all, exists by force of the constitution that no act of congress can impair.

There were, Field also said, likely to be serious consequences to this kind of ruling. If enslaved people had standing as citizens to sue their masters in court, the premise of the "Fugitive Slave Law would undoubtedly become of little value, and this may probably be a strong argument against allowing black men to sue as citizens."[9]

If Dred Scott had standing as a citizen to sue his owners, the question of whether he was free by reason of living in a free state remained. "The American cases," Field contended, "are nearly uniform in holding that a removal of a slave by his master into a free state makes him free forever."[10] The Northwest Ordinance of 1787 outlawed slavery in new northern territories and had been reaffirmed by the Missouri Compromise of 1820. But the Missouri State Supreme Court, now dominated by proslavery justices, was moving toward rulings that hinted both the Northwest Ordinance and the Missouri Compromise were unconstitutional.

Five US Supreme Court justices supported Sanford's claim and two dissented in their decision of March 6, 1857. Benjamin Robbins Curtis of Massachusetts, who, like Samuel Knox and Pardon Dexter Tiffany, attended Harvard Law School and was a student of Joseph Story, offered a powerful dissenting opinion. Curtis was adamant that birth in the United States was linked to citizenship, and, therefore, Dred and Harriet and their children were unequivocally US citizens. Curtis did not say that being citizens meant that persons of color were entitled to civil rights and full equality under the law.[11]

Although most of the concurring justices ruled on the technical grounds of residence in a free state or territory to deny the Scotts their freedom, Chief Justice Taney, in his separate concurrence opinion, honed in on the central question that Field raised in his correspondence with Montgomery Blair. Taney of Maryland, an old ally of Andrew Jackson and a close friend of Francis Preston Blair Sr., was deeply committed to keeping Black Americans outside of the polity. Taney took the most extreme position possible: that the Northwest Ordinance and the Missouri Compromise were unconstitutional because they denied slaveholders due process and their property rights and, in a shocking pronouncement, said that persons of African descent had no rights to citizenship in the United States. When the Constitution was written, Black persons "had for more than a century before been regarded as beings of an inferior order, and altogether unfit to associate with the white race, either in social or political relationships; and so far inferior, that they had no rights which the white man was bound to respect."[12]

The Scott family's freedom was about to be won outside the province of the law. Sanford died in an insane asylum a few weeks after the US Supreme Court's decision. Emerson's widow, Irene, was now the wife of Calvin Chafee of Massachusetts, and holding the Scotts in bondage was an embarrassment for abolitionist Chafee. When the Springfield, Massachusetts, newspapers highlighted the Chafees' ownership of the Scotts, Samuel Knox's brother-in-law Reuben Atwater Chapman, a future Massachusetts Superior Court Justice, helped the Chafees draw up a quit claim transferring the ownership of the Scotts to Taylor Blow in St. Louis. (Irene Emerson Chafee refused to agree to the transfer until she was paid the back wages Dred and Harriet had earned as hired-out enslaved people, and she was awarded about $700 in the St. Louis courts.) Taylor Blow, recently recovered from a case of excessive drinking and converted to Catholicism, was evidently sympathetic to a man who had been his boyhood companion.[13]

With Chapman's help, Taylor Blow manumitted Dred Scott on May 26, 1857. Dred was nearly sixty when the decision was rendered, having lived longer than the average male enslaved person. Slim and about five and a half feet tall, he was said never to be a very sturdy person and was picking up jobs around St. Louis as a porter at hotels and offices. Roswell Field secured Dred a job at the Barnum Hotel, where he became a local celebrity. Dred died in 1858, leaving Harriet and her daughters on their own. Taylor Blow arranged for Dred's burial at Wesleyan Cemetery in St. Louis and when Wesleyan was closed, moved Scott's remains to the Catholic Calvary Cemetery, which permitted the interment of owners' enslaved persons. Harriet is said to have died in 1876 and was buried in a new African American Greenwood Cemetery in Hillsdale, a St. Louis suburb.

Samuel Knox and Reuben Atwater Chapman were closely allied in their stern religious and, by now, abolitionist views. Chapman had been John Brown's lawyer when Brown lived in Springfield, Massachusetts, between 1846 and 1849. Chapman renewed his acquaintance with the fiery radical when Brown returned to Springfield in 1851 to organize Black community resistance to the enforcement of the Fugitive Slave Act. As a federal marshal, Chapman was required to seize fugitives and return them to their owners but announced that he would refuse to do so. He helped organize the Emigrant Aid Society in 1854 to bring New Englanders and their rifles to Kansas in the wake of the Kansas-Nebraska Act of 1854 and the Democratic Party's endorsement of "popular sovereignty." When Brown faced the gallows for inciting a slave revolt at Harpers Ferry (now in West Virginia), in 1859, he wrote to his former attorney and asked him to come to Virginia. Chapman sent his sympathies but did not go south. Many years later, Samuel Knox's daughter Hannah could recall her father pacing the floor the night before the morning of Brown's execution.[14]

John Brown's raid, his execution by the Commonwealth of Virginia, and the new notoriety of the Scott family were dramatic narratives that seized the nation's imagination at the end of the 1850s. The front page in *Frank Leslie's Illustrated Weekly* features an interview with the Scotts at home in St. Louis, describing Harriet at the ironing board, pursuing her trade as a laundress. Photographs from a St. Louis gallery were duplicated on the front page in engravings, the piece highlighting the images of Dred, Harriet, and their daughters, the women dressed modestly in respectable middle-class clothing, and Dred in a suit jacket, white shirt, and bowed tie. While the text uses racist language and is condescending, the illustrations present another view: Americans with very dark skin looking like counterparts of a proper white family anywhere in the United States.[15] The new realism of the illustrated weeklies *Harper's* and *Frank Leslie's* would soon transform reporting from the front lines of the Civil War.

Roswell Field played a major role in the Dred Scott case and sided with the Unionists when the Civil War began. His Republican colleague Samuel Knox was doing what he could to further the Congregationalist and Presbyterian gospel that slavery was a sin and required a national reckoning. The New Light Presbyterians in the Kerr and Knox congregation hired Truman Post from the East in 1847 and changed the church's name and affiliation to the

First Trinitarian Congregationalist Church, allying them more closely with the doctrine preached at William Greenleaf Eliot's Church of the Messiah.

Much to the annoyance of Eliot, Samuel Knox joined the radical antislavery political faction in both Massachusetts and St. Louis, the faction dismissed by moderate Republicans and Democrats as "Charcoals" or "Black Republicans," and used his eloquent oratory to rouse others to the cause, as his disdainful brother-in-law Pardon Dexter Tiffany reported to his wife in the spring of 1858:

> The election is approaching and the people are getting quite warm. Sam'l Knox went to a political meeting and made a speech for the Black republicans and I send you the enclosed notice in which the opposing paper speaks of him . . . but I think he is about as fond of being abused in the papers as he is of abasing others. He may take pleasure in such things. He told a man today that he intended to speak every night if they asked him.[16]

Knox's public stance, which echoed William Lloyd Garrison's and Frederick Douglass's demand for the immediate abolition of slavery, was countered by Eliot's moderate, and more popular, position that gradual emancipation would be the best public policy. A Congregationalist in public and in personal practice a Unitarian, William Greenleaf Eliot was the most influential and popular Protestant minister in St. Louis. But he thought radical reform hindered the common good and developed elaborate self-justifications for his public silence on slavery.

His economic interests and stature in the community may have helped determine his position. Wealthy businessmen, slaveholding families, and political conservatives attended his church and viewed the antislavery views of Knox, Field, and New Englanders like Chapman as extreme. Eliot's elaborate Gothic-style Church of the Messiah, built at a cost of $105,000 with a $5,000 organ from Boston, was dedicated in 1851. Paying off the debt was a decades-long project, requiring the renting of pews, the sale of his sermons in book form, and frequent guest preaching in other pulpits.

"Go slowly" was his constant message. In 1849 he encouraged Senator Benton to introduce a bill "providing for the gradual emancipation of our slaves, say in a course of ten, twenty, or thirty years, upon some system which would protect the interests of all parties as far as possible. . . . I believe that all great changes in the social system, to be well made, must be gradual."[17] He would not abandon this position until the beginning of the Civil War.

Probably under pressure from some of his congregants to "say something" in light of the Dred Scott decision in 1857 and the increasingly abolitionist position of Unitarians in New England, Eliot delivered his sermon "Social

Reform." He had recently withdrawn from the Western Conference of Unitarian Churches over a proposed referendum condemning slavery. The pulpit, he said, was not the place to discuss controversial topics. Parishioners come to services "already weary of strife, and desirous of hearing words of peace and rest; to retreat from newspaper warfare and congressional harangues. . . . We must behave *under the laws of the land*, to do our own humble part to increase the sum of happiness. . . . In a large and prosperous society such as this, in a city so wonderfully active, and growing so fast . . . there is enough to do."[18]

Eliot's position, for different reasons, was echoed by other factions in Missouri, factions that did not view slavery as a matter of morality but in economic and practical political terms. As the slavery expansionist Democrats floundered and the Whigs collapsed, prominent white men, once Whigs or Democrats, furthered their political careers with new political affiliations that hinted at a conservative antislavery position based on "free labor." By the mid-1850s they were trying on the label Free Democrats and leaving behind the Know Nothings and Nativists, who had condemned the immigrants these future Republicans relied upon for their growing power in Missouri and in the nation.

Edward Bates, one of the prominent founders of the state of Missouri in 1821, left the Whigs and was briefly a Know Nothing but then saw both a moral principle and a main chance in the new Republican Party, as did Henry Taylor Blow, now a well-to-do miner of lead and manufacturer of lead-based products. Blow began his terms in the Missouri State Senate from 1854 to 1858 as a Whig but changed his party to Republican and represented Missouri at the Republican Chicago Convention in 1860, which nominated Abraham Lincoln. But none were more crucial converts to the new party than the Blairs: Francis Preston, Montgomery, and Frank. Frank Blair was elected to the Missouri House of Representatives from 1852 to 1856 and a term in the US House of Representatives in 1857. Lincoln met with him in Springfield, Illinois, in 1857, approved of the dashing redhead, and began a partnership with the Blair family that would lay the groundwork for Lincoln's journey to the White House.[19]

The Blairs held considerable sway in politics with their powerful presence as Democrats in Maryland, Washington, DC, and Missouri. They were perhaps the most influential political family in the nation, with ties to the legacy of Andrew Jackson and his Missouri protégé Senator Benton. Benton did not win reelection in 1856, a blow to Missouri and Illinois Democrats like Stephen Douglas who supported "popular sovereignty" in Kansas and Nebraska. Bates and the Blairs could see that the Democratic Party was in crisis and that the promotion of what they described as "free soil, free labor, free men" was a more viable path to their political future.[20]

Free Soil advocates opposed the westward expansion of slavery made possible by the Kansas-Nebraska Act. In their Address to the Democracy of Missouri, Frank Blair and Montgomery Blair argued that slavery should be allowed to remain where it already was but not extended into new territories that were bound to become states. Slavery was not, as abolitionists claimed, a moral or religious question but an economic and political one: "Domestic slavery is pernicious. . . . It retards the growth and prosperity of communities . . . to say nothing of the aristocratic tendencies and degradation which it attaches to labor." Slavery was, above all, a hindrance to the future of white laborers in what should be an ever-expanding nation of equal opportunity for whites, including white immigrants.[21] Frank Blair saw the gain to be made by promoting Free Soil at political rallies, and he quickly became a favorite of German and Irish immigrants in St. Louis. The Kansas-Nebraska Act of 1854 was the tipping point that pushed many Germans in Missouri over the edge of their tolerance for any new policies that would hinder their economic prospects west of Missouri and toward an antislavery posture.[22]

Frank Blair laid out his family's position with sweeping policies that would solve the slavery question, extend US influence throughout the Americas, and—of, perhaps, the most emotional concern to the Blairs—prevent further race mixing in the United States. Frank Blair delivered an address to the US Congress in 1858 that argued for acquiring territories in Central and South America, sending emancipated Black citizens there, and then holding these regions as a "Dependency of the United States."[23] The promoters of a Honduran Inter-Oceanic Railway had just distributed a prospectus to all US senators in hopes that federal funding would be granted for the building of a route across Honduras from the Atlantic Ocean to the Pacific Ocean, providing another route to the goldfields of California.[24] William Walker's insurgency in Nicaragua and other "filibuster" adventures in Central America fueled expansionist dreams of penetrating the small and, to American observers, disorganized countries of the region.

As Frank Blair acknowledged, many of those interested in Walker's filibustering style of expansion were seeking to extend slavery but claimed the Blair plan would accomplish the opposite. While some might think the task of transporting so many people to another region impossible, he pointed to the example of several millions of immigrants who had come to the United States from Ireland, Britain, and Europe in a staggering mobilization of capital and transportation. Why not send formerly enslaved people to an even less faraway destination, to South America or to the Caribbean?

The Blairs viewed colonization as a critical piece of any gradual emancipation policy, linking it to racial purity in the United States. Whites in both the new Republican Party and the old Democrats condemned the moral crime of amalgamation. Douglas attacked Lincoln in the Illinois Senate debates over his seeming leniency on social integration of the races and the sexual race mixing that might result. Lincoln responded, saying in 1858 that "a separation of the races is the only perfect preventive of amalgamation," and, with a reference to his negative position on popular sovereignty, commented, "If white and black people never get together in Kansas they will never mix blood in Kansas." But, he added, "Separation, if ever effected at all, must be effected by colonization."[25]

Wherever and whenever Black activists and their white allies tried to move African American rights forward, they encountered the sexual component of the national discourse about race, epitomized in the term used here by Lincoln, "amalgamation." This existential question towered over American politics and sectional conflict and would persist well into the twentieth century.[26] The ending of Reconstruction, the Jim Crow decades, and the segregation battles of the 1950s were all influenced by paranoia of what would be dubbed "miscegenation" in 1864. The long-lasting presence of these ideas should warn us that they never lost staying power among certain groups of white Americans and that the Blairs represented a significant sector of the electorate in the nineteenth century.

Even as narratives of the enslaved and abolitionist speeches depicted and decried the sexual assault of Black women, prominent whites in social reform movements and national politics in the 1850s assumed that intermarriage or sexual relations between Black people and white people should be avoided, perhaps forbidden. The Blairs were adamant about their solution to this problem: deport Black Americans, with fabulous predictions of what deportation would accomplish. In a speech at Cooper Union in New York City in early 1860, Frank Blair resummarized his position. Slavery would "work out its destiny by degrees, under the shield of the Constitution, the negro [*sic*] race receding before the skill, economy, and self-impelling power, of free labor" in the United States. A new kind of racial imperialism would foster a rebirth of vigor in the lackluster southern Americas. Somehow the "colored people of this continent" would "carry freedom" to the tropics, "where the white race languishes through successive generations, passing into mongrels and utter decay."[27]

Lincoln promoted colonization in his State of the Union addresses in 1861 and 1862. The House Committee on Emancipation and Colonization, headed by Representative Frank Blair, recommended in July 1862 that Congress allocate the incredible sum of $20 million to deport formerly enslaved people and begin compensating slaveholders for their lost property. That same year Congress authorized $60,000 for colonization projects, still a very large amount in the federal budget at mid-nineteenth century.

The importance of the Blairs' decision—as it turned out temporary—to leave the Democrats and to throw in their lot with the new Republican Party cannot be overemphasized. Lincoln, arguably, would not have been nominated, elected president, or maintained the Union in his first administration without their help. The Blairs were key spokesmen for the border states, states that had to be placated lest they leave the Union and join a secessionist confederacy. Lincoln made the Blairs prime movers in his first administration.[28] Francis Preston Blair, ensconced in Blair house in Lafayette Square, could stroll to the White House and give advice to Lincoln, whether he wanted it or not. Frank Blair was down the Washington Mall at the Congress of the United States. Montgomery Blair was in the cabinet as postmaster general. The Blairs' ultimate disappointment in Lincoln as he grew into the presidency and moved toward the Radical Republicans would leave the Blairs embittered and ferocious in their tirades against Republican "tyranny." It would not take them long to return to the Democratic Party but still holding the position that the Union should be preserved.

With the help of the Blairs, Lincoln was elected President of the United States in November 1860, as talk of secession in the South was already underway. Newly freed dressmaker Elizabeth Hobbs Keckley from Saint Louis heard secessionist talk in the highest of circles. After enrolling her son, George, at abolitionist-founded Wilberforce College in Ohio, Keckley went to Baltimore to teach young "colored women" the art of dressmaking—as well as illicit reading lessons—but could not earn enough money to sustain herself. She moved to Washington, DC, in mid-1860, where she relied on referrals from old St. Louis clients to open a thriving business and design elaborate dresses for the wives of prominent politicians in the nation's capital. Often at the home of Varina and Jefferson Davis, US Senator and future President of the Confederate States of America, Keckley recalled that "the prospects of war were freely discussed in my presence."[29]

Mrs. Davis urged her to come South when the Davis family left Washington in early 1861, but Keckley refused and was hired by Mary Todd Lincoln, who wore a Keckley-designed dress to Lincoln's inauguration. Keckley was an intimate member of the Lincoln household in the White House, where she witnessed the death of the Lincolns' son Willie, the despair of the president in the early years of the war, and the aftermath of Lincoln's assassination.

In St. Louis, where Keckley purchased her family's freedom, Black leaders positioned themselves for a pivotal conflict that might end slavery. Moses Dickson, founder of the secret insurrectionist Knights of Liberty, changed his strategic plan as abolitionist sentiment grew and Civil War was imminent. He tried to dissuade John Brown from launching the Harpers Ferry raid in 1859 and disbanded the Knights and the idea of Black revolution, urging its members to join the Union Army as cooks, teamsters, and servants to white officers.[30] James Milton Turner, who as a boy attended Reverend John Berry Meachum's Mississippi River steamboat school, enrolled in antislavery Oberlin College for a semester, returned to St. Louis to support his family, and joined the Union Army as a body servant for a white officer. Many of the ex-Knights, Dickson included, would enlist in the Union Army as soon as Colored Troop regiments were formed.

Prominent white families in St. Louis also saw the possibility of war on the horizon. William Greenleaf Eliot, trying to convince himself that conflict could be avoided, said that though "political affairs at the South look badly . . . the noise will end in a sputter. South Carolina and Massachusetts are the mischief makers." Pardon Dexter Tiffany, who several times represented slaveowners in civil suits attempting to reclaim their "property," wrote to his wife, Hannah, in Worcester, Massachusetts, that "the people of the East have no idea of the magnitude . . . of this revolution and the real fear and terror . . . it inspires. . . . I confess I see but little chance to save the Union & what the horrors of a dissolution may be no man can tell—There must be some concession by the north or there will be a terrible time for the whole country."[31]

Henry Taylor Blow and his wife, Minerva, were steadfast Unionists from the beginning. Henry visited Lincoln in October and told Minerva that "he was delighted with [Lincoln] and thinks him one of the purest men living." Henry wrote to his children in November 1860 that he had an abiding faith in that "love of liberty that banded the original states into a brotherhood and united them under a 'constitution' *so glorious*, that . . . it must *endure*. . . . Remember my children that every part of this glorious Union is *our heritage*." In December Minerva ruefully observed, "Friends are divided in every sentiment, and even relations are estranged."[32]

By January 1861 a confederacy of secessionist states was underway, following the lead of South Carolina in December, and in February, a rebel government formed. Minerva Blow saw her social world, centered in the Presbyterian Church, collapse. Although she thought Union sentiment was strong, "many despise the Republicans. This party you know does not embrace many of our circle. . . . We are compelled to listen to many absurd reproaching things said by them." Henry Blow defied the critics by flying an American flag on top of his house. When Jessie Benton Fremont arrived in St. Louis in July with her famous husband, General John C. Fremont, she would say that "to be with the North and for Freedom" was "unfashionable."[33]

With Fremont's inspiring command of the Upper Mississippi before him, William Greenleaf Eliot, with much agonizing in his journal, finally took a firm public position on the preservation of the Union. His "Loyalty and Religion" sermon delivered on August 17 addresses the "struggle to determine whether we shall remain in the Union or go out of it." "My convictions are too strong to be repressed," he announced, "and the only thing left for individuals to do is to choose on which side they will stand." He had attempted to create a church that was "intertwined with the prosperity of St. Louis" and listed in detail all the good the Church of the Messiah had done "in various works of benevolence and charity, not less than the sum of $50,000 annually." He knew he would alienate some and put his church in jeopardy. But "the love of country, loyalty, patriotism, is the foundation of all social virtues, the corner stone on which society is built. . . . It stands next to religion; and the man who betrays his country can hardly be true to his God."[34] He did not mention slavery.

There were consequences for William to his Unionist stance. Some church members walked out before he finished his sermon, and he lost the donations of Southern sympathizers. Prominent St. Louis citizen and Eliot family physician Dr. William Carr abandoned the church, as did other "secesh" proponents. William cut back on the church's expenses and his own salary and lowered the rate of pew rentals. He was able to use his St. Louis political connections to continue his "Nigrita" school for Black children in the church basement but white Methodists, Baptists, and Presbyterians were splitting into Northern and Southern factions with slavery at the heart of their differences.

Lincoln took office in March in a dissolving nation. The loyalty of the remaining border states—Missouri, Kentucky, and Maryland—was of preeminent concern, and the secession of Virginia in April was a terrible blow. To further his moderate, and often Blair-driven, goals, Lincoln urged the border states in March 1862 to enact gradual, compensated emancipation bills. Congress passed the District of Columbia Compensated Emancipation Act in April 1862 and ended slavery in the nation's capital. Loyal slaveholders were to receive $300 for every enslaved person they held in bondage, and those who were freed were offered $100 if they would leave the United States and join Black colonies in Haiti or Liberia. These incentive carrots had little success with either slaveholders or enslaved people. But this was the Blair plan: gradual emancipation, compensation, and colonization.

The military organization of pro-Union and prosecession factions began in the spring of 1861 in the border states. Frank Blair was an early and vociferous proponent of raising pro-Union militias to secure St. Louis and Missouri for the Union, and hundreds of Irish and Germans in Missouri would join the Union forces. Blair was named a colonel of the First Missouri Volunteer Infantry, later to be the First Missouri Light Artillery Regiment of the US Army. The governor of Missouri, Claiborne Jackson, sympathized with the secessionists and Jefferson Davis, who was plotting to send troops from Baton Rouge, Louisiana, up the Mississippi River to take the federal arsenal at Liberty, Missouri, on the outskirts of St. Louis.

The federal arsenal at Liberty, now dubbed Fort Jackson, was the second largest in the United States, "the arms depot of the nation's western empire," furnishing the US Army with supplies used to decimate Native American peoples of the West.[35] Fresh from these "Indian Wars," General Nathaniel Lyon, with the help of volunteer rank-and-file troops, many of them German, seized Fort Jackson and secured the federal arsenal on May 10, 1861. General Fremont, recently returned from his triumphs in California, was named Commander of the Department of the West by Lincoln and arrived in St. Louis in late July.

On August 4, 1861, Fremont declared martial law in Missouri. His quixotic and imperious style led to charges by his critics that he was autocratic and corrupt. General Lyon was at that moment trying to defeat Confederate militias west of St. Louis. Probably passing for white, Keckley's son, George Kirkland, who had taken the last name of his white father and his mother's rapist Alexander Kirkland, enlisted in Lyon's regiment, and both Lyon and George Kirkland were killed at the Battle of Wilson Creek on August 10, a victory for secessionist sympathizers that gave them control of Springfield, Missouri, and most of the state's southwest. But the federal arsenal was secured, and Ulysses S. Grant put in charge of pushing Union control down the Mississippi, a plan that would ultimately lead to a critical Union victory at Vicksburg, Mississippi, in the summer of 1863. The arrival of martial law with protection for Black citizens in St. Louis meant that free Blacks could storm the courthouse to obtain business licenses and post bond to secure papers authenticating their free status. Eliza Scott, daughter of Harriet and Dred, was eighteen in April 1861 and applied for her papers, as did drayman Griffin Brander.[36]

Frank Blair, who had firm ideas about what should be done militarily and in part because he saw the crisis in Missouri as a way to further his own political and military career, opposed the appointment of Fremont and attacked his style of command immediately, sending his "evidence" of abuse of power directly to President Lincoln. Blair had not foreseen that Fremont's popularity in a wide swath of the German antislavery factions would lead to widespread criticism of Blair's leadership among the Free Democracy Democrats. The Blair family's resentment increased to white-hot anger as Fremont arrested, briefly, Frank. Blair was trying, in the chaos of the early Civil War, to hold on to both his position in Congress and his military appointment.

Fremont was trying to manage the growing numbers of Black people fleeing slavery and seeking protection behind Union lines. Estimates of these new arrivals in St. Louis, many of whom were white refugees, varied between thirty thousand to fifty thousand people. A similar migration was taking place on the outskirts of Washington, DC, where escapees from Virginia and Maryland were voting with their feet to leave slavery. The hard proof of this migration was reflected in the St. Louis census figures. The African American population grew by 600 percent between 1860 and 1870 but was still not enough of an increase to compete with the Irish, the Germans, and the whites who abandoned the South and left for St. Louis.[37]

Something had to be done with the Black families flocking to Union Army camps. Officially, they were contraband, meaning they were property of the enemy that could be seized during times of war. Men were put to work building military installations and assisting army regiments with trenches and battle fortifications. Although contraband women were not considered as desirable as the men, some found work as laundresses and cooks. But Fremont was going much further in his martial law proclamation (known as the Fremont Proclamation) of August 30, 1861. Citizens who took up arms against the Union Army were now subject to court-martial and their property to confiscation. Rather than designating property held in enslaved people as contraband, Fremont declared that all enslaved people of disloyal owners in states that had seceded were to be emancipated immediately, with no mention of compensation. Ironically, Missouri, a border state that had not left the Union, would be exempt from these strictures, and the Missouri enslaved would be, for the moment, still enslaved.

The ruling was technically illegal because it violated the US Second Confiscation Act and its provisions for judicial review, but more broadly because constitutionally the federal government could not outlaw slavery in slave states. Ending slavery, except as a temporary military necessity, would require amending the Constitution. Lincoln feared, as was confirmed by politicians he knew in the border states, that both the confiscation of slave property and the arrest of slaveholders would further alienate those he relied on to support the Union. The Fremont Proclamation so alarmed the Kentucky state legislature that Lincoln feared the commonwealth might leave the Union, and then "we can not hold Missouri, nor, as I think Maryland. . . . We would as well consent to separation at once, including the surrender of the Capitol."[38] In the end Lincoln's diplomacy saved Kentucky and other border states for the Union. The president cancelled the Fremont Emancipation order and removed the general from his command in early November 1861. But the idea of immediate emancipation was only on hold, not forgotten, and was gaining in popularity in the North.

Montgomery Blair began corresponding with African American leader Frederick Douglass as early as the fall of 1861 to convince him of what the Blair family believed was the necessity of colonization. Douglass, who had railed against "colonization cant" since 1851, remained incredulous that such a thought would even be entertained by the Lincoln administration. Blair used the old race canard of Thomas Jefferson's and the pseudoscientific theories of Harvard University's Louis Agassiz to argue that Black people could never adapt to the North American climate, were unable to measure up to the standards of the white race, and would be happier elsewhere. Lincoln stressed the notion in his conference in 1862 with Black leaders that since Black people would never be viewed as equal citizens by whites, they should seriously consider going elsewhere.

Douglass flatly refused any "discussion of 'confining different varieties of men to different belts of the earth's surface' as 'chimerical in the extreme.'" "We are Americans by birth and education," he said, "and have a preference for American institutions. . . . That we should wish to remain here is natural to us."[39] As the critical year of 1863 went by, Lincoln began to see this point of view more clearly. His colonization schemes in both the Caribbean and South America fell through, and the ill-advised Haitian Ile-á-Vache mission resulted in disaster and death. As the Civil War intensified and Black leaders weighed in at the White House against what they defined as "deportation," the discussion of employing Black troops intensified. Lincoln abandoned attempts to sponsor colonization by executive order, and congressional sponsorship of colonization fizzled.

The implacable Blairs still wanted to take history in another direction. There was talk in Lincoln's cabinet of forcibly deporting formerly enslaved people, but Montgomery Blair for the moment chose a somewhat seemingly more temperate—and politically expedient—path. In speeches he delivered in Cleveland, Ohio, and New York City in the spring of 1863, he argued that the secessionist states should be brought back into the Union as soon as possible with the carrot stick of compensation. He also promoted the creation of what can only be characterized as labor concentration camps for African Americans. Confiscated enslaved people should be assembled in army encampments "in a state of probation" and after the war put to work to build harbors, canals, and even a transcontinental railroad. But the ultimate measure should be deportation. Otherwise, there would be a permanent process of "amalgamation" and a nation of "mongrel races."[40]

The Blairs' plans were going awry. Frank Blair was holding on to his seat in Congress while also serving as a Union officer. Samuel Knox ran against him for his House of Representatives seat in Missouri in November 1862 as a Radical Republican arguing for immediate emancipation. Knox was a strong advocate of temperance as well and in his lawsuit *Knox v. Blair* charged that Blair brought in unregistered voters, many of them Germans, from the Benton army barracks and plied them with "free beer and whisky." Knox's mother-in-law, Hannah Kerr, had often complained of drunken disturbances on Election Day, and this was really nothing new.[41] Knox also charged that the "oldest German newspaper in St. Louis," supposedly "a radical abolition paper," endorsed the conservative Republicans and went all out for Blair.

Knox's charges were heard by the US House of Representatives Committee of Elections. The committee decided that Blair "was not duly chosen" at the election and awarded the Missouri seat on June 13, 1864, to Knox, who had little time left in the term to serve in Congress on the Committee of Military Affairs. The more important consequence was Frank Blair's expulsion from Congress, largely on the grounds that he had held two federal government positions at the same time. Montgomery Blair pleaded with President Lincoln on his brother's behalf, but Lincoln refused to intervene. Montgomery was by the time of his brother's bad luck on his way to leaving the Lincoln cabinet, resigning in the fall of 1864. The Blairs would soon condemn Radical Republicanism in every venue they could find.

Lincoln courted the border states by nullifying Fremont's emancipation proclamation but had not reckoned on its popularity in much of the North with abolitionists, German Americans, immigrants, and Radical Republicans, who were hailing it as the beginning of the end of slavery. And the president still faced the problem of what to do with refugees flocking to border-state cities, Washington DC, and Union Army camps. He drafted a preliminary Emancipation Proclamation in July 1862 and said that the enslaved people of traitorous slaveowners in areas held by the military in slave states would be "forever free of their servitude, and not again held as slaves." Pushed forward by the Radical Republicans in his cabinet, the Northern antislavery press, and abolitionists in Congress and seeing no other way forward, Lincoln issued a preliminary emancipation proclamation in September to take full effect on January 1, 1863.

Lincoln evolved from a position that initially blamed the Civil War on the presence of Black people in United States to the far more generous, even noble, ideas of liberty and equality in the Gettysburg Address in 1863 and the second inaugural address of 1865. He was feeling his way forward in a step-by-step set of new strategies, the Emancipation Proclamation among them, and he was also changing his personal beliefs about race. In his meeting of August 14, 1862, with a delegation of Black leaders to discuss colonization, he peevishly argued that it would be best for the Black population to leave the United States because there could never be an equality of the races. There were real physical differences between Black and white people that could not be overlooked. He dwelt on the harm that slavery had caused for whites—"its evil effects on the white race"—and the fact that white soldiers were giving up their lives in battle for a cause that was not really their own. "But for your race among us there could not be war. . . . I repeat, without the institution of Slavery and the colored race as a basis, the war could not have an existence."[42] But when he defended his Emancipation Proclamation to his friend James C. Conkling in August 1863, who had argued he would not fight a war to "free negroes," Lincoln retorted, "Some of them seem willing to fight for you." The victories in July at Vicksburg and Gettysburg had hopefully turned the Civil War to the Union's side. The bravery and heroism of Black soldiers in their own regiments were changing Lincoln's mind on race. Peace might eventually come to the United States, and if Black soldiers "stake their lives for us, they must be prompted by the strongest motive—even the promise of freedom. And the promise being made, must be kept."[43]

Lincoln knew that an intimate member of his household, Elizabeth Keckley, had lost her soldier son at the early Battle of Wilson's Creek that had saved Fort Jackson for Unionist sympathizers in the border state of Missouri. Keckley was a steady presence in the Lincoln household during the illness, final days, and death from typhoid fever of ten-year-old Willie Lincoln in February 1862. The weight of the war, the terrible losses of dead soldiers, and his own grief in the White House were making Lincoln a more somber and thoughtful man, and the Emancipation Proclamation may have reflected not only a wartime political necessity but his growing empathy for Black Americans, perhaps sparked not only by the pushback from Douglass over colonization but also by his personal relationships with people of color in Washington, DC, among them Keckley.[44]

Lincoln proclaimed in the brief Emancipation Proclamation of January 1, 1863, that "persons of suitable condition, will be received into the armed service of the United States to garrison forts, and other places, and to man vessels of all sorts in said service."[45] The possibility of opening the door to Black troops was out in the open at the highest level of government. There was no mention of colonization or compensation, although Lincoln's second inaugural address still held out the promise of compensation to loyal enslaved holders. The Emancipation Proclamation was in most ways similar to Fremont's policy. It would, as had Fremont's dictum in Missouri, apply only to the enslaved of disloyal owners in slave states. This was fine print that most abolitionists—and people of color—ignored. The abolitionist Radical Republicans and Horace Greeley of the *New York Tribune* seized the moment to pronounce slavery dead. While some state legislatures flirted with compensation to loyal slave owners, none adopted them. Lincoln's evolving position on emancipation and the recruitment of Black troops led to a rift with the Blairs and Edward Bates, Lincoln's attorney general. The Radical Republicans in his cabinet, William H. Seward and Edwin McMasters Stanton of New York and Salmon P. Chase of Ohio, were increasingly influential, and the president's reliance on border-state politicians—and the Blairs—was waning.

There was now no stopping the tide of human beings freeing themselves, whoever their owners were. Black men in Missouri and elsewhere wanted the option of joining the Union Army and ridding themselves of the "contraband" label policy, which often resulted in forced labor on plantations and in Union Army encampments. Until the summer of 1863 the war went badly for the Union, and conscription policies for badly needed new troops led to the infamous draft riots by poor whites in New York City. More troops were needed, whatever the color of their skins.

In St. Louis William Greenleaf Eliot noted in his journal that Black citizens were celebrating in the streets as the Emancipation Proclamation was announced and that there was a demonstration outside the Germans' Turnervarian Hall at the corner of Market and Tenth Streets. The reputation of the antislavery Turnervarians was not lost on the Black community in St. Louis. Some Turners fought on the antislavery side in Kansas and in St. Louis rented their hall to Black groups for special events.[46] John Anderson led his African Baptist congregation on a march from their Eighth Street building in a snowstorm to Turner Hall, where he delivered a speech of thanksgiving. It is entirely possible that Harriet Robinson Scott and her daughters and the Griffin Branders were in attendance; this was their congregation. The judicial arguments the Scotts' case had evoked could now be contested in earnest. Black men and women knew they were citizens and would find more and more avenues for expressing their civic will.

# 4 Civil War in the Valley of the Mississippi

As Abraham Lincoln assumed the office of the presidency in the spring of 1861 and the Civil War began, St. Louis and the State of Missouri were central to the efforts of the US Army Department of the West. A border state with enslaved people was now occupied by a US government considering emancipation. General John C. Fremont was in charge of Union forces in the Valley of the Mississippi in July but having blown up Lincoln's gradual emancipation strategy was replaced by John Schofield in November 1862. With disagreements over how to interpret the president's preliminary Emancipation Proclamation and what should constitute the war effort in their region, leading citizens in Missouri with influence in Washington, DC, jockeyed for leverage over the appointment of generals, the "contraband" property under their jurisdiction, and the handling of the shocking reality of the wreckage of plantation life downriver, where the lives of both Blacks and whites were in ruin.

The refugee crisis was one of astonishing proportions. Black people freeing themselves tried to reach Washington, DC, or St. Louis, where the federal government was in charge and where they hoped to find official emancipation and paying work. By 1862, ex–St. Louis resident Elizabeth Keckley was settled in Washington and was the dressmaker for Mary Todd Lincoln. On her way through city streets with a friend, she encountered a charitable event to benefit sick and wounded Union soldiers. She asked, "If the white people can . . . raise funds for . . . suffering soldiers, why should not the well-to-do colored people go to work to do something for the benefit of the suffering of the blacks?" She suggested to her Union Bethel Church congregation that they form "a society of colored people to labor for . . . unfortunate freedmen." Forty congregants established a contraband relief association (CRA), and similar organizations appeared in Boston, New York, Philadelphia, and Baltimore, the major centers of free Black life in the North.[1] When "colored troops" were mustered up, the CRAs became the Ladies' Freedmen and Soldiers' Relief Association. Mary Meachum, the wife of African Baptist Reverend John Berry Meachum, was the president of the local group in St. Louis. Managers of Freedmen's Hospitals found these associations particularly helpful.[2] The Sisters of Charity and the Sisters of Mercy provided nursing and hospital services in St. Louis and aboard the steamboats bringing patients upriver, with some Unionists in St. Louis questioning the sisters' attentions to Confederate patients as well.

What kind of gainful employment could be put in place for ex-slaves was the paramount economic question, with a strong belief held by both Black and white leaders that self-help and productive labor were the keys to a healthy postwar world. But those beliefs often got in the way of what unclothed and unfed refugees, often suffering from typhoid, diphtheria, tuberculosis, or smallpox, really needed: a long-term plan of substantial help from the federal government.[3] Enslaved people from plantations wanted labor that paid wages and, when dreaming big, plots of land that would belong to them. Most could not read or write—the same was true of many poor whites—so schools and intensive education efforts were priorities of both Black and white reformers. Confederate sympathizers in St. Louis jockeyed for funding and institutions to support white refugees in the city, some of them former plantation owners and slaveholders.

Influential whites with charitable instincts worked alongside but not necessarily with Black organizations and churches to ameliorate the growing crisis of wounded and dead Union and Confederate soldiers and whole families of displaced persons. Several thousand victims of war required hospitalization or burial. Black and white refugees from farms and plantations downriver were destitute as war came to their doorsteps and arrived at Memphis or St. Louis only with, often, the clothes on their backs. The battle of Pittsburg Landing, or Shiloh, Tennessee, on April 7, 1862, left 1,735 Union soldiers to bury. And there were nearly eight thousand wounded, who were sent to St. Louis on steamboats and carried through the streets on stretchers to hospitals. The largest facility in the city was managed by the Catholic Sisters of Charity, but they were unable to take in all the patients. Many of the wounded were sent to Benton Barracks, where conditions were deplorable in the early months of the war.

Unitarian William Greenleaf Eliot, longtime builder of civic institutions in St. Louis, would step in to organize the effort to provide a vast system of medical services for the valley of the Mississippi. He was worn out by 1861, physically and spiritually, from his ambitious pastorate at the Church of the Messiah. Having alienated Southern sympathizers in his congregation, he cut back on services and convinced church elders to hire substitutes for 50 percent of his duties. Finding an influential role in the great cause of the moment was most important to him. He plunged into building organizations to meet the growing consequences of combat and began planning a new university he hoped would be the best of its kind in the West.

Fremont's wife, Jessie Benton Fremont, encouraged the establishment of a sanitary commission in the West to parallel the US Sanitary Commission in the East, now headed by Frederick Law Olmsted. Eliot had already envisioned something like this, and by September 1862, a Western Sanitary Commission (WSC) was in place, with Eliot and four other commissioners, all Church of the Messiah parishioners, and all men, to manage freed people's services and camps downriver, hire surgeons and nurses, and find suitable locations for hospitals in St. Louis. (It seems not to have occurred to Eliot to make this a more inclusive endeavor by contacting any of the now well-established Black churches or women's volunteer societies in St. Louis.) Pushing back against Olmsted's attempts to merge the WSC with the US Sanitary Commission, the WSC board maintained its independence and leased buildings and solicited donations, many of which came from Eliot's and others' contacts in New England. These efforts provided a patchwork of medical and supplementary aid for the growing number of freed people in St. Louis and contraband persons stuck in camps along the Mississippi. Antislavery women from the Northeast were ready to join the relief efforts or to teach the rudiments of literacy in makeshift schools for freed people, and their services were quickly accepted.[4]

Wayman Crow's friend and Church of the Messiah congregant James Yeatman took charge of WSC operations in the Mississippi Valley war theater. Yeatman, a Tennessee planter turned sour on slavery, arrived in St. Louis in 1842, manumitted his remaining enslaved people, invested in banks, sold iron, and promoted railroads. Baptist minister Galusha Anderson said that Yeatman "was eminently just . . . had large administrative ability, and to crown it all, a great heart."[5] When Olmsted visited St. Louis in 1863, his report spoke highly of Yeatman's leadership.

The ambiguous status of the still technically enslaved "contraband" on seized plantations and farms in the early years of the Civil War left Black families in limbo. Some army commanders were tempted to return individuals to their owners, others provided aid as they could, and most seized the opportunity to put Black male refugees to work. In the spring of 1863, some white "slavecatchers" approached Benton Barracks to reclaim several Black men, now impressed laborers. A brawl erupted when white workers questioned this request, with one of the slavecatchers brandishing a knife, and the provost guard arrested them and led them out of the barracks.[6]

With the exceptions of Benton Barracks and a downtown hotel converted into contraband quarters, promptly burned to the ground by secessionists, contraband camps and villages were not in the city proper but along the Mississippi River between Cairo, Illinois, and Natchez, Mississippi. Forty thousand people, one WSC agent recalled, "were in a country stripped by the ravages of war, with no demand for labor excepting in a few localities without means of providing for food, clothing, and shelter."[7] The desire to reach urban centers was universal but for many impossible.

Conditions in the camps often depended on their physical location. Those on the higher bluffs of the Mississippi had salubrious air and reasonable sanitation conditions while those on islands, often chosen as sites to prevent Black women and children from going into Memphis or St. Louis but also to protect them from kidnapping by slavecatchers, had more disease and fewer amenities. Yeatman reported that Camp Shiloh had six hundred residents in 1863 who were self-supporting and would not need special aid. The men worked in the engineering corps (a fancy label for heavy labor), and the women earned income from washing for a neighboring fort and the Freedmen's Hospital. Elisa Mitchell from Oberlin, Ohio, was the sanitary agent in charge of the hospital, and she had been joined at the Shiloh camp by two women schoolteachers.[8]

But in the Helena, Arkansas, encampment, nearly fifteen hundred people were drawing rations from the federal government and in desperate need of clothing. Small pox was epidemic, and within a month of their arrival, half of the refugees died. Maria R. Mann, daughter of educator Horace Mann, wrote home from Helena with "terrifying scenes of suffering and death," and said that "women were frequently reduced to prostitution by the want of food and clothing."[9]

US Secretary of War Edwin McMasters Stanton sent General Lorenzo Thomas to the region in the spring of 1863 to organize chaotic conditions in the Mississippi Valley. The War Department was assuming that able-bodied Black men would be impressed as laborers or soldiers. Both Thomas and WSC agent Mann argued that Black families should be encouraged to return to abandoned plantations so that they could feed themselves and prevent the collapse of the agricultural economy. This policy was put into effect by the summer of 1863 and became an essential piece of resettling some of the displaced and also serving as a bulwark against possible Confederate advances coming upriver.

Officially, "contraband" became freed people once their prior owners were deemed disloyal, a technicality that broke down almost immediately. Large numbers of enslaved people were simply leaving their plantations in search of freedom as the Union Army neared. Despite the desire of ex-enslaved people for land of their own, only radical abolitionists and some in the command of the Freedmen's Bureau talked of giving them their own acres. "The mobilization of land and labor in the Mississippi Valley," Louis Gerteis concludes, "came not out of moral concern for the freedmen, but as a matter of military policy."[10]

Yeatman argued the early conditions in freed peoples' camps were not really those of freedom, as many of the men (and women) were essentially impressed laborers. He was furious over the low wages, the standard being $10 a month, often not paid at all. He reflected on the cruel irony of Lincoln's "Emancipation" measure:

> This negligence and failure to comply with obligations have greatly disheartened the poor slave, who comes forth at the call of the President and supposes himself a free man, and that by leaving his rebel master he is inflicting a blow on the enemy. . . . But how is it with him? He is seized in the street and ordered to go and help unload a steamboat . . . or sent to work in trenches. . . . He labors for months, and at last is only paid with promises, unless perchance it may be with kicks, cuffs, and curses. . . . Something should be done . . . to correct these terrible abuses. . . . The President's proclamation should not thus be made a living lie.[11]

Men in contraband camps pleaded for more pay and a chance to put on the Union uniform, backed up in mass meetings in the East by Frederick Douglass, Frances Watkins Harper, and Philadelphia orator Anna Dickinson, who all argued that once armed and contributing to a Union Army victory, Black men should demand full citizenship and voting rights. Conservatives like the Blairs, with Montgomery still in the cabinet, were adamant that Black men should not be given arms. Many prominent Republicans continued to resist the recruitment and enlistment of Black men.

William Greenleaf Eliot still believed that freed men and women were not yet prepared for full freedom and citizenship. He consistently advocated for gradual emancipation along with intense education efforts. But he came to understand that a gradual pace of freedom would never fly with the Black citizens of Missouri. He welcomed Lincoln's preliminary Emancipation Proclamation in 1862, wrote letters to the editors of St. Louis newspapers, arguing that slavery must die in Missouri, and gave new sermons on the theme that "the days of Slavery [are] numbered. . . . In this State, Freedmen only question quick or slow. As quick as Justice & kindness to Blacks will allow."[12]

Putting guns into the hands of Missouri Black men, he admitted, was terrifying to him. He reveals in his journal how far he was from granting real racial equality and how psychically disturbing the picture of armed Black men was: "No armed negroes—not wanted—not good, not trustworthy—barbarous—their motives of revenge." He was conjuring up the old tropes of the Denmark Vesey and Nat Turner slave rebellions.[13] But education was something Eliot backed wholeheartedly. Eliot and Yeatman established an American Freedom School at the Ebenezer Church in 1863 for refugee enslaved and Free Blacks, but an arsonist set the school on fire within two days of its opening. The school was moved to another site and remained open for the duration of the war.

Lincoln resisted the recruitment of Black troops but came to realize its military necessity whatever its political dangers. Soon after, "I was," Lincoln wrote to Albert Hodges, a Kentucky newspaper editor, "in my best judgment, driven to the alternative of either surrendering the Union, and with it, the Constitution, or of laying strong hands upon the colored element. I chose the latter. . . . It shows a gain of quite a hundred and thirty thousand soldiers, seamen, and laborers. We have the men; and we could not have had them, without the measure." In an earlier but pointed letter to James C. Conkling of Illinois, Lincoln said, "You say you will not fight to free negroes. Some of them seem willing to fight for you; but, no matter. Fight you, then exclusively, to save the Union."[14]

The most imminent danger to civic order was from white men who could not afford to pay substitutes for their service. Draft riots in New York City raised the specter of mutinous Irishmen and other poor whites resisting their draft notices and taking their rage out on Black people in lynchings, arson, and the destruction of an orphanage. The need of Grant and William Tecumseh Sherman for more bodies to feed the war machine was ever growing, and Lincoln urged Secretary of War Stanton to make "a renewed and vigorous effort . . . to raise colored forces along the shores of the Mississippi."[15]

By the middle of 1863 the specter of Black men with guns became a reality, even if the initial idea of the US Army was to use refugee men as workhorses and guards to free up white soldiers for fighting. While some Union officers believed Black men would never be good soldiers and resisted sending them to the front, others held back Black soldiers from major battles out of fear they would be captured by Confederate troops and shown no mercy. The disastrous battle at Fort Pillow, north of Memphis, in 1864, where Black soldiers trying to surrender were beaten and killed, showed just how full of revenge Confederates might be.

Immigrants in Missouri answered the call to join arms, especially the Germans, but the Irish came along, too. Irish troops in Missouri served in the Seventh Infantry Regiment, known as "the Fighting Irish," and were attached to Fremont's Army of the West in the summer of 1862. Colonel Peter Joseph Osterhaus organized the Twelfth Missouri Infantry Regiment in the summer of 1861, made up mainly of German recruits with some from Illinois. The Twelfth Missouri Infantry was at Wilson's Creek in 1861, the siege of Vicksburg in 1863, and in the final push to Atlanta in 1864.

There was intense interest in the Black community in joining the Union Army. Elizabeth Keckley's son had already died at the Battle of Wilson's Creek. James Milton Turner, who was a young student at Meachum's African Baptist Church and then went to Oberlin College in Ohio for a year, was working as a porter in St. Louis in 1860. He offered his services to Nathaniel Lyon and Frank Blair at Camp Jackson in 1861, became the body servant of a prominent Union officer from St. Louis, and was also at Wilson's Creek. He was part of most of the first battles of the Mississippi Valley and was wounded at Shiloh in 1862, leaving him with a permanent limp.[16]

At the beginning of the Civil War, 115,000 enslaved persons were in Missouri, and most of them lived in the "Little Dixie" strip across the Missouri River from east to west, north of Columbia. Black people in the northern counties slipped away into Kansas, and Black men joined regiments to fight for the Union. Henry C. Bruce, an enslaved man in Chariton County left in charge of his owner's (and his father's) farm, recalled that Union Army recruiters from Iowa competed with those in Missouri to attract "colored troops." Both Iowa and Kansas welcomed Black men as willing and unwilling recruits into all-Black regiments. In 1862 Kansas US Senator James M. Lane organized the First Kansas Colored Volunteer Infantry, primarily staffed by Missourians.

Henry Bruce left Missouri for Leavenworth, Kansas, in 1864 and avoided serving in the Union Army altogether, preferring to work for a brick contractor to support his newly wed wife. But in Little Dixie's Howard County, just northwest of Columbia, close to Bruce's home in Chariton County, Missouri's Black men flocked to recruitment centers. Altogether, 39 percent of military-age Missouri Black men served in the military. "The sheer volume of black—and particularly slave—enlistment in Kentucky and Missouri," says Aaron Astor, "transformed much of the labor force into a vital weapon in the Federal Government's counterinsurgency campaign against rebels." Runaway Jacob Anderson of Lafayette, Missouri, joined the Union Army on November 28, 1863, served in the Sixty-Second Missouri Regiment of Colored Infantry, and became a sergeant and a member of the Honor Guard, his stripes proudly kept by his grandchildren.[17]

The first Black troops in Missouri were mustered in at Benton Barracks in June 1863 where the initial living conditions were dreadful, and adequate food, clothing, and bedding in short supply. Many men had no shoes. Within a year, a third of the recruits died of smallpox, pneumonia, or tuberculosis, diseases as widespread at the barracks as they were in contraband camps. New replacements arrived, and by the end of the year, there were two regiments of Missouri Colored Infantry, the Sixty-Second and the Sixty-Fifth. In total eighty-four hundred Black soldiers were enrolled in Missouri regiments by the end of the Civil War.

Some white officers commanded Black regiments and were often cruel taskmasters, but some officers came from antislavery backgrounds, believed in their men, and insisted they learn to read and write. Abolitionist Richard Baxter Foster of New Hampshire, a graduate of Dartmouth College, was a schoolteacher of Black children in Iowa and then followed John Brown to Kansas. Foster joined the Union Army in 1861 and volunteered in 1863 to lead Missouri's Sixty-Second Regiment of Colored Infantry. His co-officer David Branson used both carrots and sticks to increase literacy in the Sixty-Second Regiment, demoting those who refused to study and giving preference for promotion to those who could read. When a soldier was seen playing cards, he was placed in public view with a book, "there to learn a considerable lesson in reading and spelling. . . . No freed slave who cannot read well has a right to waste the time and opportunity here given him to fit himself for the position of a free citizen," Branson announced. Gold pens were distributed to sergeants who wrote the best by the Fourth of July 1865. Both the Sixty-Second and the Sixty-Fifth would be among the Colored Troops with the highest literacy rates in the US Army.[18] By the end of the war, soldiers in two Black Missouri regiments had collected $5,000 to fund a Lincoln Institute for African American students, shepherded initially by Foster, in Jefferson City, Missouri.[19]

As casualties mounted and disease raged, efforts to attend to the sick and the dying were launched by authorities and volunteers in and around St. Louis. Privileged white women in St. Louis, led initially by Anna L. Clapp and with their Ladies' Union Aid Society, tried to provide necessities and services for Union soldiers at Benton Barracks. Like their counterparts in the Confederate South, these women welcomed the idea of service, which could be dangerous. Two members of the Union aid society were frostbitten while attending soldiers on the front in Tennessee in the winter of 1862. Largely Presbyterians and Unitarians, most of these women had antislavery sentiments.[20]

The WSC secretary described these women's self-appointed duties: making hospital garments on treadle sewing machines, distributing sanitary supplies and reading materials provided by the US Christian Commission, consoling the wounded and writing letters to their families, and praying with many who did not survive the night. Eliot appreciated these volunteers but believed that only a professionally trained nursing force could provide the regimen of nursing and sanitation that a properly run hospital required. A near-military response in organization would be indispensable.

Eliot and his wife, Abby, befriended Jessie and John Fremont early in the war, and Jessie put them in touch with Dorothea Dix, by then the commander of nursing for the US Sanitary Commission in Washington, DC. Dix visited the Eliots in August 1861, and they were more than enthused about her suggestions. In a letter for the *Missouri Republican* drafted largely by Jessie, Eliot announced, "Miss Dix, our American Florence Nightingale, will be here this week. . . . Amateur . . . nursing is not enough for the stern realities which war has already brought among us." In his letter "Appeal to the Public," he promoted Dix's philosophy: "The hardest battle is fought in the hospitals, and *these women are the best soldiers.*"[21]

Hospitals were commissioned in Tennessee, Kentucky, Mississippi, Arkansas, and Louisiana. A fleet of hospital steamboats housed others. By the spring of 1864 the WSC supported fifteen hospitals in and around St. Louis, with its largest facility of more than two thousand at Benton Barracks. Over four years of Civil War, the WSC raised and distributed $4.5 million, largely from donations, to keep its enterprises afloat.[22] Along with its counterpart, the US Sanitary Commission, the WSC changed medical practice and its organization in permanent ways for the rest of the century. The WSC engaged in bold, new experimentation in treating Black patients and refugees as American citizens in need of health care and education, even if these efforts at improved race relations were halting and impermanent.

Emily Parsons, trained at Massachusetts Hospital in Boston, was one of the qualified nurses who served at Benton Barracks. Parsons, thirty-eight years old in 1862, had already worked at military hospitals in New York State. According to her father, she was nearly blind in one eye, somewhat deaf, hobbled by a badly set broken ankle, and received glowing reviews from her male superiors. Initially assigned to a hospital steamboat making its way from Vicksburg to St. Louis, she both found wounded soldiers and commandeered contraband workers aboard.

Parsons, a devotee of Dix, understood from the beginning that she was to organize and administrate, not do hands-on nursing. Whitewashed floors and walls, sanitized privies and wards, and clean sheets and hospital uniforms were the elements of most concern to her. She tried to enforce her rule that all patients bathe and put on hospital garb. She taught nursing and then assigned it to her workforce: "I hire *young* nurses; they are more willing to follow directions, more energetic, and stronger."[23]

This near-military ideal was balanced by her empathy and close reading of human nature. On the steamboat up the Mississippi, she "received one of our new laundresses, a contraband, with one pretty little boy; she wants to go to St. Louis, where she can get employment. When the doctor saw her he did not at first think of taking the child; but, when he understood, he said to me, 'The boy may come too.' I wish you could have seen the poor woman's face. She . . . has lost her husband: her boy is her all."[24] Black men, women, and children were clamoring aboard steamboats and any kind of river transportation upriver they could find to freedom. Charles Davis, his wife, and their two sons hitched a ride from Arkansas to St. Louis, where Davis settled his family and went to work on the steamboat *Marble City*.[25]

Upon reaching Benton Barracks Hospital, a former site of the Horse and Cattle Fair, Parsons was put in charge of the care of several thousand patients. She directed all of the nurses, of which more were male than female, and brought Black nurses into the hospital for the "colored wards." In her words these nurses were not just attending the sick, they were teaching them to "read, write, and in some instances, to cipher. The poor colored men are very grateful and anxious to learn; it is very touching." Black nurses wanted corn bread and bacon, not boiled beef and tasteless toast. Parsons herself attended "our poor colored soldiers. . . . They are as pleasant to take care of as white soldiers, and the wards are as nice, both with regard to comfort and order."[26]

Parsons had ideas about race that now might be seen as shortsighted and condescending. She delighted in "the queerest little pickaninnies," a trope of Black children that evoked Harriet Beecher Stowe's character Topsy in *Uncle Tom's Cabin*, but she also convinced a surgeon to operate on a child with a cleft lip. Her constant fixation on "whitewashing" as a cure for dirt and disease, and her frequent use of the term in general, might be construed as a subconscious effort on her part to make her "colored" patients "more white," but these were known techniques for combatting hospital germs.

Parsons's sympathy with her patients grew stronger over time. In the aftermath of the Union siege of Vicksburg in July 1863, her duties encompassed the entire swath of humanity affected by the Civil War: "I am rather busy now: I have to look after refugees, contrabands, soldiers, both black and white, and keep my senses." She welcomed the assistance of the Colored Union Society, whose members were being ejected from streetcars or forced to ride outdoors on platforms. She was won over to the most radical views of the antislavery movement:

> I used to think the statements of abolitionists extreme and that their views were sometimes irrational; now I wonder that people acquainted with the

> facts can keep any bounds at all. . . . I do believe that is one reason that this hospital for colored soldiers has been permitted to be established . . . for it is doing more than taking care of their bodies; it is bringing to the surface facts, and establishing precedents face to face with the enemy. It is storming the citadel.[27]

Nursing staffs, the Black and white Union aid societies, and the WSC organized a grand Mississippi Valley Sanitary Fair for two weeks in May 1864. Sanitary fairs were being held in most big cities in the North to raise funds for hospitals and freed people, and St. Louis responded in kind. Women sewed, knitted, and crafted items to be sold at booths, often set up in a large arena with military guards and lavish public entertainment. It was a society event as well as a fundraiser. Appoline Blair, Frank's wife, was the director of the Women's Sanitary Fair Committee in St. Louis, and Minerva Blow, Henry's wife, was on the flowers and horticulture committee. Minerva wrote to her husband in February that "the great Sanitary Fair is occupying the attention of the people, and all seem more willing to aid in this effort, than in any previous one for the same object."[28]

The St. Louis Fair offered a skating rink, a band, and restaurants. "The Germans," Galusha Anderson reported, "were given a large space in the building, where they patriotically sold lager beer, and a host of people patriotically drank it," despite the condemnation of temperance attendees. The proceeds of the sanitary fair in St. Louis, according to Anderson, were nearly $555,000. Parsons helped to organize the fair, and her equanimity and sense of social justice were evident in its execution. Black troops were assigned to do guard duty, committing some of their "meagre wages to aid refugees and freedmen. . . . It looked like a revolution when we saw, in a slave State," said Anderson, "white women of high social standing, without complaint or a murmur, sell articles to colored purchasers." There were a few objections to this "abrupt change from the old order of things, but on the whole the sentiment toward the colored people was humane, reasonable, and liberal."[29]

One of the objections Anderson was obliquely referring to may have been a publicized incident at the fair. A Presbyterian minister invited two Black clergy to dine with him at the café and were refused service by several white women before another stepped up to wait on them. A *Missouri Republican*'s cartoon caricatured the Black men and described their server as "a homely white woman wearing spectacles" while a table of "attractive young white women" look on with disdain, surely a reproof to the Yankee women like Parsons who had come from the North with antislavery sentiments to help with the war effort in Missouri. But the Fair invited both patriotism and sentimentality and may have been a high point of race relations in St. Louis.

With its freedmen's camp, Black troops, and a hospital with Black women nurses, the barracks' Civil War complex might be seen, as Walter Johnson has said, as examples "of Black . . . self-care and self-determination." But, as he underscores, these bureaucracies had white superiors and a chain of command that prioritized white Union soldiers and saw segregated hospital facilities with fewer resources for Black people as unquestioned practice. Black troops and Black patients were on the bottom of the military and medical pile.[30]

As the Benton Barracks hospital transitioned in 1864 to treating refugees and fewer soldiers, conditions deteriorated in the face of overwhelming dirt, poverty, and malnutrition. Pneumonia, measles, and smallpox ran wild. Parson's diary begins to express dismay at the scope of problems even good nursing could not solve. She had a recurrence of malaria and became too ill to work and returned home to Cambridge, Massachusetts, in August 1864. But she maintained her ties with the WSC, sending packages of clothing and garden seeds to St. Louis. After recovering from malaria, she took up the instruction of nursing duties at the newly established Cambridge Hospital at the corner of Hampshire and Prospect Streets.

Not only were the hospitals and camps flooded with Black and white refugees but also several thousands of migrants who were coming to the city looking for shelter and employment. The population of St. Louis soared during the Civil War, mainly due to the arrival of whites and free Blacks from the South and more European immigrants. The Black proportion of the population of St. Louis had been losing ground during the mid-nineteenth century, and this trend continued in the 1860s. Women outnumbered men, a sex ratio common in most antebellum American cities for both poor whites and African Americans.[31] As more Black men were seized as contraband and enlisted in the Union Army, wives and children tried to reach St. Louis, joined by wives of Irish and German Union recruits looking for work and trying to feed their families. Union commander Samuel Curtis took control of the Missouri Hotel to house Black women refugees in the spring of 1863 and sent women and children, willing or unwilling, to midwestern states, where employers, mostly agricultural ones, welcomed an infusion of vulnerable laborers.[32]

With an internal slave trade that was alive and well as the war began, unfortunates separated from loved ones had no other choice than to turn their faces toward the future and hope for the best, to find employment in and around St. Louis as they could, and focus on keeping their children safe. Black couples like Griffin and Catherine Lucas Brander were among the many free Blacks and ex-slaves who longed to make their marriages legal in the eyes of the law and blessed by pastors in their churches.

In the middle of wartime hostilities, Protestant ministers Galusha Anderson and William Eliot encountered newly freed people and wrote about them later. Both ministers came into the Civil War with what they considered to be beneficent views of runaways escaping to freedom. But they were also running households with a now limited pool of servants for hire, and both men seized the opportunity to "do good" for runaways by employing them as household labor. Anderson hired two "contrabands." James Jackson, age twenty-five, "split the wood, brought in the coal, kept the yard in trim, ran errands, and cared for the horse and carriage." He learned the rudiments of reading and married "an excellent colored woman." Harriet, a former field hand, was a "black as ink" woman hired to do the laundry and other household chores. Anderson summed up her situation in what must have been a common feeling for recently freed people earning cash wages, eagerly learning to read and write, and attending, as Harriet did, AME churches: "She was happy in her new-found freedom. To receive week by week money for her labor made her cup of joy brim over. The dawning consciousness that she belonged to herself and had a right to what she earned filled her with unspeakable gladness."[33]

Eliot was heading full bore into a long-held optimistic plan: establishing a first-rate university in St. Louis, one that could rival the best institutions in the Northeast. After convincing a stingy parishioner to donate a large parcel of land northwest of the center of St. Louis for Washington College, Eliot sold his downtown home on Eighth Street in 1856 for $12,000 and rented the three-story Beaumont Cottage, residence of a former governor. Beaumont Place was in the city limits but had a rural feeling that contrasted with the "noisy and disturbed city." Left unsaid by Eliot was the same motive driving many of St. Louis's native-born residents—like the Kerrs, Knoxes, and the Tiffanys—fleeing from an inner city now dominated by German and Irish immigrants. Eliot intended the Beaumont property to be an anchor for the site of a new Washington Institute and wanted to downsize his household expenses. The roomy house was close to Camp Jackson, Benton Barracks; in the early military action of the Civil War, the Eliots could hear cannon shots being fired and saw troops passing by.[34]

The Eliots were in what they considered to be tight financial circumstances with William's reduced salary from Church of the Messiah. Faced with more care of animals and landscaping work than they could manage, they decided to find a "manservant" in 1863, "if we could find one at low wages." According to Eliot, Abby went into town and asked the butcher she frequented if he knew of anyone. The "Dutch" butcher had just greeted an escapee named Archer Alexander, now about fifty years old. The shopkeeper asked Alexander to carry Mrs. Eliot's order in a basket to Beaumont Place. Here was a golden opportunity for a laborer to take charge of their domain. The "boy" agreed to take care of the grounds, attend the animals, and plough a field for planting. He was given a bunk in the stable.

William Greenleaf Eliot soon grasped that Alexander was a fugitive. Alexander had a dramatic story of himself, claiming to have interrupted a plot by secessionist sympathizers in St. Charles County to destroy a bridge over Lick Creek to slow down Union Army troops pacifying rebels west of the Missouri River. Eliot attempted to buy Alexander from his owner, Richard Pittman, for $600, intending then to emancipate him, but Pittman refused the purchase. Eliot then took the case to a US Army officer, who issued emancipation papers on the grounds that Archer Alexander belonged to a rebel. But within a few months a posse of slavecatchers invaded the garden at Beaumont where Alexander, now known by the family as "Archie," was at work and entertaining William's youngest children, who had grown to love him: Christopher, age seven, Edward, age five, and one-year-old Rose, attended by her nurse. Archer was kicked and beaten as he was carried away. The children were terrified and traumatized.

A vivid account of the cruelty of slavecatchers, Eliot's recounting is a reminder of how vulnerable all African Americans were at any time and in any place to kidnapping, how very small children might witness a horrific event, and why drayman Griffin Brander never stopped carrying his free pass, which he kept until the day he died. But as with most everything else we know about Archer Alexander, his story passed through the mind and pen of Eliot in *The Story of Archer Alexander from Slavery to Freedom*, published in 1885. Some of that account, written two decades after the Civil War encounter, is fact and some is fiction, written at a time when Eliot was in declining health and summing up his own past and legacy.

Alexander had a story worth telling. That story was typical of early nineteenth-century adults who as children were born into slavery in Virginia, lived lives with pressures to procreate, faced forced migration, and were enmeshed in the economy of the internal slave trade. Archer was born in 1810 or 1811 on a Virginia plantation, his parents enslaved persons of plantation owner James Alexander. Archer told Eliot that his father, Aleck, knew how to read, and that when Archer was ten, Aleck was sold away from his family for spouting principles of the Declaration of Independence. In 1829 James Alexander and his brother-in-law James McClure, later joined by a cousin, William Campbell, left Virginia for Saint Charles County, Missouri, an area already made famous by the travels of Lewis and Clark and the growing legend of Daniel Boone. St. Charles township, just across the Missouri River from the northern edge of the city of St. Louis, had been the state's capital before it was moved to Jefferson City in 1826.

The McClure and Alexander families owned twenty-three African Americans, the extended Black Alexander family among them, and made a good investment in potentially productive real estate. The Virginia transplants convinced local prominent Scottish Presbyterian stonemasons to train their enslaved laborers to build brick houses, among them the magnificent Campbell House on Boone Lick Road. Archer Alexander most likely learned his bricklaying and building skills while working on this structure. But both McClure and Alexander died of cholera in the early 1830s, and William Campbell was made executor of the estate. Campbell hired out the estate's laborers to pay for the upkeep of the family orphans, some of whom returned to Virginia and took inherited human property with them. The Black Alexanders lost track of extended family kin, siblings, and children as their white owners sold or exchanged them or relocated with them elsewhere.

The precarious lives of Black men and women attempting to build families in slaveholding counties like St. Charles have been documented by scholar Diane Mutti Burke. With small slaveholdings the norm, men and women formed marital relationships in "abroad" style, that is, spouses lived on different farms, and as long as these unions were not interrupted by the auction block or husbands and wives were not transferred to other relatives in wills, these relationships proved to be "remarkably stable, surviving for many years." "Owners' deaths were moments of extreme anxiety," because, as in the case of the McClure and Alexander families, the settling of estates "resulted in the dismantling of slave families."[35]

Archer Alexander was the husband of Louisa, owned by James Naylor, a nearby German postmaster and stagecoach driver. The Alexanders had ten children and were raising them in St. Charles. But Louisa and the children belonged to Naylor, raising legal difficulties that impaired their mutual freedom. Archer was obviously considered to be a valuable and skilled worker and was sold and resold to several owners, ending up in the hands of David Pittman and then his son Richard, among the largest slaveholders in St. Charles County before the Civil War.[36]

Historians of local history and family trees have filled in some of the missing links in Archer Alexander's story. Alexander, who has recently been recognized in St. Charles County as a Civil War hero, did alert Union Army authorities to a meeting in which David Pittman plotted with other "secesh" rebels to destroy a bridge across Lick Creek and then was made an outlaw by Confederates. But other questions remain. Eliot claimed Alexander was illiterate, and whatever skills he acquired in freedom were rudimentary. But Alexander worked in a St. Louis brickyard as a hired-out worker in the 1830s. He knew his way around the city before he ran away. His father knew how to read, and Alexander had at the very least picked up the rudiments of reading street and storefront signs. When his wife, Louisa, had delivered to him a letter saying that her master would not release her and the couple's small children to join Alexander in St. Louis, might it be assumed that both she and Archer were somewhat literate? Did his choice of a German butcher shop close to where he had worked previously in a brickyard mean that he was seeking help from an Underground Railroad family to leave Missouri for Illinois?

The importance of the brickmaking economy in early Missouri and its centrality to the lives of its workers cannot be overemphasized. St. Charles, with its port access to the usually lazily flowing Missouri and vast clay and sand deposits, had become a center of the making of bricks, with St. Louis soon following in small-scale production. By midcentury more than fifty clay mines were in St. Louis, where clay was dug up, molded, and fired in local neighborhoods.[37] In a coincidence that tells an instructive story of the determinants of class and race, William Eliot's second-oldest son, Henry Ware Eliot, the father of poet T. S. Eliot, accumulated enough capital to become a partner in the innovative Hydraulic-Press Company and retired a wealthy man. Alexander remained a wage laborer for the rest of his life, but Eliot saw him as an accomplished "jack of all trades," recognizing that he had skills not found in every "hired hand."[38]

Immigrants and their sons would take over most sectors of the laboring classes in the manufacturing and masonry industries in the late nineteenth century, but at midcentury in Richard Pittman's mind, Alexander was too valuable a property to allow to escape in St. Louis. After the slavecatchers' raid at Beaumont Cottage, Pittman probably arranged for them to retrieve Alexander and take him to a St. Louis jail, where he was to be sold to another owner in Kentucky. But Eliot had enough important contacts in St. Louis that he was able to intervene, freeing Alexander and bringing him to the WSC offices. It was agreed that Archer would go across the Mississippi to nearby Alton, Illinois, where a strong antislavery community could provide him with protection. (Eliot often preached there.)

The only mention of Alexander during the Civil War in Eliot's journals and letters is a brief one in a November 1863 letter to Eliot's son Thom. Archer's wife, Louisa, had returned to her former master in St. Charles County to retrieve some of her belongings and died there. "The Colored folks all 'suspicion,'" wrote Eliot, "[of] Foul play, but it is not at all probable."[39] Eliot was leaning back on his inherent trust of whites of his class and disdain for the "tales" of Black people. The depth of this new disaster on Alexander and his children must have been devastating, unreported by Eliot, but the Alexander family's rapid acceptance in the Black community in St. Louis is clear in Eliot's offhand comment. Once the Gradual Emancipation Act was passed in Missouri, and he received an emancipation certificate, Alexander returned to work for the Eliots before establishing his own household in St. Louis with his second wife.

By the fall of 1863 the pace of the Civil War had become the all-consuming obsession of most citizens, Black and white, in Missouri. Sons of several prominent St. Louis families joined the armed services, including those of US Attorney General Edward Bates. Of his sons, John served in the Union Army, Fleming was in the Confederate Army, and Charles was at West Point. The two oldest boys of the Eliot family, Thomas and Henry, were both Union soldiers, and William Eliot's brother Frank Andrew Eliot died at the battle of Charlottesville in May 1864. Alexander's son James, still living in Virginia, escaped from slavery and was one of the early armed "contraband" soldiers who died at the Battle of Hilton Head in North Carolina in 1861. Elizabeth Keckley's son also died early, in the conflict at Wilson's Creek, as did Friedrich Muench's seventeen-year-old son, Berthold.

African American regiments from Missouri companies were dispatched to Louisiana, and the Sixty-Fifth was sent on to Texas near the end of the Civil War. Still under the command of white officers Colonel Theodore Barrett and Lieutenants Colonel David Branson and Richard Baxter Foster, 250 men of the Sixty-Second stationed at Brazos Santiago on the Rio Grande fought at the Battle of Palmito Ranch and suffered thirty casualties before an orderly retreat on May 13, 1865. This is said to be the last battle of the Civil War, and on June 19, slaves in Texas were finally told that they were free.[40]

The sons of Henry and Minerva Blow and of Samuel and Mary Knox were too young to serve in the Civil War. But in the late 1850s the Blows' oldest daughters, Susan and Nellie, were sent to a prestigious private school for girls headed by Henrietta Haynes in New York City, where they were both fine students in academic subjects. Susan Elizabeth Blow was more interested in books and her lessons than any other activity since childhood. She resisted learning how to sew and studied for so many hours that her parents and teachers ordered her to make at least one dress and to take afternoon naps to rest her eyes, strictures she agreed to reluctantly. As Susan and Nellie saw their New York City schoolmates face the divide over the Lincoln presidency and Southern secession, with many of the Southern students leaving for home, the family decided Susan and Nellie should return to St. Louis for the duration of the war. The Blow girls were being guided in their studies at home in Carondelet by their neighbor William Taussig.

Susan fell in love with a young Union soldier, a relationship her parents discouraged. She resisted proposals from other men, never married, and found companionship and comfort with women friends and other intellectuals in St. Louis. In Germany in 1870 she studied philosophy, most excited by the work of Friedrich Frobel, who was devising a new approach to the education of children based on "learning-through-play." She was an advocate of the experimental public kindergarten movement and opened the first kindergarten in the United States in Carondelet in 1876. Susan, along with Dix, Parsons, Keckley, and the Yankee schoolteachers, were examples of the exciting new avenues opened for women's work and civic duty as a result of the Civil War.

Citizens of St. Louis welcomed the end of the Civil War with jubilation, despite the storm cloud of potential postwar policies hanging overhead. Grave political and social questions needed to be decided. Despite the misgivings of many whites about immediate emancipation, the Missouri legislature, controlled by Republicans and moderate Democrats, abandoned the gradual emancipation law drafted by William Greenleaf Eliot and voted for the immediate abolition of slavery on January 1, 1865, a few weeks before the Thirteenth Amendment to the US Constitution was proposed in Washington. In February the Missouri state legislature, now dominated by Radical Republicans and led by Martha Blow's husband Charles Drake, passed legislation allowing the former enslaved who had cohabited to be married legally by justices of the peace, with the names of their children recorded as legitimate. Catherine Lucas and Griffin Brander were married on January 29, 1867, by Henry H. Highland, now pastor of John Anderson's Central African Baptist Church, and received a formal certification in 1879 of their union.[41]

Leading Black citizens of St. Louis, among them Moses Dickson and Lucy Delaney, were already on to the next steps of full-fledged citizenship, forming an Equal Rights League in the fall of 1865 with hopes of obtaining voting rights for men and promoting state-funded education. In the fall of 1866 the Lincoln Institute in Jefferson City welcomed its first students, many of them the children of formerly enslaved persons.

Slaveholders in Missouri saw their property in human beings vanish with no monetary compensation and watched in horror as African American men were armed. Sometimes whites resorted to violence when they saw Black men in uniform or contraband heading for enlistment sites.[42] Many whites still harbored Confederate sympathies and had committed treasonous acts. Should men who had been disloyal be allowed to vote? There was the question of public schools. Would white families be forced to send their children to school with those of African Americans? A momentous revolution in social and political life was about to take place. The thinking of powerful whites during the Civil War and its aftermath shows that their often predetermined, unconscious views of race and gender would create both new possibilities for progress and old patterns of exclusion.

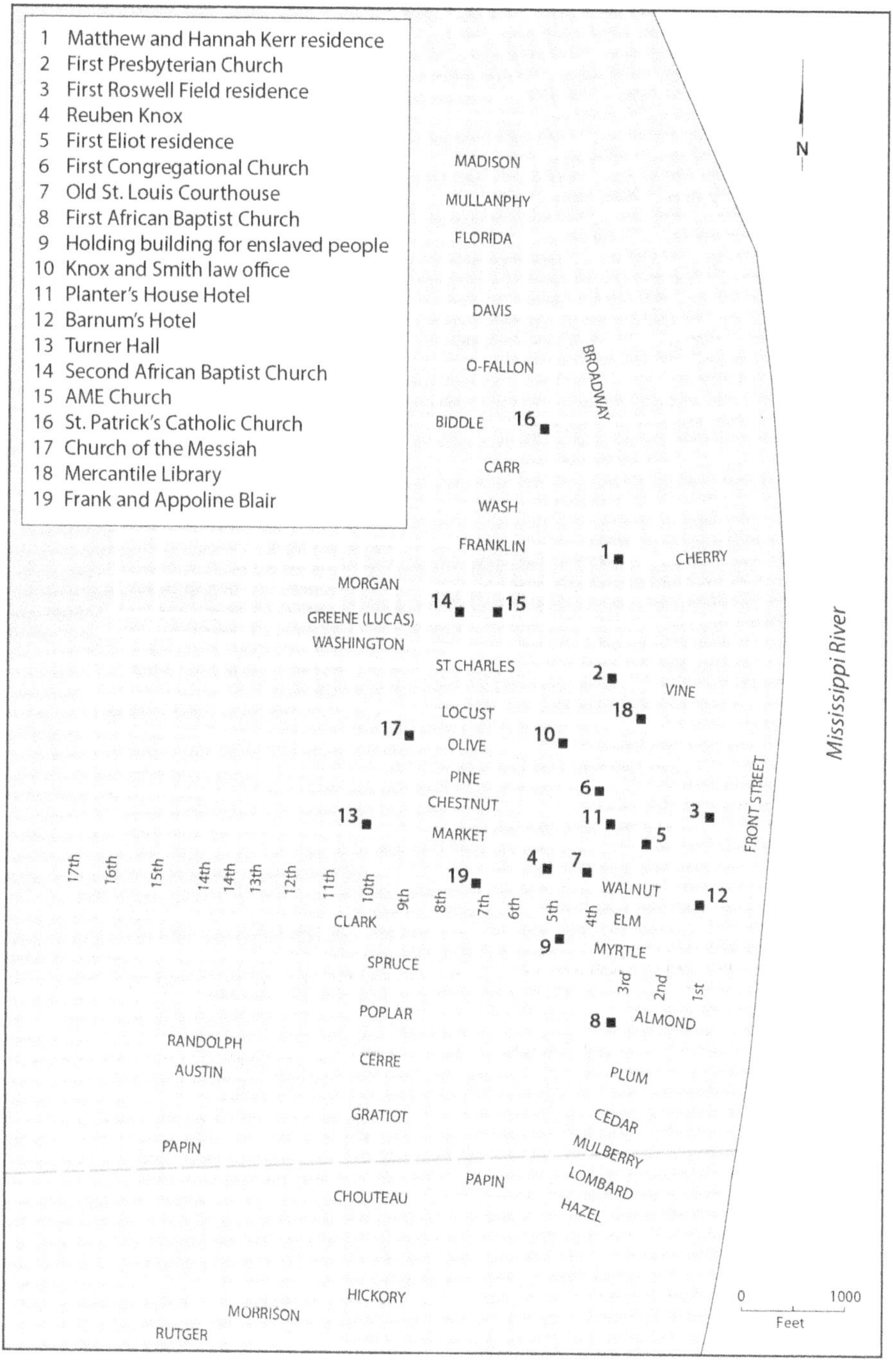


Map of central St. Louis, 1850 to 1860. Composed by Bill Nelson.

Collier White Lead Works, ca. 1855. PO 900-12876-01. Courtesy of Missouri Historical Society.

Henry Taylor Blow (1817–1875), ca. 1870. Hand-painted photograph. Identifier N38662. Courtesy of Missouri Historical Society.

St. Louis Levee, 1852. Photograph by Thomas Easterly. Identifier N17070. Courtesy of the Missouri Historical Society.

African Americans unloading cotton bales from a riverboat, ca. 1900. Photograph. Identifier N22534. Courtesy of Missouri Historical Society.

Minerva Blow with daughters Susan and Ella, 1849. Portrait in oil. Identifier N36053. Courtesy of Missouri Historical Society.

Unidentified St. Louis African American woman. Date unknown. Daguerrotype by Thomas M. Easterly. Identifier PO250-17335. Courtesy of Missouri Historical Society.

William Greenleaf Eliot, 1850. Daguerreotype by Thomas M. Easterly. Identifier N17201. Courtesy of Photographs and Prints Collection, Missouri Historical Society.

Edward Bates, lawyer, U.S Attorney General in the Lincoln administration. Library of Congress.

Montgomery Blair, lawyer, postmaster general in the Lincoln administration. Library of Congress.

Archer Alexander, ca. 1870. Photograph by J. A. Scholten. Identifier N11598. Courtesy of Missouri Historical Society.

Emancipation Monument, Lincoln Park, Washington, DC. Dedicated 1876. Sculpture by Thomas Ball. Photograph, from stereograph format. Library of Congress.

Catherine Brander, ca. 1870. Griffin Brander Papers, Missouri State Historical Archives.

Susan Blow, kindergarten pioneer and Hegelian philosopher, ca. 1870. Identifier N38666. Courtesy of Missouri Historical Society.

Engraved portrait of Elizabeth Keckley, frontispiece. *Behind the Scenes or Thirty Years a Slave and Four Years in the White House*, 1868. Identifier N23872. Courtesy of Missouri Historical Society.

John Mercer Langston of Ohio and Howard University Law School, ca. 1870. Library of Congress.

The family of Helen Davis (*fourth from right, back row*) with her son Joseph (*far left*) and her daughter Julia (*far right*) in 1919. Courtesy of St. Louis Public Library.

Julia Davis, standing in front of the books she donated to the St. Louis Public Library, presents a check for further acquisitions in African and African American history and literature. Courtesy of St. Louis Public Library.

African American girls gather after school near Sumner High School in 1917. Photo by Charles Clement Holt. Identifier 147056. Courtesy of Missouri Historical Society.

Black Lives Matter protest at the Emancipation Monument, June 20, 2020. Photograph by Tracy Meehleib, Library of Congress.

# 5 What Rights Should All Citizens Have?

With universal and immediate emancipation, validation of their marriages, and legitimization of their children, Black citizens of St. Louis next fought for better education and the right to vote. They founded an Equal Rights League in 1865 to further these causes. The league had to convince powerful white men who controlled the political process in Missouri and in Washington, DC, to address the Black community's goals to make any progress. These white men—and women in their families—were, in fact, contemplating what steps they might next take to enhance—or not—the status of all citizens in civic life and the body politic. Edward Bates, Montgomery Blair, Frank Blair, William Greenleaf Eliot, Henry Taylor Blow, and Henry's brother-in-law Charles Daniel Drake began to make public declarations of where their families stood on these questions.

An evolving definition of citizenship framed their positions, with an incident off the coast of New Jersey in 1862 that posed again the question of who could be a citizen. David M. Selsey, a free Black master of a commercial vessel, was detained and his ship inspected for contraband goods. The fine print of US naval law required all shipmasters to be US citizens. Secretary of the Treasury Salmon P. Chase asked Attorney General Bates, his co–cabinet member, to write a legal opinion as to whether free African Americans could be considered citizens, now in question in light of US Supreme Court Justice Roger J. Taney's assent in the Dred Scott decision of 1857.

Bates found this an interesting question. He began by saying he could not find a definition of what constituted a citizen in the Constitution or in a large body of legal opinion: "eighty years of practical enjoyment of citizenship, under the Constitution, have not sufficed to teach us either the exact meaning of the word or the constituent elements of the thing we prize so highly." He analyzed the most extreme statements of Taney, who argued that even when born in the United States, "persons of color" had no claim to citizenship. Bates's view was that everyone born in the United States should be considered a citizen and that there was nothing in the Constitution to bolster Taney's argument: "what can there be in the mere color of a man . . . to disqualify him for bearing true and faithful allegiance to his native country, and for demanding the protection of that country?" And these, moreover, "constitute the sum of the duties and rights" of natural-born citizens of the United States. He argued that Selsey deserved the protection of the United States on the grounds that he was "a free man of color."[1]

With the Emancipation Proclamation on the horizon and the women's rights movement gaining momentum, Bates felt compelled to ask whether citizenship automatically entailed voting rights. Certain classes of citizens—children, women, propertyless men, and felons—had, historically, been denied voting rights by states of the United States. Voting rights, said Bates, should be determined by the states, not the federal government, and in a long entry in his diary in 1864, he discussed whether citizenship entailed full equality to all men, as the Declaration of Independence had seemingly announced, and decided that it did not.[2] But citizenship, he wrote, was a national right that could not be denied by any state of the United States.

Now in the shadow of the more Radical Republicans Chase, Edwin McMasters Stanton, and William H. Seward, Bates and Montgomery Blair would leave Lincoln's cabinet in 1864, and while Bates retired quietly to private life, perhaps disappointed that he was not named a Supreme Court justice, he did not publicly condemn the president. But the Blair family used Montgomery's resignation and their condemnation of Radical Republicans to begin a savage campaign against Lincoln and the Radicals that would last through the end of Reconstruction and beyond. The Blairs agreed with what seems now to be the startling views on race Taney, a personal intimate of the Blair family, presented in the Dred Scott decision. The Blairs believed in compensation for slave property to loyal slaveholders and were above all committed to deporting Black people from the United States to privilege white men's labor and prevent "amalgamation." Arming Black men and granting voting rights to them seemed out of the question.

The Blairs, Francis Preston Blair and his sons Montgomery and Frank, helped organize the Republican Party as a border-state enterprise with Lincoln as candidate for president (although they hoped Frank Preston Blair would be the nominee). They viewed the Republican Party and its 1860 nominee as their creation, and Lincoln as a man who once elected president they would guide and even control.[3] As the Civil War began, they had significant positions of power in Congress, in the cabinet, and in Blair House, where patriarch Blair had access across Lafayette Square to the White House. But they underestimated Lincoln as a strategist, a man guided not only by his own moral convictions but also with the ability to change his mind as events outran his original plans.

Lincoln and the Blairs had not anticipated the power of the idea of emancipation once it became a near reality and the once outrageous views of the abolitionists almost mainstream. No less a personality than successful Missouri politician Benjamin Gratz Brown, cousin and former ally of Montgomery Blair and Frank Blair Jr., was in touch with William Lloyd Garrison by 1863, applauding the American Anti-Slavery Society for its arousal of "this nation to a sense of the sin of slavery" and pronouncing that no one should consider the Fugitive Slave Act embedded in the Compromise of 1850 to be legitimate.[4]

Responding to this new sensitivity, Montgomery gave highly charged and partisan speeches in New York and Cleveland in the spring of 1863. He laid out how emancipation might work in the interests of loyal slaveholders and conservative Republicans. States now out of the Union should be readmitted as soon as possible. Colonization "in the Tropics" was essential to ridding the United States of African influence and an inferior "blood line." Emancipated slaves should be drafted into the army as heavy laborers or held in camps to rebuild the country, even to work on a transcontinental railroad and widen the Erie Canal. Echoing William Greenleaf Eliot's refrain, Montgomery suggested that the secessionists, led by John C. Calhoun, and the abolitionists, guided by Wendell Phillips, were to blame for the disruption of what had been a harmonious nation. But going much further than William Eliot, Montgomery Blair declared that "True Constitutionalists" would "repudiate the idea of equality . . . in regard to citizenship that . . . would make our government one of mongrel races."[5]

The Blairs launched a public campaign to promote their position. In October 1863 Montgomery gave addresses on the family turf in Maryland, disguised as support of the president's policies but really with an eye on what was going on at that very moment in Missouri in Radical Republican meetings. The "Revolutionary Schemes of the Ultra Abolitionists," now being pushed by the "coadjutors of Presidential schemers in St. Louis and throughout Missouri," said Montgomery, "are endeavoring to throw that State in the caldron of revolution, that it, too may be annihilated" and made into "a 'clean slate' on which Congress may write the laws it pleases."[6]

Frank Blair was about to be ousted from his seat in the House of Representatives, replaced by Radical Republican Samuel Knox of St. Louis, and to return full time to his military duties in the West. Before he departed, Blair gave two lengthy speeches on the floor of Congress in 1864, echoing his brother Montgomery's views but with personal diatribes of invective directed at Radicals in the Congress, including Thaddeus Stevens of Pennsylvania, Henry Winter of Maryland, and his one-time St. Louis friend and fellow Presbyterian congregant Henry Taylor Blow.

In these diatribes, Frank Blair argued that the suppression of the rebellion was nearly over and former rebel states should be reincorporated into the nation. It was not too late for the Congress to fulfill the president's original promise that loyal slaveholders in the border states be compensated for their loss of property in slaves. But he admitted this moment of possibility had probably passed. Two other policies were now paramount. Ex-slaves should be "transplanted to some of our vacant regions, if remote colonization cannot be effected in such an emergency," with "the southern frontier of Texas" as a possibility for Black resettlement. (Texas, now out of the Union, was, evidently, not to be consulted on this matter, Mexico viewed as blank space.) Blair claimed that President Lincoln favored amnesty and forgiveness for most Confederates. Blair's racial politics, echoing the Taney assent in the Dred Scott decision, was clear. Blair said that Black Americans "never can enjoy freedom, equality, civil rights, or even safety of property or person unless separated from the dominant race."[7]

Frank Blair's speech evoked immediate rebuke, but he persisted in piling on invective. His speech in Congress nearly three weeks later began with a condemnation of Radical Republicans in Missouri, accusing them of retaliation and revenge. Blair attacked Henry Blow as a former Know Nothing who hated the Irish and would seek to diminish their voting powers. But Blair's most profound disagreement with Blow and Winter was with their views on race. They would dare to arm Blacks, which, as Frederick Douglass and Phillips had argued, might be the first step toward granting the franchise. They opposed colonization, a policy at the heart of everything the Blairs hoped to accomplish.

These views were amplified when Frank Blair ran for vice president of the United States on a ticket with presidential candidate Horatio Seymour of New York in 1868. The voting campaign employed vicious rhetoric that linked greater equality for Black men to political chaos and the rape of white women. That kind of rhetoric was now being employed by Ku Kluxers and other vigilantes in the former Confederacy to justify violent assaults on Black families and Black and white Republican men—and their families—who dared to vote or run for office. The Republican ticket triumphed in 1868, and Ulysses S. Grant would run again in 1872. But this dark current of hatred and endorsement of violence against people of color would always lie beneath the veneer of American politics, spouting up whenever Black civil rights movements made strides forward.[8] In St. Louis, for example, in reporting the huge multiracial protests and a crowd estimated at five thousand along the waterfront during the great railroad strike of 1877, the St. Louis *Missouri Republican* "imaginatively reported 'distressing scenes of terrified women, rudely handled by brutal negroes.'"[9]

Not having ever resorted to this kind of rhetoric, Missouri US Representative Henry Taylor Blow began his national prominence in 1860 when he made a speech in nomination of Lincoln at the Republican Convention in 1860. He was appointed minister to Venezuela by the new president in the fall of 1861, where he lived in a hotel in Caracas and was out of his depth because he did not speak Spanish. He stuck it out for a year, longing to return to the heart of the conflict in the United States. He was not impressed with South America, echoing in his dismissal the widely held cultural constructs of the Blairs and many others and often repeated in prospectuses for colonization: "This country, tho' beautiful as Paradise, has become like Paradise desolated by Sin, the People have forgotten even their rights, and with a consequent demoralization, are without a hope in the future."[10] Blow had most likely been asked by the Lincoln administration to explore the idea of arranging for the deportation of some US Black people to Venezuela, but he made no mention of it in letters to his wife, Minerva. In the Lincoln cabinet, both Montgomery Blair and Edward Bates were still arguing for the forced deportation of contraband slaves to somewhere "in the Tropics," a position the president would reject emphatically soon after Blow came home.[11]

Blow returned to the United States in time to run for Congress in 1862, and he was elected and then reelected in 1864. In the aftermath of John C. Fremont's removal and his replacement by Lincoln with General John Schofield in the summer of 1862, Blow and other Missouri men, including Drake, Blow's brother-in-law, visited Lincoln in the White House to convince the president that Schofield was not up to the task because he was not sufficiently antislavery.[12] By then the Blairs and the Blows were not on speaking terms, with Minerva Blow reporting that rifts between a minority of Unionists and a majority of proslavery congregants had arrived with bitter enmity among Presbyterians in St. Louis. Edward Bates, on a visit to St. Louis in the summer of 1863, reported to a colleague that "our society is slivered into splinters—all the active rebels are one, and many of them are dead; but their families and friends are still here, discounted and sulky."[13]

Henry Blow, still flying an American flag over his house in Carondelet, followed up on his visit to the White House with a plea in a letter to Lincoln urging him to make the Civil War a war to end slavery: "We will ensure a destiny more brilliant than imagination can conceive, if we are faithful to the great idea of the Revolution and proclaim at once our intention to place the Republic on the just and enduring basis of freedom."[14]

What should constitute that freedom had yet to be decided. Charles Sumner of Massachusetts and Thaddeus Stevens of Pennsylvania were the most radical representatives in the US Congress in the 1860s and had a significant proportion of constituents who agreed with their views on granting the vote to Black men. Blow was in a far more tenuous political position. He was among the most radical of the Republicans in Missouri in articulating a more generous view of the future of Black Americans but one rooted in constructions of race believed in by most whites and certainly most white Missourians. In his ongoing discussion with Frank Blair on the floor of the House of Representatives, Blow condemned colonization: "We are content to let them remain where God . . . placed them, and with a more elevated sense of justice, to ameliorate their condition . . . and elevate them as speedily as possible on the soil . . . enriched by the heat of their brows through years of unrequited toil."[15] Blow endorsed the recruitment of Black men as Union soldiers and sailors and described as "disgraceful inhumanity" the massacre of Black soldiers at Fort Pillow.

But there were still leaps in logic to be made for Blow to see Black people as equals. He had already formed relationships with Germans as servants and friends and abandoned live-in Black help in his home. In his own mind he had the best of motives. Blow, like William Greenleaf Eliot, believed that slavery in Missouri had largely been a benign institution. Henry, Taylor, and Martha Blow had been young children with Dred Scott in Virginia, Alabama, and St. Louis, and the Blow siblings arranged the manumission of the Scotts. Perhaps drawing on this familial past, Henry Blow asserted in Congress that "from my earliest years I have known the race well."[16]

In tropes echoing those that dominated contemporary fiction, journalism, and pseudoscientific speculations, Blow could not see African Americans as a class of fully developed human beings. They were "trusting," "contented with little," loved music, were exceptionally pious, and craved "warm sunshine." He dismissed fears of amalgamation, arguing that most Black people were not really "black": centuries of race mixing had already occurred. Nothing dreadful had arisen as a result, and white blood lines remained "superior." More important, people of color would inevitably migrate to warmer climates (Missouri was supposedly too cold for them) or die from "scrofulous" diseases like tuberculosis, thus avoiding too much racial intermixture. Blow, drawing on his observations in his brief stay in Caracas, amplified his derogatory comments about South America, placing indiscriminate interracial sex between whites, Indigenous peoples, and Blacks at the heart of the region's supposed political instability.[17]

Blow had most likely read Samuel Gridley Howe's 1864 report "Refugees from Slavery in Canada West" for the Freedmen's Inquiry Commission. Howe was a New England abolitionist, and his wife, Julia Ward Howe, wrote the poem that was put to music in the "Battle Hymn of the Republic," by 1865 a patriotic anthem. Most of Blow's ideas about race echoed Howe's conclusions, which were based on theories popular among intellectuals, such as Louis Agassiz at Harvard, that placed whites at the apex of and Africans at the bottom of the pyramid of the world's humankind. The report was given even-greater authenticity with copious notes taken from the Canadian census (although Howe admitted the figures were unreliable) and interviews with Blacks and whites in the cities and towns that served as sanctuaries for fugitive slaves who left their homes in the United States during the 1850s. Howe claimed that Blacks in these towns longed for old homes in the South, never adjusted to Canadian cold weather, and, as they aged, were sickly and died at higher rates than whites. Blacks in Canada, he concluded, would die out eventually or, more likely, once the Civil War was over, migrate to the deep South.[18]

Historian of science Stephen J. Gould, who a century later inherited Agassiz's old position at Harvard, has shown how this "mismeasure of man" dominated white Western thinking for centuries. As health experts emphasize, poverty, crowded housing, and lack of decent food are the mix that make tuberculosis thrive, and most Canadian Blacks were impoverished and leading lives of hard labor in inadequate housing. The myth of inferiority linked to tuberculosis would later be applied to American Jews and Italians in urban neighborhoods where disease due to unhealthy environments was widespread. Many in St. Louis believed, without real evidence, the rumor that Dred Scott had died of consumption like his former white owner Emerson. It is not surprising that Blow turned to current experts to justify the feelings he probably already had about Black people.[19]

Henry Blow, a wealthy business owner and US Representative, had intertwined interests—the personal and regional—he was bound to promote. He embedded his views on race in an agenda for lawmakers in Washington and in his own state by suggesting how to approach the "reconstruction" of the postwar society and economy. He had cast his lot "with the great, free West." No state other than Kentucky, he believed, had suffered and given more to the cause than Missouri, with St. Louis at the center of the western conflict. It was of critical importance to Missouri and the Mississippi Valley that rivers, ports, and commercial enterprise be restored as quickly as possible. He argued for a speedy readmission of both Arkansas and Louisiana into the Union to cement this revival.[20] Edward Bates was thinking the same thing, writing to a friend that in St. Louis "the general tone is . . . hopeful . . . now that the river is open—trade will revive, tranquility be . . . restored."[21]

Because the State of Missouri had not left the Union, its legislators and voters, not the federal government, were in charge of their own "reconstruction" plan for the future. Blow noted that the 1865 constitutional convention of Missouri was at the very moment of his congressional address meeting in St. Louis, with the question of Black rights being debated. He agreed with Bates that voting rights should be left to the states and that it was not, at this time, advisable to grant the suffrage to African Americans in Missouri and elsewhere. He advised, "Secure them freedom, schools, and churches, the way to wealth . . . and we simply discharge an enlightened Christian duty." Likely with an eye on his region's white population, he argued that granting Black suffrage would alienate whites who had sympathized with the Southern cause, as well as immigrants who were becoming naturalized citizens.[22]

With so-called copperheads (a term applied by their enemies to Democrats) and Confederate rebels in political disarray, the Radical Republicans in Missouri won control of the state in the election of 1864, with an eye above all on resuming river commerce to restore the economy of St. Louis. They convened a new state constitutional convention in 1865. Drake drafted the document submitted to voters for ratification. Slaves were to be emancipated immediately with no compensation to their owners. School boards would be required to provide education for African American children. By 1866 a St. Louis Board of Education for Colored Schools governed three district schools with 437 Black students, inciting constant handwringing from Democrats over what they deemed wasted taxpayer money.

For many Black children, privately funded and Catholic parochial schools continued to be better options. In 1865 William Greenleaf Eliot invited his niece from New Bedford, Massachusetts, Ida N. Eliot, to teach at a new St. Louis high school for Black students he founded in the basement of a building at Eighth and Locust Streets.[23] His vision for the future was almost always to be accomplished by education and cultural refinement.

The new Missouri constitution instituted a "test oath" required of all potential voters, with teachers, lawyers, and ministers singled out especially, to swear that they had not committed disloyal acts during the Civil War. Judges were to ensure that those who served on the bench would qualify under the terms of the test oath. This purging of the professional and former ruling class throughout Missouri met with resistance but managed to endure a statewide ratification of the new constitution. These were extreme measures, but even Presbyterian moralist Charles Drake could not bring himself to put voting rights for Black men in Missouri in the new document. The measure would have been defeated if he had.[24]

The strictures eliding the participation of large numbers of white men in Missouri put the Radical Republicans in charge of most of Missouri's state government for the near future but with policies that were untenable in the minds of the general population in the long run. Five years later, in 1870, when an inadequate provision of the Fourteenth Amendment to the US Constitution was replaced by a provision of the Fifteenth Amendment that dictated voting rights for all Black men, Black men in Missouri were supposedly able to vote, and some did help keep the Radicals in power. But African American male voters never made up enough of a proportion of voters in St. Louis or in the state to determine the outcome of elections, and violence and voter intimidation discouraged those who were eligible and further diluted the power of the Black vote.

Other disturbing developments were in store for the Radical Republicans. By 1865 fractures erupted between the Protestant white Radicals and the Germans, who had long cooperated in the antislavery movement in St. Louis. German men saw Drake as a fanatical advocate of temperance, and as anti-immigrant; he did, in fact, like Samuel Knox and his in-laws, the Kerrs, see drinking as a public hazard and a personal sin. The Germans in St. Louis resembled white Presbyterians on the larger question: they condemned slavery but could not take the steps necessary to grant full equality.[25] Once white Democrats were able to rejoin the voting public, the more liberal views of this coalition would be eclipsed well into the twentieth century.

Two new constituencies challenged the assumptions the Drake constitution and Radical Republicans in Missouri had made about voting rights. The Black leaders who formed an Equal Rights League petitioned the state legislature for a hearing of their demands for suffrage. And in 1867, in the wake of the ratification of the Fourteenth Amendment, a handful of women organized a woman suffrage movement in Missouri. The Fourteenth Amendment created discontent in the women's rights movement all over the North because it put, for the first time, the word "male" in the US Constitution. Most Black leaders and their white allies argued its other provisions were linchpins of Black citizenship and civil rights and the expansion of civil rights for the foreseeable future. Let women, they said, wait their turn to secure voting rights. With the passage of the Fourteenth Amendment, persons born in the United States were now unequivocally defined as citizens and must be afforded equal protection and "due process" of the law. The federal government could intervene if individual states restricted the basic rights of their citizens and did not afford them "due process of law."[26]

The Black community's most outstanding citizens organized the Equal Rights League in 1865. Moses Dickson transformed his revolutionary Knights of Liberty into a peaceful Masonic order, the Knights of Tabor, and was also the pastor of the influential St. Peter's AME Church in St. Louis. J. Milton Turner, wounded Civil War survivor, was forming a Lincoln Institute in Jefferson City. H. McGee Alexander, chairman of the Equal Rights League, was a prominent Freemason in St. Louis who had worked with Reverend John Anderson to bring the principles of Prince Hall Freemasonry from Boston to St. Louis. Blanche K. Bruce, younger brother of Henry C. Bruce (both were sons of a prominent white landowner from Chariton County, Missouri), would become the first Black US Senator from Mississippi while managing his large plantation on the delta of the Mississippi River.

These kinds of Protestant ministers, Union soldiers, mixed race persons with some white privilege, and Freemasons in Missouri, as elsewhere in the border states and the Midwest, were the first Black civil rights leaders in the region after the Civil War. They asserted that voting rights "rightfully and logically belong to us as freedmen, and as those who have never deserted the flag of our common country in the hour of its darkest peril."[27] In early 1866 they brought lawyer and orator John Mercer Langston of Ohio, a Knights of Tabor brother of Dickson, before the Missouri House of Representatives. Langston was the first "colored man," as he described himself, ever to speak in the state's capitol. "I am here," he declaimed, "to ask you to adopt the proper Constitutional measures for the amendment of your organic law, by the erasure of the word '*white*' wherever it occurs, therein, and thus make *manhood*, not color, the basis of suffrage."[28]

In his analysis of constitutional history and the law, Langston laid out the logic of the founders, the opinions of Bates, the dissents in Dred Scott, and definitions of citizenship long held in the United States. Being born in the United States, paying taxes, swearing allegiance to the nation, and serving in its defense constituted citizenship. The Taney decision in Dred Scott was "a national apostacy" that could not stand because it used the color of a person's skin to deny full citizenship. In his own state of Ohio, potential voters had to prove they were 50 percent white. As a result, all people of color were labelled mulattos and denied the right to vote, serve on juries, and bring lawsuits against whites. Ending slavery should have changed everything: "We are no longer things, but persons. We are no longer beasts of burden but men. To-day we can say, *my self, my body, my wife,* and *my children.*"[29]

The cloak of manliness that citizenship, military service, and voting rights settled on men impeded both Black and white men's willingness to consider women as voters or in the professions, where they were still largely excluded from medicine, the law, and the clergy. But white women's rights reformers and Black women abolitionists understood immediately that the arguments of someone like Langston could apply to them. In 1867 white women Anna L. Clapp and Virginia Minor, who had both served in the Union Aid Society on behalf of the Western Sanitary Commission during the Civil War, formed a Missouri Woman Suffrage Association in St. Louis.

Why did Clapp and Minor feel able to pursue this new way of organizing women in St. Louis? The atmosphere among elites in St. Louis was encouraging to white women as a class. Minor and her husband, Francis, came to St. Louis from Virginia in 1845 and, despite their backgrounds in slaveholding plantation families, were Unionists during the Civil War. The first convention of the suffrage group, with Minor as its president, was held in 1869 in the St. Louis Mercantile Library, established two decades earlier by Wayman Crow and William Greenleaf Eliot and graced with the art of up-and-coming young sculptor Harriet Hosmer. Crow had opened his home to New Yorker Hosmer when she studied anatomy at the McDowell Medical College just before the Civil War. He was a sponsor of her early career and commissioned several sculptures for the Mercantile Library, including a version of Hosmer's most famous work, Queen Zenobia in Chains, one of many marble statues created as metaphors of slavery—and in Hosmer's statue—of defiant womanhood—at midcentury.

Eliot was invited to address the first meeting of the Missouri Woman Suffrage Association but declined, sending a letter of encouragement instead: "I believe now, as I have for fifteen years, that the question of female suffrage is only one of time." Every woman should have "equal opportunity and right of self development, and her sphere of influence should be limited only by her natural ability." A year later he endorsed women's right to vote but, like many Republican conservatives, insisted on a literacy requirement, a stricture that would have a significant impact on potential Black voters and along with poll taxes and Jim Crow would seriously impede voting access in the South.[30]

Entering the professions and gaining the right to vote were inextricably linked for woman citizens. By 1870 Missouri had the state's first woman lawyer, and in 1871, Phoebe Wilson Couzins of St. Louis was graduated with a law degree from William Greenleaf Eliot's Washington University. In next-door Illinois, Myra Bradwell trained in the law but was denied a license in 1869 on the grounds that she was married; another woman lawyer who was not married was denied admission to the Illinois bar on the grounds that she was "a woman." Bradwell's case went to the Supreme Court of the United States. Her argument was that as a person and a citizen who qualified for practicing the law, she deserved "equal protection" and "due process" and that Illinois could not deny her a license to practice law. In its 1874 decision the Supreme Court turned down her claim, with Justice Joseph Bradley ruling that, among other considerations, "the constitution of the family organization, which is founded in the divine ordinance, as well as in the nature of things, indicates the domestic sphere as that which properly belongs to the domain and function of womanhood."[31]

This kind of exclusion, based on a biological imperative, bore a striking similarity to the logic used in Taney's Dred Scott decision: the genetic makeup of entire classes of people could keep them from full citizenship. Bradwell's attempt to use the Fourteenth Amendment for women's rights would soon be repeated in the Virginia Minor case. As soon as the Fourteenth Amendment was ratified, women's rightists argued that the word "male" in its text enabled Black men to vote but did not disqualify women necessarily. They mobilized women in 1872 to vote for the reelection of Ulysses S. Grant. The Minors' registrar in St. Louis, Reese Happersett, would not allow Virginia to register. The Missouri courts ruled that Virginia could not sue Happersett because as a married woman, she had no legal standing. Her husband sued on her behalf, but the state superior court ruled the case was moot anyway because as a woman Virginia Minor was not eligible to vote. With this twisted logic in place, the Minors took their case to the US Supreme Court, where it was decided in 1875. The ruling agreed that women were persons and citizens but not necessarily voters. The Bradwell and Minor decisions were as significant as Dred Scott—and as it turned out—more long-lasting in keeping a broad class of citizens from voting and joining the professions.[32]

As these Supreme Court decisions affecting women's status were debated, Black citizens of greater St. Louis attempted to gain access to political decision making and continued the building of community in churches, schools, and Masonic orders. Henry Blow had followed through on the commitment he made in his Reconstruction speech to "enlightened Christian Duty." In 1868 he signed over a piece of his family's vast property in Carondelet to an AME delegation headed by Pastor Dickson and seven Black trustees, who described themselves as "just emerged from slavery . . . without means. We want to make good citizens and give our children a Christian education."[33] Some of these AME founders appear in the 1870 census, in US military records, and in St. Louis city directories. George Kilpatrick served in the Thirty-Fifth US Colored Infantry and was twenty-six years old in 1868. The city directory of 1873 found John Sides living on Thirteenth Street, occupation laborer. Aaron Russell was listed in the city director as a porter for the Life Association of America, living on Olive Street; the taker of the Census of 1870 in St. Louis recorded both Russell and his wife as unable to read or write. The cornerstone for the AME church was laid in 1869 on the former Blow lot, the ceremony officiating it conducted by Black Freemasons. Dickson named it Quinn Chapel, after William Paul Quinn, who had organized the AME congregation in Cincinnati, Ohio, and converted Dickson's parents to Methodism.

Dickson, former leader of the Knights of Liberty, and his wife, Mary Butcher Peters Dickson, were now major leaders of a peaceful but determined civil rights effort in St. Louis. The Dicksons turned their secret society, the Order of Twelve, into the Knights and Daughters of Tabor in 1872 and made it a self-help engine for the Black community. The goals of the Taborites were the "getting of homes and acquiring wealth" through "Christianity, education, morality and temperance and the art of governing, self-reliance and true manhood and womanhood." By 1869 four African American Masonic lodges were in St. Louis and seventeen in Missouri altogether. Dickson traveled to Arkansas, Iowa, Kansas, and Mississippi to organize new lodges that became pillars of their communities and recruited "colored teachers" for the "colored schools" in Missouri. He was named an elector at large for the Republican Party in 1872.[34]

Charlton H. Tandy, born free in Lexington, Kentucky, in 1836, also saw Freemasonry as a path to prosperity and new freedoms. Tandy claimed to have been a conductor on the Underground Railroad helping slaves cross the Ohio River after he came to St. Louis in 1857. He worked as a porter for Kennard's carpet store and as a coachman and a waiter. He enlisted in Company B of the Thirteenth Regiment of Colored Troops, achieving the rank of captain by the end of the Civil War, and helped to establish the Lincoln Institute in Jefferson City, Missouri. Using the help of white Republican friends like Benjamin Gratz Brown, he was employed as a messenger in the US Customs House in St. Louis, a post he held for seventeen years, using the patronage system to advance to other commissioned offices in government. He exhorted eligible Black voters in St. Louis to vote for Republican candidates and ran for (and lost) the office of Missouri state senator. Considered a "great orator," he lectured on the history of Black leaders of the past at the St. Louis Mercantile Library, an indication that whites such as Eliot and Crow perhaps saw him as an intellectual equal.

In 1870 a dramatic shift in the political winds arrived in St. Louis, when Liberal Republicans Brown and ambitious German immigrant Carl Schurz, along with Tandy, assailed the effects of the so-called Drake Constitution of

1865. The test oath was now depicted as a restriction of free speech and an impediment to widening the voting public. Amnesty for former Confederate sympathizers was popular, and when a new constitution was put to Missouri voters, an amendment repealing the test oath was ratified by a margin of eight to one. Schurz and the other Liberal Republicans hoped they might now take the political lead in Missouri, but there were both local and national forces conspiring to undermine their political legitimacy. The Grant administration was riddled with corruption, most white citizens of Missouri aligned with the Democrats, and Black voters could not make up the difference as a voting bloc. A new Missouri state constitution in 1875, without any test oath for voting, ensured the influence of Republicans would be thwarted for decades to come. The 1875 constitution also made clear that the great swath of rural Missouri was not going to tolerate the more liberal politics of the city of St. Louis.

The white Protestants who had made up the core of antislavery and unequivocal support for the Union now found themselves on the outside looking in. The Radicals had no choice but to retreat to the sidelines of politics. Samuel Knox left Congress after serving part of the term he had contested and then retired to the practice of law in St. Louis. He was drawn into the scandal of the Whiskey Ring, a corruption scheme based on the patronage positions of old allies of Grant in St. Louis. These schemers took bribes from distillers hoping to avoid the federal excise tax on liquor, bribes they used for their own enrichment and a political slush fund for Grant's reelection in 1872. William McKee, editor of the St. Louis *Missouri Globe Democrat*, also used the funds to buy up and consolidate several Missouri newspapers. Part of a defense team requesting a pardon for McKee, Knox argued that the jurors assembled for the trial had recently held "rebel" views and should not have been allowed to serve and "that no juror was summoned from counties that were republican." Knox's allegiance to old values like the test oath, in this instance, demonstrates how blind he was to the new political order that had evolved quickly under Grant, with excessive use of patronage and corruption that alarmed political purists like Schurz. Knox's daughter Hannah remembered going with her father to meetings in the lobby of the Willard Hotel in Washington, confabs soon dubbed in the popular press as "lobbying." Hannah grew up with contempt for lawyers and as a young woman joined the Knights of Labor and became a suffragist.[35]

Radical Republican influence in Missouri was about to be decimated. Charles Daniel Drake was elected from Missouri in 1867 to the US Senate, where he was an impassioned supporter of Radical Republican measures and voted to convict in the impeachment trial of President Andrew Johnson. But in 1870, facing defeat for his next reelection and with the rise of the Liberal Republicans and the clamor of Democrats bound to undermine his stern position, Drake accepted an appointment as chief justice of the US Court of Claims and died in 1885. Henry Blow served on the Senate Joint Committee that drafted the Fourteenth Amendment but declined to run again in 1867. Named ambassador to Brazil by President Grant in 1869, Blow was accompanied by his daughter Susan, who learned Portuguese quickly and assisted him in drafting trade agreements with the Brazilian government. Henry and Minerva took their children to Europe in 1871 and were barely at home for years at a time in their lovely home on the bluffs overlooking the Mississippi in Carondelet. Minerva and Henry died within three months of each other in 1875. Susan continued to make a name for herself as a pioneer in the German philosophy of kindergarten.

Old age was catching up to most of the longtime Civil War influencers in Missouri. Edward Bates returned to St. Louis after leaving the cabinet in 1864, where he had opposed Lincoln's new alliance with Chase and Stanton. Bates disapproved of the test oath in Missouri and the new constitution of 1865 and died in 1869 in the bosom of his large family in St. Louis. Having crusaded against the Radical Reconstruction agenda and returning to the Democrat Party, Frank Blair was only in his early fifties when he took Drake's place as US senator in 1871 but suffered a stroke in 1872 that left him partially paralyzed and in poor health. He was defeated for reelection by the Missouri legislature in 1873 and died in 1875. Montgomery Blair, ever the Democrat, continued to operate from his base as a powerful lawyer in Washington and became engaged in the dispute over the presidential election that required a dodgy compromise to make Republican Rutherford B. Hayes the president and to end Reconstruction by withdrawing federal troops in the South.

The city of St. Louis had long been seen by the much-larger geographical body of St. Louis County as a center of dubious social policies and a waste of taxpayer money. The liberal sentiments of the New Englanders and their Protestant churches had not gone unnoticed in the more rural and traditional communities of outer St. Louis County, whose "freeholders" controlled local government. There was a steady undermining of the St. Louis municipal government by the county bureaucrats, who appointed city officials, managed the courts, and collected taxes on top of those paid in the city itself, making it difficult for St. Louis to support adequate public schools and infrastructure improvements. The political corruption that was rampant on the national stage in Washington was evident in St. Louis County as well. The local arrests of those involved in the Whiskey Ring scandal of 1875 made that clear.

As the Civil War came to an end, African Americans from the countryside in Missouri and from southern states, especially Kentucky, Louisiana, Tennessee, Western Virginia, and Louisiana, migrated into both the city of St. Louis and its outer rim, St. Louis County. Whatever its drawbacks, St. Louis continued to attract new communities of "colored people" who sought jobs and housing in a "cosmopolitan" border-state city. The US Census of 1880 counted more than 176,000 white native-born citizens, 59,000 Germans, and 32,000 Irish in St. Louis and St. Louis County. A St. Louis newspaper commented on the growth of the Black population from 5,000 before the Civil War to 22,000 by 1880, assuring readers this was no cause for alarm: "The growth of the city has been so wonderful during the last ten years that this great influx of colored people, which might have been a source of annoyance, remained almost unobserved."[36] The erosion of African American jobs as immigrants and Southern whites took them over was a never-ending trend as the century came to an end and made rising in station for Black families ever more difficult.

The bitterness of James Thomas's observations in his memoir describes just how painful everyday racism had become in his long and mostly successful life in St. Louis. Thomas settled in St. Louis in 1857, married into great wealth, and succeeded more than most other Black people in St. Louis. He had bitter words at the turn of the new century for what he viewed as the popular "classification" of American races: "White man first, 'Injun' next, Dog next, Nigger last." "The Negro," he wrote, "has had up-hill work from the start." He could not obtain a real education, apprentice in a trade, or belong to a union, and "if he has a job of some kind, there is always a white man at his elbow ready to take his place for a little less money." If a Black person did accumulate property, whites would "use some means to reach it and destroy it."[37]

This was both true and not always true in St. Louis. Griffin Brander had no formal education, but he worked steadily as a drayman on the waterfront, obtained yearly licenses from the city of St. Louis, bought his own house, and supported his family with his income. He paid his taxes and bought insurance. The AME and Baptist churches and the Freemasonry lodges of St. Louis preached a gospel of self-help and betterment through education, the building of schools, and agitation for civil rights. Some Black families were sending their children to high school, creating small businesses, and buying property for homes and businesses. Janitor John Davis and his wife, Helen, lived on Wash Street and were congregants at the Central Baptist Church. They would launch their children into middle-class jobs through education, hard work, and community support.

As they were in Philadelphia and Baltimore, upwardly mobile Black men and women in St. Louis were on the forefront of civil rights agitation. As the city and the county of St. Louis expanded, more streetcar lines were built. As in Philadelphia and Baltimore, streetcar conductors refused to seat Black women inside the cars or did not even stop to pick them up. Neptune and Caroline Williams filed a lawsuit against the Bellefontaine Railway in 1867 charging that a "conductor had pushed Mrs. Williams, pregnant and carrying an infant in her arms, from a car as she tried to get aboard." The court hearing their case banned discrimination on the streetcars. But some conductors continued to refuse to pick up Black passengers, and many white riders continued to refuse to ride inside cars with an "inferior" race. In May 1867 Frances and Taylor Watson boarded a car, he standing on the platform, she going inside to sit down. In protest, most of the white riders left the car and walked alongside it.[38] Making a judicial pronouncement and getting people to accept it are two different things.

Tandy organized a boycott of the cars by Black citizens in St. Louis in 1870 and to make his point one day grabbed the reins of one team of horses and forced the conductor to halt his car. Tandy was arrested and thrown in jail. But he had enough prominent contacts in St. Louis to get himself out of jail and effect a change in official railroad policy on the cars. Now a part of the Liberal Republican "establishment," he continued to round up Black votes for the Republicans, at times threatening to take them over to the Democrats if the interests of Black voters continued to be ignored. He had to be content with nibbles of patronage and small victories for Black people in St. Louis here and there. He was caught in the struggle between the good and the possible, as most politicians are.[39]

The new constitution of 1875 did not alleviate the second-class stature of the city of St. Louis. St. Louis County continued to "manage" the affairs of the metropolis and view it as a den of all things rural whites disliked: too many Black people, too many immigrants, too many Republicans. The constitution eliminated the test oath, and Democrats took control. But one demand of African Americans in St. Louis was heard. A new public high school, named after Charles Sumner, would provide learning beyond elementary school for Black children. Within a few decades, with input from Black leaders and qualified teachers and progressive moves to better locations, Sumner became one of the best high schools for Black teenagers in the region.

The "reconstruction" of St. Louis along radical emancipationist lines was coming to an end, just as the federal enforcement of the Civil Rights Act of 1866 and the Fourteenth and Fifteenth Amendments were winding down in the South. Many of the whites who had championed abolitionism and expanding rights for Black people—to a certain extent—were either dead or in reclusive retirements. The abandonment of the goals and accomplishments of Radical Reconstruction would begin almost immediately in 1876, with new framings of slavery in the upper South and depictions of freed people about to take hold that seemed to render them incapable of the duties of full citizenship. William Greenleaf Eliot would be at the heart of this reinterpretation, echoed by historians and social scientists, in the interests of what they saw as the importance of the reunification of the United States, with a watered-down version of citizenship for African Americans that was white American dogma by 1910.

# 6 “Nothing of the Horrors of Slavery”

Conservative Republicans and the Democrats in Missouri, some who had served in the Lincoln administration and the US Congress, led the groundswell to end Radical Republican control of the state in 1875. What might be surprising is that the political allegiances of strident Democrats and self-righteous Republican factions were starkly different, but their underlying assumptions about race were not. Both sides could not perceive of African Americans as persons yet capable or even ever deserving of full citizenship.

White antislavery reformers initially seized ownership of the history of what had taken place during the Civil War and Reconstruction in Missouri. They created a story of the end of slavery that could underpin their boosterism of a vibrant city on the Mississippi River with thrilling prospects ahead. A rosy glow of the “peculiar institution” crept into this narrative for decades after the end of Reconstruction. The message of the story was that it was best for slavery to be forgotten and that it had largely been a benign institution in the border states and a dying institution in the upper South. As scholar David W. Blight has so forcefully demonstrated, this focus on forgetting the real past was widespread among elites in white communities throughout the United States.[1]

Some of these elites were in Protestant churches, the backbone of the white antislavery movement in St. Louis, and they had welcomed emancipation. Congregants supported the Reconstruction policies of the Grant administration but, tired of corruption in Washington and Missouri and continued disorder in the deep South, concluded it was time for “reunion and reconciliation.” Presbyterian Edward Bates, who left his post as attorney general of the United States in 1864, was disgusted by the lengths to which Radical

Republicans in Missouri used the test oath to keep many male citizens from voting and to maintain what they viewed as a righteous Republican regime with the state constitution of 1865. After Roswell Field and Samuel Knox visited him in June with Republican friends from the Northeast, Bates disdainfully wrote in his diary that Governor Fletcher of Missouri "must be a very mean *little* man, and under the influence of very poor advisers (I hear that Knox and Field are his chief counselors at law)."[2]

Bates was in the bloc of former Whigs and moderate Republicans who opposed the new constitution, dubbed the Drake Constitution, because Charles Drake, Henry Blow's brother-in-law, drafted the document and pushed it over the finish line. Among its most unpopular provisions was the lifting of tax relief for Catholic Church properties. Some Radical Republicans described the Catholic hierarchy in Missouri as "a 'money-getting and money-making machine' which had not been paying its share of taxes."[3] Elijah Lovejoy, the antislavery journalist who was lynched in Alton, Illinois, before the Civil War, despised Catholics as much as he did slaveholders and drunkards. These views did not sit well with Irish and German voters in Missouri, who joined moderate Republicans and Democrats in a growing chorus of criticism of the 1865 constitution, and in ten years it would be gone.

By 1875 the Radical Republicans who "reconstructed" Missouri without the granting of voting rights to Black men were out of power, unable to convince the next generation to continue their strategy of maintaining control by denying the vote to former Confederates and Confederate sympathizers and requiring loyalty oaths of a wide swath of public figures. Republicans made modest gains in the funding of African American public schools and vocational education in line with their conviction that progress grounded in literacy and economic mobility would eventually—at some unknown date in the future—lead to full citizenship for Black people.

The deaths of Union soldiers on the battlefields of the Civil War cried out for remembrance with permanent markers at Vicksburg, Gettysburg, and Washington, DC, as sculptors and artisans labored to express human emotion in stone. Antislavery communities erected monuments to honor Union soldiers, President Lincoln, and what they viewed as his greatest accomplishment, the Emancipation Proclamation. Formerly enslaved woman Charlotte Scott, now living in Marietta, Ohio, sent $5.00 to James Yeatman during the Civil War with the hope that the Western Sanitary Commission would honor Lincoln as the Great Emancipator. The Colored Troops of Missouri and Tennessee made donations for the statue and with contributions from others had reached a total of $21,000 by 1873.

Numerous artists' careers might be furthered with a commission like this one, commissions that would culminate in Augustus Saint-Gaudens's frieze of the Fifty-Fourth Black Regiment led by Robert Gould Shaw in Boston and in the Lincoln Memorial by Daniel Chester French in Washington. Wayman Crow of the Western Sanitary Commission had long promoted the career of sculptor Harriet Hosmer, a friend of his daughter, who studied anatomy in St. Louis before the Civil War. She worked up a model of an elaborate tableau with numerous figures and motifs depicting slavery, emancipation, and the Black soldier, topped by the catafalque of Lincoln. Hosmer and Edmonia Lewis, a Chippewa Black woman, both had European studios in Rome. Lewis celebrated emancipation with a statue of two recently freed people, a standing Black man and a Black woman on one knee beside him as he points upward, without any presence of Lincoln. Lewis was achieving fame in her own right. Black St. Louis residents James Thomas and his wife, Antoinette Rogers Thomas, sat for Lewis and received her busts of them in 1873 and 1874. Hosmer's statue was the WSC's first choice—they had not considered Lewis—but it was too elaborate and expensive to make with the funds they collected.[4]

Abigail and William Eliot went abroad in the fall of 1869 and visited studios in Rome and Florence to find another artist. William wanted Yeatman to abandon the Hosmer version of the statue, describing it as "in honor of everybody & therefore of nobody. . . . Pour cold water on it, if you can." He was most impressed in Florence with a work by Thomas Ball of Massachusetts, of "Lincoln and a slave . . . the African's type well maintained without overdoing." The *St. Louis Daily Democrat* was thrilled with the visual message of the tableau: "We see nothing of the horrors of slavery: except the symbolic chains which have fallen from the slave's hands, while the freedman is a vigorous, strong athletic man . . . whose face is full of gratitude, as he looks up, seemingly in thanksgiving to God that the great boon of freedom has been conferred."[5]

The US Congress donated the pedestal for a sculpture to be installed near Capitol Hill in Lincoln Park, and work on the monument began. The Western Sanitary Commission asked Ball for modifications of his initial design by freeing the kneeling figure's right hand from its shackle and, most important, at Eliot's suggestion, making Archer Alexander's face the model for the kneeling Black man. With photography now a useable and transportable medium, Eliot sent a photograph of Alexander to Ball, who reworked the head of the man in his statue under the beneficent gaze of Lincoln to resemble Alexander.

The Emancipation Monument was dedicated in April 1876, with President Grant, his cabinet, and members of Congress and the Supreme Court in attendance. John Mercer Langston, who argued before the Missouri state legislature for Black voting rights, was now the dean of Howard Law School and led a procession from the Howard campus to Lincoln Park. Frederick Douglass was invited to speak, an acknowledgment of his status as the most prominent leader of the Black community. As he gave his speech he was in a tough spot, personally and politically. He could recall, vividly, being summoned to the White House to explore Lincoln's and the Blairs' plans for "deportation." He had seen in his adult lifetime the tortured evolution of Lincoln from conservative Illinois antislavery politician to a president who made reluctant calls for emancipation and the enrollment of Black troops, largely as military measures.

"Abraham Lincoln," Douglass said, "was not, in the fullest sense . . . either our man or our model. In his interests, in his associations, in his habits of thought, and in his prejudices, he was a white man." Nor was Douglass pleased with the statue. But he was willing to say that Lincoln "was at the head of a great movement, and was in living and earnest sympathy with that movement." In a letter to the Washington, DC, *National Republican*, Douglass argued for a more dignified statue to be built sometime in the future: "The negro here, though rising, is still on his knees and nude. . . . What I want to see before I die is a monument representing the negro, not *couchant* on his knees like a four-footed animal, but erect on his feet like a man."[6] A few such renditions began to appear in the coming decades but were vastly outnumbered by those of fallen Confederate and Union generals and their white soldiers.

The election season of 1876 was well underway by the time Douglass spoke in Washington. In the riverfront city of Cincinnati, the Republicans nominated Rutherford B. Hayes of Ohio. The Democrats, who failed miserably in 1872, saw a new opportunity for success in civil-service reformist candidate, Samuel Tilden, governor of New York, who was nominated in June in St. Louis at the party convention. The return of Democratic Party control of the state of Missouri in 1875 guaranteed a robust celebration at the first national party convention held in St. Louis, the "gateway city." It was the kind of event city boosters Yeatman and Crow envisioned in what 1876 election historian Roy Morris has characterized as "a nod to northern patriotism, and also, perhaps, a wink to those who had worn the gray."[7] In his address to the Merchants Exchange of St. Louis in 1875, Crow bragged that "in a little more than a half century Saint Louis has passed from a border trading post, scarcely yet Americanized, to a metropolis . . . [whose] population [has] increased to nearly a million, . . . contending for a foremost rank among American cities."[8] Symbolizing St. Louis's progress on a number of fronts,

Phoebe Wilson Couzins, the first woman to graduate from a law school in the United States, spoke before the convention in the opening ceremonies. The daughter of the St. Louis chief of police, she had attended Washington University and was now a talented orator.

The Democrats were about to nominate a reformer who would be popular among Liberal Republicans intent on civil-service reform and restoring the vision of honest government. Tilden led the fight in New York to overthrow the Boss Tweed machine and seemed an ideal candidate. But he was also spearheading a political movement committed to overturning Reconstruction and Radical Republican influence in the South by arguing for "home rule," coded language that approved of eliminating Black men and Northern Republicans, dubbed "carpetbaggers," from voting and holding office in Alabama, Arkansas, the Carolinas, Florida, Georgia, Louisiana, Mississippi, Texas, and Virginia. Tilden campaigned alongside Horatio Seymour and Frank Blair in their losing battle to take the White House in 1868, a campaign laden with racist slogans and diatribes against so-called miscegenation at every opportunity. There were the usual references in Tilden's network to protecting white women from Black men, mantras repeated on the ground by Ku Kluxers in violent attacks on Black voters and their families in the South. But many Northern voters were tired of Reconstruction news, and "waving the bloody shirt" no longer worked as well as it once had in rallying votes for the Republicans.

William Greenleaf Eliot would go through a personal journey that mirrored this national longing for reform and ambivalence about Reconstruction as he considered the politics of 1876. In early October he wrote to his son Thom, "If the 'United South' & the half-principled doughface northern Democrats prevail, we shall have trouble of which no fellah can tell." He collected clippings headlined "The Situation in South Carolina," describing "rifle clubs" assaulting Republican voters and Grant's military response. He concludes, "The election of November 17 is of vast importance. A 'United South' with a northern plastic supplement, means a renewed Rebellion against Law and Order."[9]

The Hayes-Tilden election, as Eliot thought it would be, is a turning point in the nation's history. By a narrow margin, Tilden won the popular vote with the highest turnout of eligible voters up to that point in US history. (Voters did not include, of course, all women and many Black men, who were openly intimidated and prevented from voting in the Midwest and the South.) The reporting of electoral college votes to the US Senate before the assembled US House of Representatives now set the stage for a struggle over who would be president, with electors from Florida, Louisiana, and South Carolina claimed by both Democrats and Republicans. State electoral commissions, mostly controlled by Republicans, reported widespread fraud. South Carolina, for instance, had recorded more than 100 percent of eligible votes for Tilden.

In Washington, Democrats controlled the House of Representatives, Republicans the Senate. With no possible resolution between the two bodies over how to proceed, Congress created a bipartisan electoral commission to make a recommendation. Montgomery Blair was one of the lawyers who assisted the Democrats in making their case and arguing for Tilden. Deadlocked for weeks, a backroom deal bypassed the commission and settled the dispute at the beginning of March. The electoral college vote would go to Hayes, and in exchange Hayes would return federal troops to their barracks in the South, leaving Republicans and Black voters with no protection from violence and intimidation. Hayes was inaugurated on March 5, 1877, and any semblance of electoral integrity in the South was now gone.

Having gone abroad in the fall of 1876, Abigail and William Eliot returned to the United States through New Orleans on their way home to St. Louis. Both the Blows and the Eliots, like many prosperous families in St. Louis, often went to New Orleans for better weather and recreation, an easy steamboat ride downriver. Eliot preached at the Unitarian church in New Orleans in the mid-1870s for extra income, where there was a vacancy in the pastorate and a disorganized congregation. The Eliots' eldest son, Thom Eliot, a Unitarian church minister in Portland, Oregon, was experiencing headaches and blurry vision. His church caught on fire in 1873 and required rebuilding. Thom and his family came home to St. Louis in the summer of 1876 so that his eyes might rest while he looked for another position closer to St. Louis. William thought he might be able to install Thom in the Unitarian Church in New Orleans.

In spending time with Unitarians in New Orleans and considering his interest in promoting his son's career, William had to walk the same fine line with his congregants that he did in St. Louis during the Civil War. Unitarians in Louisiana had been part of the Confederacy, and they were now seeing a political order in which Black men assumed new, and to many whites, disturbing responsibilities. In a March 1877 letter to President Hayes, widely printed as an editorial in Northeastern newspapers, Eliot outlined his assessment of the political situation in Louisiana. Worth underscoring is Eliot's long-held conviction that emancipation should have been gradual and that literacy should be a requirement for voting. Some of this could be put down to upper-class snobbery, but some of it was based on Eliot's disdain for Black people, a people who should be lifted up but who were not yet ready for full citizenship.

In his lengthy letter to Hayes, made public in newspapers in St. Louis, Boston, and New York, Eliot began, "I am quite well acquainted" in New Orleans and "mix freely with all classes." Having been in the city over the previous two years as a visiting preacher, he thought he could offer realistic impressions of the "color line," which, in his view, was more sharply drawn than ever. Eliot visited both houses of the Louisiana state legislature and concluded, "I should not be willing to trust my interests" to the men who were in control. "A *large* majority . . . is composed of colored people," and "the white members, if I may judge by appearance and manners, are a very second rate sort of men." He could understand why "property holders and educated people" would not want to be "under the control of such bodies of men." Most whites in the city believed that those governing them had been unlawfully elected. The "mothers and wives" of the city were especially "outspoken and bitter," and the "whole social influence in all circles, especially the highest, is in favor of strong and summary measures."[10]

Eliot's suggestions were to solve the electoral dispute by putting the Democrat governor in control and allowing whites to reclaim the legislature. The current situation, holding the white citizens of Louisiana hostage with federal bayonets and under Black and so-called carpetbagger rule, Eliot thought, would never accomplish reconciliation between Confederates and Unionists. A return to local control was preferable to the "social war of races" that would inevitably follow a continued federal presence. He reminded Hayes that there were thousands of men in state militias "with the belief that their cause is just." They were anxious to overthrow the Republicans, and most of the South agreed they should. Eliot admitted that the spirit of the Fifteenth Amendment would be in jeopardy if such a coup took place and that Black men would be discouraged from voting for years. But over time, Eliot argued, "as the colored people advance in thrift and intelligence," full voting rights would be entertained by whites. "If an educational test or qualification for voting could be secured by an Amendment to the Constitution, we might reasonably look for enduring peace," he said.[11] No such literacy law was even being considered in Missouri, and where it was safe to do so, more Black men were voting after the passage of the Fifteenth Amendment. James Milton Turner and Charlton H. Tandy were rounding up Black votes for the Republicans and attempting, unsuccessfully, to run for the state legislature. They were largely treated with disdain by the white Republican establishment.[12]

Eliot's view of corrupt and incompetent government dominated by Black men and white carpetbaggers took hold in the American imagination and lasted well into the twentieth century. In his 1934 book *Black Reconstruction*, W. E. B. Du Bois painted a more nuanced picture of so-called Negro rule in Louisiana. There was no way of really estimating how many Black men served in the government. Many of them were of mixed race and, like state senator P. B. S. Pinchback, might have passed for white but chose to present themselves as "colored." "These colored leaders," says Du Bois, "had a task of enormous difficulty. . . . Some looked white, some black, some born free and rich, the recipients of good education; some were ex-slaves, with no formal training. They were faced with an intricate social tangle among the whites." They never gained a majority in the legislature, which remained under white control.[13]

Du Bois showed that Reconciliation was far from peaceful in a state where racial violence was already the norm. The state of Louisiana was in a continuous state of internal warfare from the end of the Civil War to the end of Reconstruction, with "open intimidation and murder" enforced by well-armed secret groups, such as the White Camelia and the Ku Klux Klan. These groups paraded nightly to support the Democratic Party ticket before the 1868 election, with Seymour and Blair receiving a lopsided victory in Louisiana. With the election of 1876 on the horizon, these militias were out in force, the violence even more extreme, with, in Du Bois's view, the "whipping, shooting, wounding, maiming, mutilation, and murder of women, children and defenseless men."[14]

These militias were the very groups that Eliot believed might bring peace and stability to New Orleans. A systematic campaign in Northern newspapers, amplified by cartoonish depictions of lolling legislators with their feet on the desk, eating fried chicken and watermelon, convinced many Northerners that Black legislators and their white allies were a menace to democracy. Tropes of reunion and reconciliation, with an assumed undercurrent of the belittlement of Black people, were a given as the election of 1876 took place.[15]

Hayes probably received many letters like the one Eliot wrote to him about the need to end Reconstruction in Louisiana, but William Greenleaf Eliot was an important witness. He was originally from New England, a minister with a sterling reputation, a former administrator of the Western Sanitary Commission, a friend of Dorothea Dix and the Fremonts, and perhaps one of the most well-known citizens of St. Louis outside of Missouri. Hayes assumed the presidency by agreeing to end federal occupation and campaigned with slogans urging reunion. Letters like Eliot's underscored Hayes's already held views and gave them moral credence. As Hayes took office, the Louisiana business class bribed the Louisiana state legislature, dominated by Northerners and Republicans, to disband, and the Democrat Party gained control. On April 14, 1877, the federal troops returned to their barracks, and white supremacy was enshrined in Louisiana.

Radical Reconstruction ended in the same way in most of the South: violence perpetrated by secret armed groups; an end to public schools for Black and poor white children; intimidation at the voting booth; and terrible poverty for rural populations, exacerbated in later decades by the boll weevil and cotton-crop failures. The Panic of 1877 and the ensuing depression only compounded general misery in the South. In 1879 Black families from downriver responded to their desolate lives by traveling through St. Louis, intent on homesteading land in Kansas and the Oklahoma Territory. By the time families reached St. Louis, they had spent most of their funds and needed emergency relief. Estimates were that by the spring of 1879, sixteen thousand Black migrants were stranded in St. Louis, unable to cross the Missouri River and move further west. Most whites in Missouri were disdainful of the refugees, all too reminiscent of the crisis that poor people uprooted during the Civil War had created when they poured into St. Louis. The *St. Louis Globe Democrat* described the migrants as an "Ebon[y] Exodus" of foolish people who were dupes of land speculators and facing no real future in the West.[16]

The Black community of St. Louis organized an impressive relief effort. Tandy and Turner led these efforts, and Moses Dickson served as president of the Refugee Relief Board. Black churches opened their doors to provide temporary shelter. These leaders disagreed over whether to encourage migration from the South or to urge African Americans to stand their ground and stake claims to what should be their own lands in the South. Their importance in the agricultural economy was reaffirmed when some white planters and farmers with armed force tried to prevent their laborers from leaving. Douglass argued that the economic engine of the agricultural South could only be advanced by Black labor and that for the immediate future it was best to stay at home.[17] A renewed discussion of moving to Liberia was entertained by some. But if migrants could not cross the Missouri, they were unlikely to afford an Atlantic passage to Africa. Black leaders in St. Louis used this opportunity to educate the St. Louis citizenry on the root of this migration: violence and intimidation directed at Black farmers and workers with the end of Reconstruction.[18] They were also creating links to organizers in Kansas to help provide for "getting started" in this, hopefully, new "promised land."

White leaders of the WSC responded to the refugee crisis as well. Eliot tapped his New England friends for funds and shipments of clothing and foodstuffs. In April he visited some of the migrants in the St. Louis camps and Black churches to assess their situation and their reasons for leaving the South. He contradicted the profile being sketched in the city's newspapers: "The majority are in apparent good health, able-bodied, expecting to work and with a little something to get along with." What they would need in the way of economic help in the future, he said in agreement with Turner, Dickson, and Tandy, was support for their lives in Kansas. Why had they left? They were headed for Kansas because "of the impossibility of bettering themselves or obtaining full benefit of freedom under the law; because they are socially kept under and despised." The end of slavery created a new consciousness and discontent, growing "out of increased intelligence and a better perception of the rights of freedom, not from mere restlessness, unwillingness to work or ignorance." The migrants were, in fact, better off than they had been ten years ago, "except that the right of *free* suffrage is practically denied to them and is sure to be."[19]

Although he never said so, Eliot was admitting in these statements that his resolution to the crisis in New Orleans in 1876 was a failure and that the end of Reconstruction only tightened the grip of the "Redeemers" on their near-captive labor force. He tried to convince General William Tecumseh Sherman to run for president in 1880, fearful that the alternatives to "firm control" would be a Republican "party politician" or "dough-face" Democrat. "The negro question is not settled," Eliot wrote in his letter to Sherman. "Loyalty is only a name in the South."[20] Eliot's fears were realized when Vice President Chester A. Arthur assumed the presidency in 1881 after the assassination of James Abram Garfield. Arthur continued the practice of leaving the Southern states to continue intimidation at the ballot box and ignore violence directed at Black citizens.

Eliot's health worsened in the 1880s, and he died in 1888. He stopped writing in his journal in 1880, suffered from constant headaches, preached infrequently, and was unable to accomplish much. He did mount an ineffective campaign against prostitution, the "social evil," recalling his popular lectures to young men on sexual purity and temperance. Reflecting on his life, he made funeral plans and insisted that no fuss be made. But he would make one last effort to strike the right balance in describing the sectional crisis, slavery in the border states, and his own attempts to combat evil masters. His sons, Edward and Christopher, and their baby sister, Rose, had been with runaway Alexander in 1863 when kidnappers arrived at Beaumont Place to seize him. Sometime in the 1880s Eddie and Chris asked their father to write the story of "Archie's" life.

The Eliot family had seen more of Archer Alexander when he returned to St. Louis from Alton, Illinois, after the Civil War and established a home with his second wife, Judy, in St. Charles, where he presumably could be in closer contact with his adult children and grandchildren. The only mention of Archer in William's personal writings (except as a model for the Emancipation monument) is a letter to his wife, Abigail, in the fall of 1872, reporting that "Archer has turned up, & is at work for me. Perhaps Judy will be a good washer for us. He comes back as poor as he went, having been cheated out of his earnings."[21] Eliot did not say how Alexander lost his earnings, but by 1872 Archer was sixty-six years old, worn down from a lifetime of physical labor and life on the move. Whether he achieved notoriety in the Black community for his uncompensated appearance as a model being freed from shackles in the Emancipation monument is unknown. But when he died in 1880, he was celebrated in a "well attended" ceremony at the new St. Peter's AME church on Lucas Avenue, and Eliot spoke at his funeral.[22]

The patronizing tone of Eliot's remarks about Alexander and his new wife in Eliot's 1872 letter were carried over as a governing style in the *Story of Archer Alexander from Slavery to Freedom*, published in 1885. When or whether Eliot wrote the entire text is unclear. Even if he authored it himself, he probably sought assistance from someone, as he was often ill. His daughter-in-law Charlotte Stearns Eliot, wife of Henry ("Hal"), was in close contact with her Eliot in-laws. Hal and Charlotte's family lived for years at a time with the Eliot parents while he struggled to establish the Hydraulic Press Brick Company. Charlotte was a Massachusetts schoolteacher before she married and in St. Louis took up pioneering social work and advocated reforms of probation laws and the prison system. She was an accomplished writer of poetry and prose and reared a famous son, the poet Thomas Stearns Eliot. In 1904 she would publish a laudatory biography of her father-in-law. She had access to Eliot's journals and letters, sources augmented by years of their personal interaction. Her biography highlighted what she perceived to be his prescient views on Reconstruction and Southern redemption, with the installation of Hayes a major turning point. It seems likely that she was Eliot's amanuensis and editor as he composed Alexander's story.

There is now no way of knowing what proportion of Eliot's writing is in *The Story of Archer Alexander* or whether it was filtered through an assistant, but it became the only widely distributed text that bears his name. Eliot portrays Archer as a strong amazing hero who had escaped kidnappers in order to report his owner's plot to destroy a crucial bridge outside Fort Jackson. William portrayed himself as a kind of antislavery hero who had once rescued an enslaved woman being assaulted in a St. Louis basement. He attached an appendix glorifying the sacrifice of antislavery journalist Lovejoy, who was lynched by a mob. Eliot positioned himself as a spokesperson for antislavery—not abolitionist—sentiment in St. Louis and argued that slavery was on its way out by the time of the Civil War.

The preface of the thin volume lays out the author's intention: not an account of the secession and Civil War but "a fair presentation of slavery in the Border States for the twenty or thirty years preceding the outbreak of hostilities." In describing the relationships between owners and their human property, "it shows things as they were, and how they were regarded by intelligent and thoughtful people at the time." There was no need to say that these "thoughtful people" were white. In the text no one other than William is given a legitimate and affirmative voice. He interprets Archer's actions and speech for him, assuming the power of master, however well intended, over the body and mind of this rescued runaway. Archer Alexander was, in William's view, "quiet, gentle and sufficiently intelligent . . . in fact he was one of the very best specimens of the negro race I had ever known." The distance that the use of the term "specimen" creates between himself and Alexander tells a great deal about Eliot's views of racial difference; it harks back to the language employed by Henry Blow and Samuel Gridley Howe, both committed abolitionists, to describe those they were trying to help.[23]

As William proceeds, he speaks for the "quiet" Archer, in the style of a "slave narrative," and in so doing, makes himself the real protagonist. As literary historian Joseph M. Thomas says, "the defining feature" of the text is that Eliot "ultimately effaces Alexander so thoroughly from the story . . . as to render him invisible."[24] The differences between William and Archer are highlighted by William's use for Archer Alexander of a supposed "Negro dialect," the language that countless other whites were employing in the nineteenth and early twentieth centuries in their depictions of Black speech. This rendering of speech infantilizes those who utter it, turning them into near-comedic figures, content with the scraps of attention more well-spoken whites are willing to throw to them. It stands in sharp contrast to, for instance, the language of resistance, direct and clear, employed by Douglass, Elizabeth Keckley, Lucy Delaney, and William Wells Brown in his first account of 1847.[25]

In his recent award-winning book *James*, Percival Everett attempts to explain this vast dichotomy between fictionalized speech and actual speech. He invents an alternative life for the character of Jim in Mark Twain's *Huckleberry Finn*, portraying an enslaved man who knows how to read and speaks dignified English. Before James and Huck flee Hannibal, Missouri, and go downriver, James, carrying a bag of books that includes William Wells Brown's narrative, instructs his family in the practice of "signifying." "Signifying" means never making eye contact with whites, never speaking first or correcting them, and above all, not letting it be known that they can read or speak proper English. James's children learn that they should always play stupid, keep their eyes downcast, and aim to please whites. He hopes these tactics will protect them to some extent. Everett writes, "And the children said together, 'And the better they feel, the safer we are.'" Daughter February translates: "Da mo' betta dey feels, da mo' safer we are."[26]

The Eliots had, almost assuredly, known Universalist and abolitionist Frances Barker Gage, who lived in St. Louis between 1853 and 1860 and had chaired a women's rights convention in Akron, Ohio, in 1850. The meeting became a historic one, largely because of the speech given by a formerly enslaved Black woman from New York State, Sojourner Truth. Gage created a version of Truth's speech that took liberties with the original text, inserting the now-famous words "Ain't I a woman?" The appropriation of Black subjects by distorting their speech was commonplace in antislavery texts, including Harriet Beecher Stowe's wildly popular *Uncle Tom's Cabin.* These texts are ambivalent: they highlight the horrors of slavery but create racially coded stereotypes of the characters who are supposed to be the protagonists of these accounts.

Eliot's story of Archer Alexander fits into this genre as the author valorizes his subject while belittling him. Once back in St. Charles after the Civil War, settled on his four-acre plot with his family, Archer was supposedly "contented, happy, and grateful. . . . A long life of slavery had unfitted him for the sharp competitions of freedom in a city life, and in many things he was only a grown-up child." When Eliot told Archer about his likeness on the Emancipation Monument and showed him a photograph of it, he, now paired forever with Lincoln, laughed and supposedly said, "Now I'se a white man! Now I'se free!"[27] Turning this expression into one of gratitude, rendered simplistic through dialect, Eliot may easily have missed what may have been an ironic or "signifying" statement by Archer, not one of longing to be white. Whatever the statement's intention, the statement was not recorded at the time in Eliot's journal or sent in a letter to any correspondent, and it might be considered apocryphal. Whether true or invented, the statement is one of the few times in the *Story of Archer Alexander* that Archer supposedly speaks "for himself."

In describing slavery, Eliot relates that he had seen in St. Louis examples of brutality that could have come from Stowe's novel, and he presents several of these from his past. But he begins Archer's life, like that of "Uncle Tom's," on a plantation with a beneficent owner whose good intentions are undermined by debt and death. Eliot returned to the theme he brought with him from Washington, DC, and Cambridge, Massachusetts, when he first moved to the West; slaveowners in the border states wanted to end slavery, were suffering from economic losses, and viewed slavery as a burden. Slavery in Missouri existed "in its mildest form," and in the border state of Virginia, where Archer had been raised, slavery was for the most part benign and was on its way out.[28] Virginians had been left with large numbers of enslaved people on unprofitable plantations, and only the worst circumstances pushed them into separating families by selling persons they could no longer afford.

In Eliot's manufactured tale, Archer grows up on a mythical plantation named Kalorama in Virginia, a "farm" with seventy enslaved people and their kindly owners. They had been forced to sell Archer's father, Alek, due to debt. Alek would be no great loss anyway, as he was a troublemaker. He had learned to read and was spouting the text of the Declaration of Independence. Archer's mother, Chloe, was bereft as her husband was sent away, and she never recovered. While Eliot thought these separations were "the most evil part of slavery," he contends most of the enslaved people at Kalorama were treated well. It was not difficult to maintain order because "the blacks are a docile and easily controlled race." When Alexander's new master in St. Charles County sold away some of Alexander's children for bad behavior, he "didn't seem to blame his master for it. The heart learns to bear inevitable burdens."[29] While Eliot had lost many of his children to death before they reached adulthood, his assumption that he could apply his own case of saddened acceptance of their loss to Archer's situation was arrogant, even flippant.

As Eliot's biography of Alexander was published, the most famous formerly enslaved person in Missouri at the turn of the century was not Archer Alexander but Dred Scott. Mary L. Barnum, widow of the man who owned Barnum's Hotel, where Scott was a porter when he died in 1858, commissioned a portrait of him based on the photograph that appeared in 1857 in *Leslie's Illustrated Weekly.* The portrait was installed in the Missouri Historical Society in 1882 next to that of Thomas Hart Benton, dedicated by Black leader James Milton Turner. In his dedication of the Scott portrait (Harriet was not mentioned), Turner said that Scott's history showed that "the Negro has been with us . . . from the very beginning of our State, and, indeed, of the nation itself."[30]

The Scott portrait was mounted in a place of honor at the World's Fair in St. Louis in 1904, meant to commemorate the Louisiana Purchase and Missouri's role in conquering the West. Of more interest to the fairgoing public than the Scott portrait was an anthropological display of the world's exotic peoples and races, with several thousand human curiosities paraded before fairgoers. Frank Boas, the renowned father of American anthropology, had given his blessing to the exhibit. "Pygmies" brought from the Congo Free State, perhaps the most outrageous and horrifying version of European colonialism in the world, were put into a "habitat" on the fairgrounds in Forest Park. Disguised as a "cannibal," Ota Benga performed for large crowds and was later displayed in a cage in the Bronx Zoo. He committed suicide in 1916.[31]

Frederick Trevor Hill, a prominent lawyer in New York, made the first attempt at a post–Civil War scholarly interpretation of the Dred Scott case with an essay written for a 1907 history of famous controversies in American law. Hill contacted Montgomery Blair Jr. for information about two cases Blair's famous father had helped to determine: the Hayes-Tilden contest of 1876 and the Dred Scott decision of 1857. Unable to retrieve much about the Scott case from the younger Blair, Hill contacted the Missouri Historical Society and engaged in an extensive correspondence with its librarian Mary Louis Dalton in early 1907. Dalton found some of the legal documents Hill needed but could not tell him much about Scott's own history. Born in 1869 in western St. Charles County, Dalton was an adult product of a life enmeshed in the Southern view of goodly masters and their "childlike" charges.

Dalton, who knew many of the elite families of St. Louis, contacted Julia Webster Blow, widow of William T. Blow, Henry Blow's youngest sibling. Julia claimed to know a good deal about Dred Scott, saying that she had often seen him hanging around the Blow family for handouts and odd jobs even after the Civil War and that the Blows had been forced to take care of him out of sentiment and their sense of duty to him. (The Scotts were self-supporting for their entire adult lives, and Dred Scott died in 1858.) In her final letter to Hill in March 1907, Dalton reiterates the post-Reconstruction version of the Southern myth of slavery: "The Blows were and are high class people. They were kind and humane masters, and this Dred Scott was no doubt a thorn in their flesh. . . . [He] had that irresponsibility and childishness which form the fundamental characteristics of the negro. . . . The key to the whole situation is that Dred was a poor worker, unreliable and irresponsible."[32]

As Hill published his *Decisive Battles of the Law* in 1907, judiciously excluding Dalton's personal diatribe, a new school of professional historians was rewriting the history of slavery and Reconstruction at Columbia, John Hopkins, and Louisiana State Universities. John Burgess, a professor of political science, brought the German seminar method to Columbia in the 1880s and it was expanded there by William Dunning. Dunning emphasized using primary sources and documents, compiling relevant statistics, and conducting interviews with living participants. A political economy approach to Southern history, Dunning's work was full of facts and figures that beefed up several profound but subjective theories that could not really be proven: slavery was an unprofitable but benign institution, and it allowed Africans to begin the process of becoming civilized under the guidance of their well-intended masters. Northern reformers undermined states' rights and had done more harm than good in their crusade to end slavery and impose Reconstruction on the South. As critic Eric Foner argues, the Dunning School "offered scholarly legitimacy to the disenfranchisement of southern blacks and to the Jim Crow system that was becoming entrenched as they were writing."[33]

Ulrich B. Phillips was the most acclaimed historian to emerge from the Dunning School. He received a PhD at Columbia in 1902 and taught at the Universities of Wisconsin, Tulane, and Yale. *Life and Labor in the Old South* is the lengthy culmination of his work and was not discredited as the primary academic work on slavery by establishment scholars until the 1950s and 1960s, even though Black historians like Du Bois and Carter G. Woodson were contesting the Dunning School as early as 1910.

The Dunning style of research and writing arrived in St. Louis during World War I. Harrison Anthony Trexler, a graduate student at Johns Hopkins who was teaching economic history at the University of Montana, was invited by University of Missouri professor Jonas Viles, a Massachusetts native and a graduate of Harvard, to do a scholarly study of slavery in Missouri between 1804 and 1865. *Slavery in Missouri*, published by Johns Hopkins Press in its University Studies in Historical and Political Science in 1914, is still in print.

Trexler set up shop in St. Louis, where he had access to the Missouri Historical Society and the Mercantile Library, and drew on information he gathered from the State Historical Society at Columbia. He used Dunning School methods to structure his study. Trexler was committed to his profession and to honest reporting and did not merely echo the Dunning School's conclusions. He included extensive statistics based on US censuses of the proportions of whites, free Blacks, and enslaved persons in Missouri. He showed that "the golden age of slave values" was in the 1850s and documented the rise in prices from newspaper ads. He was surprised to learn that during the Civil War, "the prices kept fairly high." Trexler mined the historical archives for anecdotes and opinions on the slavery question. He quoted Eliot on seeing "gangs of negroes handcuffed together two and two, going through the open street like dumb cattle on the way to the steamboat for the South."[34] He emphasized the terror that most enslaved people experienced at the prospect of being sold downriver. He admitted that when he first began his study, he had "hoped to arrive at a satisfactory conclusion as to the profitableness of slave labor" in Missouri, "but the results have been disappointing. . . . No matter what contemporaries or present-day authorities conclude the problem is not one to be mathematically settled." He was anticipating a debate that would rage among US history scholars sixty years later, when Robert Fogel and Stanley L. Engerman's *Time on the Cross: The Economics of American Negro Slavery* (1974) was critiqued for taking an unprovable mathematical approach to the conditions of slavery.[35]

Trexler, like most historians of slavery, had to use rich layers of personal remembrance, contemporary accounts, court decisions, and political statements to evaluate the many nuances of the conflicting views of masters and the enslaved. He included, in his footnotes, examples of extreme cruelties, including castrations, burnings alive, and other tortures. He had read the narratives of Keckley, Brown, and Delaney. He included references to beneficent Catholics, antislavery Protestant churches, and Black congregations. He quoted elderly "Uncle" Peter Clay of Liberty, Missouri, who said "that he went to the Baptist Church because his master did, but that after the War he joined the Methodist Church 'because the Northern Methodists stood fo[r] freedom from slavery an[d] freedom from sin.'"[36]

Trexler was able to interview many Missourians whose families had owned Black people and whose sentimental ideas about their pasts crept into his narrative. He kept coming back to Eliot to underscore his main argument: "The treatment of slaves in Missouri was perhaps exceptionally humane. All cruelty or 'unnecessary severity was frowned upon by the whole community.'"[37] Trexler's text had long quotations describing "comfortable slave quarters," "plantation singing," "corn shuckings," and "sparkling log fires," supposed examples of the humanity of slavery in the border state. But he let Thomas Summer have the last word. Summer had been well treated by his master and mistress and then endured rough conditions and hard work after his emancipation, but said, "I would rather be free and eat flies than be a slave on plenty."[38]

Most antislavery whites of Missouri attempted to criticize the conditions of slavery without alienating their extended families, their fellow parishioners, and their political allies. The antislavery whites could not help but think that most of their own fellow and sister citizens had been well intended in their management of enslaved persons in households and on farms in Missouri. These whites greeted emancipation with joy but could not see the newly freed as deserving of the same rights held by white people. But as these whites were constructing a self-serving narrative of slavery and Reconstruction, Black leaders in St. Louis and Black historians nationwide were allied in resisting the story being told about them, constructing their own, and fighting for equal rights.

# 7 "A Race without a History Is Soon Forgotten"

Radical Republican rule in Missouri ended with the ratification of a new state constitution in 1875, and in 1877 Reconstruction ended abruptly in the deep South. Democrats, many of them former Confederate sympathizers and opponents of racial equality, were now in control of state government in Missouri. The long-standing rural urban divide and Jim Crow practices were exacerbated by a political regime in St. Louis County government that robbed the city of St. Louis of self-rule and sufficient revenue from taxes. With no existing alliances between Black and white Protestant reformers to resist the return of racist practices and hierarchies, there were few ways to intervene in post-Reconstruction politics until the Progressive Era. But voices in the Black communities of St. Louis and beyond were building centers of cultural resistance and constructing a Black history that would counter the narrative of the Dunning School.

In her 1868 personal and political account of the nation's history, *Behind the Scenes*, Elizabeth Keckley offered one of the earliest of these counternarratives. Keckley examined her "thirty Years a Slave" before her purchase of her own freedom, her life as an independent dressmaker, and her "four years in the White House" during the Civil War. With help from the congregations and ministers of Black churches in Washington, DC, and New York City, Keckley helped to found the Ladies' Freedmen and Soldier's Relief Association. Her sympathies were with the North and with her people.

Edward Bates saw Lincoln almost daily in cabinet meetings in Washington, DC, but as Mary Todd Lincoln's dressmaker, Keckley was a member of the Lincoln household and, according to Keckley and extant letters to her from Mary, was Mary's personal confidant. Keckley's reminiscences, along with those of William Herndon's *Lincoln*, published in 1889, suggested that Abraham Lincoln suffered from chronic depression and that Mary was a self-centered, even deranged, wife and mother. Keckley's little book was hardly read at all in 1868, because Mary's son Robert made certain it was never sold in bookstores in New York City or Washington, DC. But it became, in the twentieth century, a major contribution to the canon of personal narratives of life in slavery.

Keckley's story opens a window into the domestic life of whites and the servants they owned or employed to do some of their most intimate tasks and into the emotions these relationships engendered. One of the difficulties in analyzing the conditions of slavery, as Trexler found in his study of Missouri, was disentangling the emotive relationships between owners and enslaved people and white employers and free Black servants. Bates's sister Sarah, on her deathbed, was so fearful for her enslaved persons' future that she freed them rather than see them in "the care" of others. Keckley was on the other side of this equation and purchased her own and her son's freedom through the income she made as one of the most prestigious dressmakers for women in St. Louis.

She carried this professional aura with her when she moved to Washington, where she made magnificent dresses and ensembles for the wives of Jefferson Davis, Stephen Douglas, Robert E. Lee, and Abraham Lincoln, eventually employing a staff of twenty seamstresses. Women confided in her, introduced her to their daughters and friends, and helped her create a successful business in Washington. Her affections for the white women—whether Southern or Northern—she had worked for in slavery and freedom and they for her is made plain in *Behind the Scenes*. The intimacies of fitting dresses and the long conversations as they were tried on and completed were enterprises that put upper-class women, at least temporarily, in the hands of their needlewomen.[1]

This concept of a "women's culture" of confidence and friendship is a foundation of feminist women's history and argues that in the nineteenth-century patriarchal structures encouraged women to identify and bond with each other, even across class and racial lines. In trying to describe her sentiments to a Northern friend, the friend chastised Keckley for saying, "You do not know the Southern people as I do—how warm is the attachment between master and slave." Keckley then devotes a long passage to the family of her former owner Anne Garland, whose daughter Nannie had been Keckley's "especial charge. She slept in my bed, and I watched over her as if she had been my own child." (Meanwhile, Elizabeth's mother cared for Elizabeth's son, George.) Ann Burwell Garland signed Keckley's and George Kirkland's emancipation papers.

When the Garlands contacted Keckley after the end of the Civil War and invited her to visit them in West Virginia, she went willingly and with excitement to see her former enslaved-holding family, who, like Keckley, had lost a soldier son. "Could my friends of the North have seen that meeting, they would never have doubted again that the mistress had any affection for her former slave. I was carried to the house in triumph . . . and placed in an easy-chair before a bright fire. The servants looked on in amazement." This distinction of class continues, in the only sentence—an ironic one—in Keckley's book in Black dialect, as the cook remarks, "I declar, I nebber did see people carry on so. Wonder if I should go off and stay two or three years, if all ob you wud hug and kiss me so when I cum back?"[2]

Keckley's intentions for her memoir are difficult to unravel. She may have hoped that her flattering depictions of Southern patrons would help it sell. But she misjudged the negative reaction her exposé of Mary would provoke in the North. As a very light-skinned Black woman, she may have wanted to show how far she had risen in the white world with her professional skills as a needlewoman. But her pleasure in again meeting—in her mind as equals—people she cared for deeply and her belief that they felt the same comes across as real and true. At the same time Keckley was undaunting in her narrative in describing the horrors of slavery for her parents, her rape and difficult motherhood, and the years of unrequited toil it took her to raise the funds to buy her little family's freedom. The intimacy of slaveholding in most of the upper South, embedded in family, sexual exploitation, and complicated biological connections, is given full expression in this early post–Civil War history, written by a Black woman recently from St. Louis.

Keckley lost most of her patrons when she published *Behind the Scenes*, and her dressmaking business floundered. Although she was publicly rebuked, it is also likely the Civil War and the economic decline that followed helped to decimate her sophisticated clientele. By 1868 she was fifty years old. She applied for a veteran's pension, due her as the mother of Union soldier George Kirkland, with the help of Elijah Lovejoy's sons in Illinois. In 1892 she went to Ohio to head Wilberforce College's Department of Sewing and Domestic Science Arts. (Her son attended Wilberforce briefly before the start of the war.) When Keckley retired, she returned to Washington, DC, to live at the National Home for Destitute Colored Women, established through the organizations she helped to found, and died in 1907 at the age of eighty-nine.

As chronicler Keckley was coming to the end of her long and fruitful life, a professionally trained Black historian was just beginning what would prove to be a significant career. Carter Godwin Woodson came to Washington in 1911, hired as a teacher at the M Street High School. Woodson's parents were emancipated persons who endured the semi-slavery of tenant-farm sharecropping before buying their farm in Huntington, West Virgina. His mother, Anna, could read, but his father, James Henry, was illiterate. Their son Carter was born in 1875 near the end of Reconstruction and attended a one-room schoolhouse a few months a year. He tried sharecropping, worked as a coal miner, and learned the rudiments of Black history from a Civil War veteran. He attended the abolitionist-founded school Berea College in Kentucky and answered a call in 1903 from the federal government to teach in the Philippines and then traveled in Asia, Africa, and Europe. When he returned to the United States, he earned a master's degree at the University of Chicago and then a PhD at Harvard University while he was teaching high school in Washington, DC.

With the help of white and Black philanthropy, Black leaders and white abolitionists were building institutions of higher learning, now known as HBCUs (historically Black colleges and universities). Gateways to college had to be expanded, as most Black communities (and white working-class communities, too) did not have schooling for children beyond the eighth grade. Establishing vocational and classical high schools was a collective race and ethnic ambition. The M Street High School was patronized by middle-class Black families whose children could afford to buy their own books and meet the rising academic standards for youth at elite Black institutions.

Woodson was an exceptionally well-qualified teacher of US history, French, Spanish, and English by the time he reached M Street. He had traveled in Europe, studied at the Bibliothèque Nationale in Paris, and was doing research for his PhD dissertation at the Library of Congress. At Harvard he faced an unsettling atmosphere as an older Black student and worked with an ambivalent all-white history department faculty dismissive of his spotty and nontraditional education. He passed the European piece of his studies easily but failed the American exam, possibly because of his views on slavery, the causes of the Civil War, and Reconstruction.

Woodson hoped to research and write on such topics as Black churches and the education of the Negro, but his attempt to bring Negro history into academia was met with contempt. The distinguished US historian Edward Channing, who had failed Woodson on the American piece of his examinations, was alleged to have told him, "The Negro has no history." The more friendly and fair teacher Frederick Jackson Turner, who came to Harvard in 1910 and was a promoter of the "significance of the frontier in American history," helped Woodson finish his degree by 1912.[3]

Like W. E. B. Du Bois, the first Black PhD to graduate from Harvard University, Woodson had no prospects of becoming a university professor in Jim Crow America. He returned to Washington and its public school system. The creation of Black colleges in the Civil War and Reconstruction eras opened jobs to Black scholars: Du Bois was at Fisk University in Tennessee, Woodson would go to Howard University in Washington, and James Milton Turner was already established at Lincoln Institute in Jefferson City, Missouri. These men were part of a circle of the Black professional class determined to demonstrate that, indeed, the "Negro has a history."

The timing of Woodson's organizational efforts was no coincidence. The newly established National Association for the Advancement of Colored People (NAACP) in its magazine *Crisis* was vigorously condemning lynching. Black leaders and sympathetic whites were responding to the searingly racist ideology of W. D. Griffith's *Birth of a Nation* (1915), playing to packed movie theaters everywhere, including in St. Louis. Woodson founded the Association for the Study of Negro Life and History in 1915 and in 1916 inaugurated an academic journal, the *Journal of Negro History*. In 1926 he promoted a National Negro History Week to take place in February of each year to encourage the teaching of Black history in schools, churches, and community centers. He urged local leaders to collect primary sources and to highlight the achievements of African American figures in the American past.

Woodson was a frequent contributor to the journal he founded, and many of his publications were pathbreaking pieces of scholarship. In 1921 he elaborated on the question Bates had raised in the early years of the Civil War on race and American citizenship. Woodson's "Fifty Years of Negro Citizenship as Qualified by the United States Supreme Court" shows in careful detail how the promise of the Fourteenth Amendment was gutted in the Slaughter-House Cases and the Civil Rights Cases and culminated in *Plessy v. Ferguson* in 1896, setting the "separate but equal" doctrine seemingly in stone. Although the Thirteenth Amendment had, technically, ended slavery, Woodson argues, without real enforcement of the Fourteenth Amendment by the federal government, the conditions of semi-slavery descended once again on most of the South. There was no possibility that literacy requirements for the vote could be met given the disdainful absence of funding for educational facilities serving the Black community. He issued a warning: The Supreme Court had "read into the Constitution so much caste and autocracy that discontent and radicalism have developed almost to the point of eruption."[4]

While Woodson welcomed the growth of a vigorous new Black middle class, he was more interested in the range of occupations that enabled ordinary Black people to buy their freedom, purchase land and property, and support their families. One of Woodson's most important publications was his 1925 *Free Negro Heads of Families in the United States in 1830* and in 1930 he published his article "The Negro Washerwoman," extolling the contributions that self-supporting laundresses, such as Harriet Robinson Scott and Sally Thomas, the mother of well-to-do James Thomas, had made to the cohesion of the Black family.

Woodson and his research staff tabulated by hand the numbers of the members of each free Black household from the US Census of 1830, some of them headed by laundresses and seamstresses. Luther Porter Jackson, another son of former enslaved parents and a civil rights leader in Virginia, extended this study in his 1942 *Free Labor and Property Holding in Virginia, 1830–1860*. These census tabulations were invaluable to genealogists and the next generation of social historians. Using similar techniques, Herbert Gutman's 1976 *Black Family in Slavery and Freedom* exploded the concept of the supposed pathology of the Black family presented in studies like the 1965 Moynihan Report. Gutman showed that it was Jim Crow practices and institutionalized racism that undermined the significant progress Black families had made as they were emancipated, navigated Reconstruction, bought land, created Black businesses, and raised their remarkably stable families toward the end of the nineteenth century.

Census statistics are indispensable for sorting out the lives of Black people and immigrants in the United States. Without many written records, although more of these are coming to light every day, historians often have no other way to assess how families lived, where they lived, what they owned, how many children they had, and whether they were literate or attended school.

Social and economic historian Leonard Curry, an earlier user of this kind of data, found that as of 1850 St. Louis was last among fifteen sample US cities in the number of free Blacks employed as artisans and tenth in his study's index of economic opportunity. The African American population of St. Louis increased from just under four thousand to more than twenty-two thousand between 1860 and 1880 but did not constitute a large enough block to negotiate effectively in the political sphere. Curry found that the high proportion of immigrants in the population of St. Louis, given the predilections of white employers and union organizations controlled by whites, could be correlated with diminished opportunities for Black men. Irish, German, and Italian arrivals outnumbered Black migrants by far, and working-class people of every ethnic background were in search of housing and schools west of Grand Avenue in St. Louis city and in towns and suburbs to the north and west. Residential housing segregation was the norm, even though some African American families moved to outlying rural areas or were already residing in them before the Civil War. One such example was Griffin Brander, who relocated from Cass Avenue near the Mississippi River across from East St.

Louis in Illinois in the 1880s to a newly purchased home on Warren Avenue in the St. Louis suburb of Clayton. His occupation as a drayman, since he owned his own wagons and teams, made him a relatively prosperous Black man in St. Louis.

Segregation grew more rigid as racial attitudes of ruling-class whites and working-class ethnics coalesced at the end of the century around Jim Crow practices in unions, political party hierarchies, and residential housing. Most Black people were packed into rundown neighborhoods south and east of Grand Boulevard in "old Saint Louis" and in Mill Creek Valley near Chouteau Pond and the railroad yards of Union Station. As Baltimore, Maryland, had done, the city of St. Louis separated from its surrounding county in 1877, initially to have more say over its own governance, a move that proved to be unwise given the permanent boundaries of the city as the county population grew. After 1875 Democrats controlled the state government and were not prone to doing the city of St. Louis any favors. On the edge of more intense industrialization and greater migration from the South, the city of St. Louis in 1877 had 350,000 residents, and the surrounding rural county only 30,000. That proportion would change dramatically by World War I. The divorce of county and city was a ticking time bomb, as the boundaries of the city were set in stone and the county saw its "suburban villages grow into cities."[5] Although some of these suburbs had Black residents who had been free or were recently freed, the political sentiment of white immigrants and Anglos was to confine Blacks in St. Louis to the inner city of St. Louis and to establish industrial zones in outer St. Louis city that decimated Black neighborhoods and the churches that were their touchstones.

Many white leaders of Missouri had said that literacy should be a determinant of voting rights but then endorsed segregated schools and refused to properly fund education for African Americans. Black leaders were universally agreed that literacy and education were indispensable for the progress of their communities. The Missouri Constitution of 1865 mandated some funds for Black schools, and a few inferior buildings with small student bodies provided public school education for several hundred Black children in St. Louis. The 1875 constitution founded a separate public school system for Black children, the schools in woefully underfunded buildings in downtown neighborhoods close to bars and brothels. James Milton Turner, Moses Dickson, and Charlton Tandy agitated for more schools and the hiring of Black teachers. A demand for a better high school was a constant theme. Charles Sumner High School, named after the Massachusetts abolitionist US Senator from Massachusetts, opened in a former white school at Eleventh and Spruce Streets but with the protests of Black citizens over its poor location was moved in 1898 to Fifteenth Street, the first "colored school" in St. Louis to bear a name instead of a number. A Sumner Normal School to train teachers of color opened in 1889.

A 1907 "Complaint . . . to the Board of Education of St. Louis" from "colored citizens," complete with photographs to make its points, is a remarkable document that survives in the Julia Davis Collection at the St. Louis Public Library. Sumner High School, by 1907 at Fifth and Walnut Streets, was in an industrial district near the waterfront next door to a biscuit factory. "It is true that a number of poor but respectable people live on this street," describes the complaint, "but it has a somber, sooty and indifferent appearance," and "every approach to Sumner is low in moral tone, a junky, bustling way, full of traffic and loungers." While domestic science and vocational education were well represented, there was no stenography and typing, and the classical curriculum was "defective," "a compromise course." The school had no summer classes, no chorus or orchestra, no library, and no gymnasium. The neighborhood of the white high school, McKinley, on Missouri Avenue, states the complaint, "is like entering another world. . . . Why should there be erected such schools for all youth except colored youth? Why should our best higher school, Sumner, be where it is, and what it is?"[6] As the petition observes, the upwardly mobile Black population in St. Louis was moving away from this downtown neighborhood to the north, where a new school for elementary and junior high students, the Simmons School in Elleardsville, could not keep up with the influx of students.

San Francisco businessman Charles Elleard purchased a large tract of land as a horticultural site north of downtown St. Louis in the 1860s. Twenty years later it was a neighborhood of modest homes owned by German, Irish, and some Black families, said to be free of the restrictive covenants in place in many other white neighborhoods. The 1907 complaint resonated with the St. Louis Board of Education and a new Sumner High School opened in Elleardsville in 1910. Business courses, so important to women's class mobility, were introduced along with a more rigorous classical curriculum.

With white flight from what was now referred to as "the 'Ville," space opened for a residential community of prosperous Black doctors, teachers, businesspeople, and clergy. Sumner, Simmons, and Dumas Elementary made up a Black school system that straddled a middle-class neighborhood and the decrepit commercial and residential neighborhoods east of Grand in old "Black Saint Louis." Black families from all over the city and from towns north and west in St. Louis County who could afford to do so were sending their children to Sumner for better prospects in life.

Discrimination in white school systems against Black teachers and professionals everywhere in the United States provided a stream of highly qualified instructors for Black schools in St. Louis, Chicago, Central Los Angeles,

Washington, DC, and Harlem. With education long regarded as a civil rights endeavor in the Black community—as well as by white reformers—the new beacon of education in the 'Ville attracted teachers and students intent on creating a professional and literate Black middle class, whose higher mission, it was understood by community leaders, would be to foster discussion of the "race question." While still at its midtown location, Washington University Law School admitted a few Black students, and Walter M. Farmer was the first to earn a law degree there in 1887. White graduates refused to walk with him at the final ceremony, so the law school dean accompanied Farmer in the procession. When the school moved to the main campus of Washington University, west of Forest Park, it did not accept Black students for decades. That part of town, home to the Eliot family, was assumed to be for whites only.

Anchored by the Central Baptist Church on Washington Avenue, still close enough to downtown to invite congregants from older neighborhoods, St. Paul's AME on the edge of Mill Creek Valley to the west and St. Peter's AME to the north, the 'Ville was the center of upwardly mobile Black life in St. Louis between 1910 and the mid-1950s. Masonic and fraternal organizations for men and women were as central to Black community life as churches and often had ties to them. The Knights of Pythias on Pine Street and the Ancient Knights of Africa on Lucas Avenue offered death and burial insurance and assistance in purchasing homes and encouraged members to frequent Black businesses. In 1887 Lucy Delaney, who would publish her narrative of enslavement in 1898, and her husband, Zachariah, organized a chapter of the Order of the Eastern Star at the "Negro Masonic Hall" on Eleventh Street. The Ancient Knights of Africa promised to be "the champion of manhood and womanhood rights . . . and to secure for its members their constitutional rights by agitation and through their legal representatives."[7] Dickson's Knights and Daughters of Tabor, which had extended its chapters into Ohio, sought to care for the "sick and disabled," to aid "widows and orphans," and "care for our old and decrepit members." Like Black churches, these organizations stressed moral codes of behavior and dress that encouraged temperance, following the law, and protecting women. A woman admitted to the Daughters of Tabor was supposed to be "a lady . . . [and] a firm believer in the Supreme Being." The Daughters of Tabor were discouraged from meeting at night so that women would not be at risk on the street. Daytime meetings would "encourage refinement, culture and purity in life and Action."[8]

Black communities like Elleardsville and the more working-class, mixed-race Mill Creek Valley, with their own civic institutions and churches, were critical to the survival of Black prospects in St. Louis. Black businesses thrived in the 'Ville, with middle-class consumers at hand—and provided jobs as well. Annie Turnbo Malone, born in 1879 to formerly enslaved parents in Illinois, attended some high school and was enthralled with chemistry. Orphaned at a young age, she experimented with cosmetic products for Black women and developed a nontoxic hair straightener that became the foundation of early twentieth-century Black beauty culture. She moved to St. Louis in 1902, opened a shop on Market Street, and trained agents to sell her Poro goods door to door. Laundress Sarah Breedlove, later known as Madame C. J. Walker, was one of Malone's saleswomen before she left for Pittsburgh, Pennsylvania, in 1908 and became a millionaire making similar products. Malone opened her combination factory and cosmetology school at the corner of St. Ferdinand and Pendleton Streets in the 'Ville in 1918, training saleswomen, producing Poro products, teaching beauticians, and offering an elegant dining room and auditorium for use by Black businessmen's and women's clubs.

Malone also financed a multistory home on Pine Street for orphaned and abandoned children. Along with Sumner High and Stowe Teachers' College, these large and impressive brick structures were material proof in St. Louis of a lively Black urban enclave with what residents thought would be enduring institutions. Created out of exclusion, discrimination, and segregation, the 'Ville, like Central Los Angeles and Harlem, was a community strengthened by family, religion, and education, conscious of its own history and identity.

St. Louis ended the Civil War with an uneven balance of women to men, a pattern that continued into the twentieth century. With a shrinking industrial economic base, the city continued to have more women's jobs than men's and developed into what one scholar has described as a "feminized" economy. Black women worked as servants, cleaners, and laundresses and in light industry, while some with better educations were entering the retail trades and finding jobs as clerks and bookkeepers in Black-owned businesses.[9]

Before the Great Depression more women than men went to and graduated from high school in Missouri (and in the United States at large). Those who took business courses might become typists and stenographers. At Stowe Teachers' College, close to Sumner High, Black women could earn teaching certificates and land jobs at Black schools. Teachers could reach the middle class and hold stable, good jobs that were usually more remunerative than typical kinds of Black employment. Women teachers who were heads of household might avoid difficult marriages and lead independent lives.

Victoria Clay Haley and Julia Davis, two Black women who graduated from Sumner, embody this profile and made indelible marks on civic life in St. Louis. Haley was born in 1877, graduated from Sumner in 1895, and attended business college in Chicago. She taught school in St. Louis until she married in 1904 and began her career as a Progressive reformer and advocate of civil rights. (As in most school systems in the United States, St. Louis required women teachers to resign when they married.) Haley was a vice president of the Young Women's Christian Association (YWCA) and served two terms on the board of commissioners of the state Industrial School for Incorrigible Negro Girls. She contributed articles to the *St. Louis Afro-American*, a weekly newspaper, wrote short stories, and was a member of the Negro Press Association. Active in the woman suffrage movement and the local chapter of the National Association of Colored Women's Clubs movement, she was divorced from her husband in 1921, an event reported in the *St. Louis Post Dispatch*, and then moved to Chicago.[10]

Nearly twenty years younger than Haley, Davis was born in 1891 and lived in St. Louis all her life. John Davis, her father, came to St. Louis from Norfolk, Virginia, in 1863 and in 1874 married Helen Mason Harris from Jackson, Tennessee, a widow with two children. Julia describes her mother "as plain as an old shoe with an abundance of common sense and wit."[11] Only four of the Davis's ten children survived to adulthood, Julia the only daughter. Her father was a janitor, and in 1900, the family lived on Wash Street in old St. Louis in a respectable but poor neighborhood near a coal dealer, several laundresses, a post office clerk, a gravedigger, a railroad porter, a barber, and a bricklayer. John collected newspaper and magazine articles about the history and achievements of Black men and women and pasted them in scrapbooks that Julia poured over as a child. Her family attended the Central Baptist Church, formerly John Anderson's and Samuel Anderson's Second African Baptist, whose current pastor, George E. Stevens, was on the committee that issued the complaint about Sumner High to the St. Louis Board of Education in 1907. Since Julia was at Sumner at the time, it is likely her parents had been in on the discussion of reporting the appalling conditions at the old Sumner High School.

Julia graduated from Sumner High School in 1909, attended Sumner Normal School, and worked as a secretary at the *Central Afro-American* from 1911 to 1913, when she was hired to teach at Phyllis Wheatley Elementary School. Her father died in 1915, and perhaps inspired by his interest in Black history and the advice of pastor Stevens, she joined Woodson's fledgling National Association for the Study of Negro History that same year. She would often refer later to the association's motto, "A race without a history is soon forgotten." She founded the Prudence Crandall study club with other women teachers in 1915 (Prudence Crandall, a heroine of abolitionists, was a white teacher in Connecticut whose girls' school was destroyed by a mob when she admitted Black students). Julia's full-time classroom activities were suspended when she married Arthur Buckner, a US Post Office clerk, in 1917. Their son Arthur Jr. was born in 1922, and his parents were divorced that same year.

Julia dropped Buckner, her married name, became Julia Davis again, renamed her infant son John after her father, and returned to teaching in 1923, becoming a beloved and steady fixture teaching junior high school–aged students at Simmons School. In 1927 she brought Black history into her classrooms, inviting Woodson to St. Louis to speak to her students. She continued her Prudence Crandall group ("the Crandalls"), describing them as "outstanding classroom teachers in the public schools . . . [and] social workers in the community."[12] Julia's parents purchased lots in the 'Ville in the 1920s, and mid-decade, the Davis extended family built two adjoining brick houses on North Market Street. The 1930 US Census places her brother John E. Davis, a postal clerk with four children, at 4246 North Market Street. Julia, her son, her mother, Helen, and her brother Joseph lived next door. Three other teachers, a porter, a carpenter, and clerks were among their neighbors.

Upper North Market Street was in the heart of the 'Ville, adjacent to other neighborhoods in St. Louis that made for a lively urban district midtown. The 1875 Missouri constitution removed taxation on religious properties, and Catholic institutions in the city were able to prosper again. The growing campus of Saint Louis University was on the southeastern border of the 'Ville and brought white students and teachers into this mixed-race neighborhood. The Black Clamorgans and Chouteaus and their descendants were welcome in the most well-off Catholic parishes of St. Louis, but in 1873 St. Elizabeth's Parish on Fourteenth Street was established to serve less well-off Black Catholics and in 1912 moved to a more pleasant building on Pine Street known to its neighbors as St. Malachy's Church.

The blocks coming up from Twentieth Street to Catholic Saint Louis University on North Grand Boulevard were known locally as Mill Creek Valley, first populated by German and Irish immigrants and, after the Civil War, Black Southern migrants seeking jobs in the railroad yards and mills close to old Chouteau Pond. Tonnage shipped by steamboats to river ports was already in sharp decline. By 1880 more than ten times as many cotton bales were shipped by rail as by riverboats. The rise of Chicago, seemingly at once, made it the center of the shipping and distribution of goods in the Midwest. St. Louis's magnificent Union Station on Eighteenth and Market was completed in 1894 but with its overbuilt railroad yards was already something of a white elephant. By the time Union Station was built, Chicago already had more railroad traffic than St. Louis.[13] In fact, St. Louis always had more traffic with New Orleans than it did with cities in the East, and in a sense this new configuration reenforced the position of St. Louis as a "border state city," not the "gateway to the west."

Begun in frame buildings downtown between Fourth and Eleventh Streets, Black Protestant congregations often moved into more substantial churches and synagogues left behind by whites moving to more prosperous segregated neighborhoods. St Paul's AME Church, the first Black congregation in the city to erect its own building, moved from Eleventh and Lucas Streets in 1890 to a brick cathedral on Leffingwell and Lawton Streets designed by Black architect A. T. Berthe. The congregation at St. Paul's was said to number more than two thousand by the 1880s, with thirty-two Sunday School teachers and four hundred students. In Carondelet, Quinn AME Chapel moved to a former public market in 1882. The Blow family had long dominated landholding in Carondelet, annexed by the city of St. Louis in 1870, but its bucolic atmosphere on a high bank over the Mississippi was being disrupted by industrial and commercial enterprises, a railroad line, and riverport landings. Downtown congregants and many others west of Grand Boulevard attended Central Baptist Church at Twenty-Fourth Street and Washington Avenue, where it has a substantial campus still.[14]

Black churches in St. Louis spearheaded the civil rights struggle, deliberately self-conscious of their history and mission of supporting public causes for the race. A self-published 1927 account of the Central Baptist Church's past, partly drafted by congregant Julia Davis, laid out a Black history of St. Louis and its fight for equality, beginning with its "heroic prophet of God," Richard John Anderson, succeeded by his son Samuel in the 1870s and 1880s. Samuel Anderson and the grandson of Reverend John Berry Meacham, founder of the First African Baptist Church, were together sent in 1858 to Eleutherian College, an antislavery school near Lancaster, Indiana, forging a unity of Black Baptist churches in St. Louis.

Samuel Anderson's career was an example of what interracial cooperation had done in the Midwest and upper South to advance racial equality. Ordained in 1863, he was asked by the Society of Friends (Quakers) in Cincinnati in 1864 to teach school and preach sermons to newly freed people in Shelbyville, Tennessee, not far from Nashville. As the story of 1864 goes, one evening as Samuel's school was closing, two white men rode up and shouted, "You niggers hike out of here." Sending the children away, Samuel tried to escape out the back door but was met by men holding "large navy revolvers" who ordered him to leave town at once. But the townspeople had heard of the assault, and Samuel could "see the crowds coming to my rescue armed with . . . guns, pistols, axes . . . and shovels . . . for the children had run crying that the Klux had taken Mr. Anderson." At a mass meeting that night, said to have been made up of both "white and colored," he was urged to stay on with the promise of the town's protection. His school survived, and he built a meeting house for worship as well. This was a counternarrative of Reconstruction that gave Black people agency in fighting off assaults by Ku Kluxers and fending for themselves that became a legend at Central Baptist.[15] The Shelbyville region was a hotbed of biracial Republican activism that would culminate in a voting registration campaign of Black men in 1867, met with fierce resentment among local whites. The first Ku Klux Klan was formally organized by six Confederate Army veterans in Pulaski, Tennessee, in June 1866.

George E. Stevens assumed the pastorate of the Central Baptist Church in 1903, and Julia Davis was baptized there in the same year when she was twelve. Stevens had a distinguished abolitionist ancestry. Born in Philadelphia in 1861, he was one of five children of Susan and George E. Stevens Sr. The family almost certainly attended the First African Baptist Church, founded in Philadelphia in 1809, where enslaved and free Black people were welcome, and partnerships with white reformers created a powerful abolitionist coalition. Black and white abolitionists who lived in the city and served in Congress, Representative Thaddeus Stevens among them, were active recruiters of "Colored troops" during the Civil War, and Pennsylvania had more Black recruits than any other state. At the age of twenty-three, George Stevens Sr. may have joined the US Colored Troops Third Regiment Infantry, heavy artillery, organized in Philadelphia in 1863 and present at the siege of Fort Wagner in 1863. George Stevens Jr. went to public school in Philadelphia and Connecticut and pursued his divinity studies at Lincoln University in Pennsylvania. Founded in 1854 as Ashmun Institute, Lincoln was renamed for the Great Emancipator after the Civil War and was the nation's first HBCU (historically black colleges and universities). Stevens was called to churches in Syracuse and Boston before coming to St. Louis, became the president of the national Federation of Colored Churches, and was said to have done "everything that meant uplift for his people . . . a front-rank fighter against segregation in this city . . . and Jim Crow Missouri."[16] Two daughters graduated from high school in St. Louis and then from the University of Illinois. His wife, Joanna Flanders, helped to organize "Negro womanhood" along with Mrs. W. D. Cook of St. Paul's AME Church and was active in the League of Women Voters.

Reverend Stevens joined Charlton Tandy in leading a political campaign against segregated streetcars in 1907, prepared reports on students of color in the public schools for the board of education, authored the 1907 complaint to the board of education from "the Colored Citizens of St. Louis," and ran, unsuccessfully, after urging from some of their parents, for the board as a write-in candidate. In a late in life interview by a teacher at Sumner High School, Stevens said that among the greatest influences on his beliefs were the ideas of W. E. B. Du Bois, Carter Godwin Woodson, A. Philip Randolph, leader of the Pullman Porters Union of the United States, and Booker T. Washington, the author of *Up from Slavery.* Stevens described Du Bois as "God's champion of righteousness," Woodson as an historian who "showed that the Negro has an honorable history," Randolph as a righteous pioneer in the cause of integrated labor unions, and Washington as a preacher of "the gospel of work."[17] It is easy to imagine the Davis family and young congregant Julia Davis absorbing these lessons in church sermons and applying them to their own activism in St. Louis. Central Baptist had a "working membership" of fifteen hundred and a "general membership" of several thousand by the mid-1920s.[18]

With the rise of the Progressive movements in the early twentieth century, Black leaders welcomed the support of white sympathizers, and the first interracial organizations emerged in St. Louis. Roger Nash Baldwin, who would found the American Civil Liberties Union (ACLU) in 1917, taught sociology at Washington University between 1906 and 1909. There he met Charlotte Stearns Eliot, daughter-in-law of William Greenleaf Eliot, and they, along with Haley, worked on reforming the treatment of juvenile defendants in St. Louis. Baldwin was both a sociologist and a social worker, the chief probation officer of the St. Louis Juvenile Court from 1907 to 1910, his national reputation created, in part, by his coauthored book *Juvenile Courts and Probation.* Baldwin was also a founder of the St. Louis Civic League, organized in 1912 to create a more functional city based on Progressive values.[19]

National organizations were emerging that might help St. Louis with its local race issues, sometimes making for uneasy alliances in the pursuit of progress. Seeking to create new branches around the United States, Joel E. Spingarn of the NAACP came to St. Louis on his western tour of 1914 at the invitation of the City Club of St. Louis, whose members were leading white professionals in business, churches, medicine, and city governance. Baldwin and Gustavus A. Tuckerman, an Episcopalian rector at St. Stephens Church and the president of the St. Louis City Club, invited Spingarn to attend a lunch at the City Club on January 19, 1914. Spingarn spoke on the colored citizen and his future and later described the reaction to his speech: "first one person after another left the room in order to show their unmistakable disapproval, until when I finished only about one-fourth of the audience remained."[20] That evening he spoke at St. Paul's AME Church and received a much warmer reception. He urged those present to form a temporary NAACP chapter until more formal arrangements could be made. Reverend W. Sampson Brooks of St. Paul's Church was elected president, Reverend B. G. Shaw, treasurer, and Haley, Baldwin's colleague from juvenile court–reform circles, secretary.

A meeting to establish a permanent NAACP branch was held the next day at Union Memorial Church, by far the most imposing and elegant Black church in town, the building a former synagogue sold to Union Methodist's congregation in 1907. Perhaps, Spingarn chose the building for the meeting just before leaving St. Louis because it was a grander building than the others, but his choices in this brief visit smacked of being as uncontroversial and as pleasing to whites as possible. At his direction a new slate of officers was selected. Spingarn argued that the most effective NAACP branches had white officers, so Tuckerman, head of the Civic Club, was made president, and Haley and the newly elected Black pastors were dismissed, creating an acrimonious divide in the community.

Tiptoeing around Jim Crow was a constant in Progressive St. Louis. Haley was active in the Republican Party, a grand matron of the Order of the Eastern Star, and president of the Federated Colored Women's Clubs of St. Louis. In 1913 a large regional conference of woman suffragists was held at a hotel that did not welcome Black guests. As an invited participant, Haley took a seat and was asked to leave but refused to do so and was supported by enough attendees that the hotel management backed down. During World War I she chaired the Colored Women's Unit of the Council of National Defense, staging a patriotic rally in St. Louis attended by more than five thousand African Americans.

Baldwin not only invited the NAACP to town but was also a member of another new civil rights organization, the Urban League, originally a Committee on Urban Conditions among Negroes, founded in New York in 1910. Chapters of both the NAACP and the Urban League were now addressing racism in St. Louis. The St. Louis NAACP tried to end segregation at the city's free symphony in 1914 and before the city council protested the showing of *Birth of a Nation* in 1915. Remarkably, the city authorities issued an injunction forbidding the showing of the film, perhaps demonstrating the muscle whites could bring to promoting some civil rights causes. But the film was shown anyway when its producers demanded access to audiences in St. Louis, and the mayor refused to reinstate the injunction.

More trouble lay ahead. A new city of St. Louis charter issued in 1914 included a common Progressive demand, the initiative. Intended to be a democratic measure that would give citizens more say over their government, one of the first initiatives was copied from a 1910 Baltimore measure that offered voters the possibility of inscribing racial residential segregation into law, endorsed by the powerful St. Louis Real Estate Exchange. Printed propaganda asked: "Do you realize that at any time you are liable to suffer an irreparable loss, due to the coming of Negroes into the block in which you live?"[21] The proposed law said that no person could move to a block where 75 percent of the residents were of another race. Signatures supporting the initiative were collected in front of theaters showing the now wildly popular *Birth of a Nation.* Baldwin was coordinator of several groups, including the NAACP, that argued against the residential real estate legislation and appealed to the courts on the grounds that it was unconstitutional. Ethnic whites in St. Louis were terrified that their property values would plummet, as they often did, when this kind of "redlining" took place. Polish American groups endorsed segregation, as did John McGuire, the white Catholic priest of St. Elizabeth's. One proponent argued, "You can count on the common people, living in homes they buy on the installment plan to be in favor of the measure." The initiative passed by a vote of 52,220 for and 17,877 against. Areas on the edge of Black St. Louis went for the bill by a margin of eight to one and in German wards by two to one.[22]

A federal court issued an injunction against implementation of the measure, and after a similar Louisville law was ruled unconstitutional by the US Supreme Court, the St. Louis law was abandoned. Well-heeled residential districts had already experimented with a more subtle solution to the threat of mixed-race neighborhoods that became common throughout the United States: restrictive covenants binding white buyers with enforceable contracts to ensure no Blacks would become homeowners in "their" suburbs.

The animosity of most midwestern whites to Black people emerged in graphic detail in the East St. Louis race riot of 1917, followed by similar orgies of white violence in Chicago and Tulsa in the next few years. Just across the Mississippi River in Illinois, the industrial city of East St. Louis attracted white immigrant workers and Southern Blacks fleeing miserable sharecropper and tenant farmer lives in the South. Commercial river traffic was still on the Mississippi, but railroad shipping was eating into the business of carrying freight to and from Chicago and to the East. With more real estate available on the Illinois side of the Mississippi, large-scale industries in aluminum, chemicals, stockyards, and steel, with access to expansive coal mines, were easy to build but spouted pollution and created ugly conditions not as common across the Mississippi in St. Louis, where civic-league beautification projects and new zoning laws were taking hold.

East St. Louis was controlled by corrupt politicians who welcomed saloons and brothels, with the police on the take for kickbacks. The proportion of Black residents in East St. Louis had grown from 5 percent in 1870 to about 10 percent by 1910. The American Federation of Labor (AFL) craft unions in East St. Louis were built on white privilege and artisanal hierarchies and excluded unskilled workers. Most Black workers were confined to the least-skilled and most-laborious jobs in unspoken but clear agreements between labor and management and were not eligible to join AFL locals. But when a major strike arose in 1917, managers used Black workers as strikebreakers and promoted the idea that if further demands were made by unions, whites would be replaced by Blacks.

In June 1917 whites went on a rampage in downtown East St. Louis, hunting down Black men, raping Black women, and even killing young children. The whites were most intent, echoing the draft riots of 1863 in New York City, on destroying Black homes and property and stealing their clothes and furniture. Rumors persisted that Black people had started the melee and were out to kill white people. Soldiers and policemen sent to bring order focused on arresting and even killing African Americans. Some victims were able to escape across the river into St. Louis on a pedestrian foot bridge, even as they were attacked as they fled.

Pockets of resistance sprang up on some neighborhood streets as roving mobs lit fires in back alleys and forced Black families out their front doors so they could be beaten or killed. Families fought back in their own neighborhoods, and some saved themselves and their homes, killing a few white invaders. This was the kind of armed defense that Ida B. Wells, the outspoken journalist and antilynching advocate, had urged her people to take in the face of mob rule. Wells and Du Bois, both at the Niagara conference that founded the NAACP, came to East St. Louis in 1917 to interview survivors. Carlos Hurd, a reporter for the *St. Louis Post Dispatch*, describes the riot:

> For an hour and a half last evening I saw the massacre of helpless Negroes . . . in downtown St. Louis where a black skin was a death warrant. I saw man after man, with his hands raised, pleading for his life, surrounded by groups of men . . . and saw them administer the historic sentence of intolerance, death by stoning. . . . The East St. Louis affair, as I saw it, was a man hunt. . . . There was a horribly cool deliberateness and spirit of fun about it.[23]

Wells and Du Bois recorded interviews with the victims and with the help of white Missouri congressman Leonidas C. Dyer, who represented the Black wards of St. Louis, convinced President Woodrow Wilson to hold a congressional hearing. Dyer was the first person in Congress to propose an antilynching law, a measure systematically defeated, on the grounds, usually, of protecting white womanhood. The US Congress finally passed the Emmet Till Anti-Lynching Law in 2020.

## Epilogue

The East St. Louis race riot, the tepid response of the US Congress to mob violence, and systematic residential segregation in St. Louis underscored what so much of the discussion about race and citizenship had entailed in the past, beginning with Taney's opinion in the 1857 Dred Scott decision, Edward Bates's Civil War disquisition, and Carter Godwin Woodson's analysis of 1921. There were to be no civil rights for Black people, scant protection for Black women against rape or of Black men accused of rape but, instead, a steady harping on the racist rhetoric of the Blairs from 1857 to 1877. People should be sent away, "somewhere," and Black men, above all, kept away from white women. Whatever sympathies whites had with the plight of African Americans, they did not want them in their homes, their churches, their schools, their unions, or their factories.

And as World War I came to an end, St, Louis had not done as well as other cities in the economic boom that accompanied militarization and a more sophisticated factory economy. In the census of 1920, St. Louis was only the sixth most populous city in the United States, behind Detroit and Cleveland in size. In a growing exodus from St. Louis, Roger Baldwin and Victoria Clay (Haley) Roland left St. Louis for Chicago, taking their ambitions and their Progressive agendas to a wider forum. Widow Charlotte Stearns Eliot left St. Louis and moved to Cambridge, Massachusetts, to be near her son Thomas Eliot (but died in 1929 while he was still in Great Britain).

Du Bois wrote an account of the East St. Louis riot for the NAACP's *Crisis*, which was keeping a daily toll of the lynchings that haunted Progressives in the North and Black churches everywhere. In his essay "Of Work and Wealth," part of his 1920 book *Darkwater: Voices from Within the Veil*, Du Bois takes the intellectual and ideological tack toward economic determinism that would culminate in his monumental *Black Reconstruction*, published in 1933.

*Black Reconstruction* was a forceful alternative to the Dunning and Phillips interpretation of the years between 1865 and 1877. Du Bois argues that Black legislators and voters made valiant attempts to remake the South into a representative democracy but faced a ruling class bent on keeping a Black labor force captive with few rights and skimpy remuneration. The corruption of capitalist greed during Reconstruction was covered over with the rhetoric of white nationalism and the justification of violence against people of color, with the white people's anathema of miscegenation always a subtext.

The turning point of 1877 had been pinpointed in Du Bois's essay. In "Of Work and Wealth," he argues that the modern era of bribing the American white working class was born in 1877 in the Great Railroad Strike and culminated in the riot in East St. Louis in 1917. Corporate owners made a bargain with white working people: to paraphrase, "we will give you a bite of the American dream, and tolerate, even encourage, your racism, because it allows us to divide the real interests of the working class and consolidate our fortunes."

Caught in the maw of ordinary life, even if they knew of and approved of Du Bois's meta-historical theories, most Black Americans soldiered on despite them, finding the strength to carry on and to fight in Masonic orders, churches, and women's organizations for their futures. As the 1920s began, Julia Davis was still living in the 'Ville, teaching at Simmons School, and raising her son, John E. Buckner, who became a well-known educator in his own right. Davis and other gifted teachers in the 'Ville produced graduates who became famous Americans and broke down color barriers, among them tennis star Arthur Ashe, comedian Dick Gregory, opera singer Grace Bumbry, and rock-and-roll musicians Chuck Berry and Tina Turner. Berry attended Davis's one-hundredth birthday party celebration, a reminder that St. Louis still fostered Black music that made an indelible impression on the American songbook.[24]

Julia Davis spent her long life fostering Black civic and church groups and collecting and promoting information about Black history in St. Louis. She began describing herself as a "researcher of Afro-American history," an epitaph inscribed on her gravestone when she died at the age of 101. She was a leading organizer of the Black History Project, its early conferences held at the Central Baptist Church. The results of the project are being catalogued at the State Historical Society of Missouri, and they are legion: interviews and oral histories, family papers like those of the Griffin Branders, and books and pamphlets in Davis's possession that detail civic and religious life in Black St. Louis.[25]

Davis retired, reluctantly, in 1961, having reached the mandatory retirement age for teaching at age seventy, and she endowed a fund of $2,500 at the St. Louis Public Library for the purchase and maintenance of the collection Negro and African Literature and Culture. Items in the collection, some of which came from Davis's father's old bookshelf, are wide ranging: John Mercer Langston's *Freedom and Citizenship* of 1883 (Langston had spoken on behalf of Black citizenship before the Missouri state legislature in 1865);

an 1876 biography of Phyllis Wheatley by William Wells Brown; the works of Herbert Aptheker, James Baldwin, W. E. B. Du Bois, Paul Laurence Dunbar, E. Franklin Frazier, Langston Hughes, and Carter Godwin Woodson. With her donation Davis declared, "For our city to hold a unique position . . . as Gateway to the West . . . it must be . . . an outstanding Cultur[al] Center where citizens . . . can find information about the contributions of all peoples, including those of African descent."[26]

The Black citizens whose lives Davis recorded in her voluminous files faced difficult odds in gaining equality in the "gateway city" after World War I. The modernization of American life at mid-twentieth century accelerated the destruction of Black life and culture in St. Louis. New federal policies could, on the surface of things, be presented as race neutral and even progressive: the federal courts' rulings on the unconstitutionality of restrictive housing covenants in 1948 in *Shelley v. Kramer*, a case launched in St. Louis; the supposed end of segregation of the public schools with the 1954 *Brown v. Board of Education of Topeka* (with its oxymoronic phrase "all deliberate speed"); and a wave of interstate-highway building and urban renewal that took down blighted buildings from 1950 to 1980 but decimated the heart of Black life in Mill Creek Valley and the 'Ville's surroundings. A web of freeways crisscrossed Black neighborhoods and isolated them in pockets of poverty. Suburbanization enclosed working-class whites and Black people in the center of St. Louis with inferior schools, declining employment, and an assault on the physical institutions that sustained community. As Keona Ervin has said, "by 1950 St. Louis was a city in free fall."[27]

Walter Johnson, echoing Du Bois, has described this tragedy as a form of "racial capitalism." "The order of the day," he writes, "was redevelopment and removal . . . a pattern which had deep roots in the city's history."[28] Middle- and upper-class Black families were able to leave all Black neighborhoods in St. Louis city for the suburbs, but poor people in impoverished ones saw their homes and churches ravaged in the name of urban renewal. Forty Black churches in Mill Creek Valley were destroyed, including St. Paul's AME and St. Malachy Catholic Churches. The north-south Interstate 70 is built over a huge Native American ceremonial mound, surrounded by trash, that had given St. Louis its earliest name, "Mound City." A downtown gentrification spree left St. Louis with a giant arch—welcoming tourists and displacing residents and important historic sites—in front of the old courthouse where the Dred Scott case was first heard. The old waterfront is no more.

Where capitalism left off and racism began is difficult to tell. Scholars and civil rights activists who argue they were inextricably linked in the history of the United States are not wrong. After 1920 the once-great city "where mighty rivers meet" lost its sense of an egalitarian self that white reformist pioneers and interracial Progressive groups tried to foster. Slavery's end, economic progress, woman suffrage, and enriched education, in and of themselves, had not opened the floodgates to a moral revolution and racial and gender justice. Left out of the white reformers' equation was not only the enduring racism of most whites in Missouri but also the determination of Black people in St. Louis, often with women leading the way, to help themselves, to demand justice, and to create a future history in spaces they could define as their own.

# Notes

*Introduction*

1. Keckley, *Behind the Scenes*, 30.
2. Blow Family Papers.
3. Keckley, *Behind the Scenes*, 21.
4. Thelen, *Paths of Resistance*, 12.
5. Foner, *Reconstruction*, 602.
6. I use the terms "African American," "Black," and "people of color" as they seem appropriate in context. The official use of the term "Blacks" to describe a population of widely different lineages is relatively recent and was not a self-identifying term for those of African descent or partial African, white, and Native American descent in the nineteenth century. Whites perceived all Black people to be "black," but within the African American community were many mixed-race people of color who might or might not have seen themselves as "black" and often viewed the term as derogatory: indeed, when most whites used the term, it was. While most persons of African descent identified themselves as part of a group that shared a common history with aspirations for the future, they sometimes rejected the term "Negro," preferring "Afro-American," and toward the end of the century adopted "Negro" and its counterpart "colored people" as more respectable labels, labels that could include persons of mixed-race origins. The contemporary use of the term "Black" implies a political and cultural attachment to the identification of race that ignores other iterations in different time periods for African Americans: Afro-American, Negro, Colored People, and African American.
7. Gerteis, *Civil War St. Louis*, 37.
8. Cronon, *Nature's Metropolis*, 296.
9. Thelen, *Paths of Resistance*, 3.

### *Chapter 1. Slavery and Freedom at the Bend of the Mississippi*

1. Hoig, *Chouteaus*, 238; Foley and Rice, *First Chouteaus*.

2. Aron, *American Confluence*, 8–17; Olsen, *Indigenous Missourians*.

3. The US census of 2020 found a .09 percent Native American/other of the population in Missouri, and 948 people in St. Louis who identified as Native American or Alaska Native American out of a total population of 301,578. More than one-third of the total identified as Black or African American. The magnificent Indian Mound of local Missouri Indians along the Mississippi is now under a freeway headed out of town, perhaps a fitting symbol for the attempted erasure of Indigenous peoples in Missouri. For a more nuanced view of Native American presence in St. Louis, see Cleary, "Destruction of the Big Mound."

4. For this argument applied in another region, see Melish, *Disowning Slavery*. As Brett Rushforth argues in his history of a similar French fur-trading community, "Pays d'en Hunt, near what would be Detroit, enslaved Indians faced an array of perils and possibilities that ranged from sexual violence and forced labor to the formation of indigenous relationships that often led to their full acceptance into French colonial society." Rushforth, *Bonds of Alliance*, 255.

5. Schmidt, "Slavery and the Shaping of Missouri." Also see Rushforth, *Bonds of Alliance*, 255–74.

6. Foley, "Slave Freedom Suits"; VanderVelde, *Redemption Songs*, 39–56.

7. Scharf, *History of Saint Louis City and County*, 880–82, 1,643.

8. Coburn and Smith, "City Sisters," 89–91.

9. Tucker, "Methodists," 92; Hill, *Historical Outlines*.

10. Peck, "Historical Sketch," 208.

11. For a helpful discussion of African Methodist Episcopal Church history, see Frederickson, *Race, Gender, and the Transformation of Labor*, 49.

12. Tucker, "Methodists," 93.

13. On the founding of the AME in St. Louis and this legal controversy, see Volkman, *House Divided*, 53–82.

14. Samuel Giddings attended Williams College and Andover Theological Seminary, "newly founded as Calvinism's answer to Harvard's Unitarianism." Ellinwood, "Protestantism Enters St. Louis," 257.

15. Joseph Phillipson of Philadelphia was an early Jewish merchant in St. Louis, arriving in 1807, and was later joined by his brother Simon. The first Jewish congregation was gathered in 1841.

16. A. N. Morris, "History," 80–91; Volkman, *Houses Divided*, 51.

17. This description of the Kerr household is taken from the 1852 will of Matthew Kerr, who died in 1857. Amy Gibson and Fanny Kerr were manumitted in the Matthew Kerr will. Gibson was seventy-six in 1851, and Fanny turned fifteen in 1853. The will is on file at the Probate Office of the City of St. Louis, a copy obtained by the author.

18. Joseph Story, recommendation, "one of the Justices of the Sup. Ct. of U.S. & Dane Professor of Law in Harvard University," July 20, 1838, Pardon Dexter Tiffany Collection, Manuscripts and Documents, Missouri Historical Society, St. Louis. The collection is hereafter referred to as PDT Collection.

19. *Bench and Bar of St. Louis*, 38–39, and Stewart, *History of the Bench and Bar*, 249–51.

20. Kaufman, *Dred Scott's Advocate*, 40.

21. Charles Daniel Drake, "Autobiography," TS, 510–11, Charles Daniel Drake Collection, State Historical Society of Missouri, Columbia and St. Louis.

22. Post, *Truman Marcellus Post*, 161, 153–54.

23. Judith Kent Green, "Conservative Voices," 338.

24. Scharf, *History of St. Louis County and City*, 359–60.

25. Woodson, *Free Negro Heads*, 170; Jackson, *Free Negro Labor.*

26. Jackson describes Shadrack Brander as "one of the leading free Negro property owners" in Petersburg. *Free Negro Labor*, 144.

27. Ashton Johnston, addendum to Griffin Brander free pass, Griffin Brander Collection, State Historical Society of Missouri, Columbia and St. Louis. Jackson found Henry Brander in his survey of wills and property deeds in Petersburg in 1860. He had purchased his property, now valued at $1,000, for $100 in 1846, the year his brother Griffin left for St. Louis. Jackson, *Free Negro Labor*, appendix 1, 239.

28. Meachum, *Address to All the Colored Citizens*, 8.

29. Emancipations, 5:480, St. Louis Circuit Court Historical Records Project, St. Louis Arch Museum. On Bates and emancipation suits, see Twitty, *Before Dred Scott*, 111.

30. "The History of the Central Baptist Church," ca. 1927, box 2, "Preliminary Inventory," 29, Black History Project Collection, State Historical Society of Missouri, St. Louis. The collection is hereafter referred to as Black History Project.

31. On the formation of this congregation, see Volkman, *Houses Divided*, 54–55, and VanderVelde and Subramanian, "Mrs. Dred Scott," 1,086.

32. Anderson, *Story of a Border City*, 12–13.

33. Winch, *Clamorgans*, 157–58, 205–6.

34. The most illuminating account of Harriet Robinson in Minnesota and her legal situation is VanderVelde and Subramanian, "Mrs. Dred Scott."

35. Bancroft, *Slave Trading*, 135–44, quote on 136; Buchanan, *Life on the Mississippi*, 85.

36. Roberts, "Crossing Jordan"; Kennington, *In the Shadow of Dred Scott*, 41–43.

37. Quoted in C. A. Gordon, *Fire, Pestilence, and Death*, 176; Miles, *All That She Carried.*

38. Quoted in Bancroft, *Slave Trading*, 137.

39. Bancroft, *Slave Trading*, 179.

40. Delaney, *From the Darkness.*

41. Delaney, *From the Darkness*, 32.

42. Keckley, *Behind the Scenes*, 9.

43. Keckley, *Behind the Scenes*, 16. Also see Hoffert, "Emancipation of Elizabeth Hobbs Keckley."

44. Keckley, *Behind the Scenes*, 20. Keckley's transaction is listed in Emancipations, 25:185, November 15, 1855.

45. Meachum, *Address to the Colored Citizens*, 31.

46. Buchanan, *Black Life*, 12.

47. Buchanan, *Black Life*, 4–5, 18–51.

### *Chapter 2. Domesticity, Immigration, and the Crises of 1849*

1. Kellner, *German Element*, 235.

2. Primm, *Lion of the Valley*, 174.

3. Duden, *Report on a Journey*, 180.

4. Browne, "Voices against Slavery," 94–95.

5. Kremer, "German Immigrants, Slavery, and Race," xvi.

6. Browne, "Voices against Slavery," 97.

7. Quoted by Primm, *Lion of the Valley*, 342.

8. For further explication of these arguments, see Nancy F. Cott, *The Bonds of Womanhood: Woman's Sphere in New England, 1780–1835*, 2nd ed. (New Haven, CT: Yale University Press, 1997); Mary Kelley, *Learning to Stand and Speak: Women, Education, and Public Life in America's Republic* (Chapel Hill: University of North Carolina Press, 2006).

9. Minerva Grimsley Blow to Henry T. Blow, February 23, 1842, Blow Family Papers, Missouri Historical Society, St. Louis. This collection is hereafter referred to as Blow Family Papers.

10. Hannah Kerr Tiffany to Pardon Dexter Tiffany, January 13, 1850, PDT Collection.

11. Mary Knox to Elizabeth Knox and Hannah Tiffany, July 20, 1854, PDT Collection.

12. Pardon Dexter Tiffany to Hannah Tiffany, July 10, 1847, and Hannah Kerr to Hannah Tiffany, March 22, 1852, PDT Collection.

13. Hannah Tiffany to Pardon, February 2, 1850, PDT Collection.

14. Abigail Cranch Eliot to mother Mary Cranch, April 3, 1838, and to a daughter-in-law, perhaps Charlotte Stearns Eliot, October 9, 1875, original emphasis, William Greenleaf Eliot Family Papers and Journals, Washington University, St. Louis. The papers hereafter are referred to as WGE Papers.

15. W. G. Eliot, journal 2:131, April 6, WGE Papers.

16. W. G. Eliot, journal 3:28, February 28, 1855; journal 6:95, January 1, 1862; and journal 6:110, all in WGE Papers.

17. McLear, "St. Louis Cholera Epidemic"; Primm, *Lion of the Valley*, 163; C. A. Gordon, *Fire, Pestilence, and Death*, 153–70; A. N. Morris, "History," 83.

18. Hannah Kerr Tiffany to Pardon, June 2 and 4, 1849, PDT Collection.

19. Hannah Kerr Tiffany to Pardon, June 21, 24, and 28, 1849, PDT Collection.

20. Hannah Kerr Tiffany to Pardon, May 31, 1849, PDT Papers. Hannah's opinion is reaffirmed by Primm, *Lion of the Valley*, 175, and Charles Van Ravenswaay, "Years of Turmoil, Years of Growth: St. Louis in the 1850s," *Bulletin of the Missouri Historical Society* 23 (1957 July), 304–24.

21. W. G. Eliot, journal 1:171, August 8, 1850, WGE Papers.

22. "Centenary Methodist Church, 1839–1842," and "List of Colored Persons in Wesleyan Cemetery, 1847–1851," both in St. Louis County Library.

23. C. A. Gordon, *Fire, Pestilence and Death*, 189; "Blacks in St. Louis History," *Globe Democrat*, February 20, 1979.

24. Hannah Kerr Tiffany to Pardon, January 1851, and Pardon to Hannah Kerr Tiffany, March 28, 1852, both in PDT Collection. On Reuben Knox, see Robert C. Thomas to Missouri Historical Society, September 2, 1967, PDT Collection.

25. Hannah Kerr Tiffany to Pardon, January 31, 1850, PDT Collection.

26. Turner, "Reuben Knox Letters," 247, 269.

27. Hannah Skinner Kerr to Hannah Kerr Tiffany, July 10, 1847, PDT Collection.

28. Hannah Skinner Kerr to Hannah Kerr Tiffany, July 2, 1852, and Pardon to Hannah Kerr Tiffany, October 15, 1858, both in PDT Collection; Arenson, *Great Heart of the Republic*, 54.

29. Williams, "Factors in the Growth of St. Louis," 13; "St. Louis Real Estate," 119.

30. Frank Blair to James Blair, July 30, 1851, box 2, Janin Papers, Huntington Library, San Marino, California.

31. Frank Blair to James Blair, July 30, 1851, box 2, Janin Papers.

32. Montgomery Blair to Frank Blair May, undated, 1854, box 2, Janin Papers.

33. C. A. Gordon, *Fire, Pestilence, and Death*, 167; Schweninger, *From Tennessee Slave*, 145, 12.

34. Pardon to Hannah, March 27, 1852, PDT Collection.

35. Pardon to Hannah, October 10 and November 11, 1857, PDT Papers. See Henry D. Bacon Papers, Manuscripts, Huntington Library, San Marino, California.

36. W. G. Eliot, journal 1, November 16, 1847, WGE Papers.

37. Twitty, *Before Dred Scott*, table A, 100–105. Scholar Kelley M. Kennington found that these lawyers charged modest fees for their freedom-seeking clients. *In the Shadow of Dred Scott*, 69–75.

38. Anderson, *Story of a Border City*, 183–85.

39. Rowan, "Henry Boernstein," 159.

40. Hannah Skinner Kerr to Hannah Kerr Tiffany, July 10, 1847, and March 22, 1852, PDT Collection.

41. Emancipations, November 10, 1835, 7:454, and July 6, 1843, 14:82.

42. Beale, *Diary of Edward Bates*, 15.

43. Holt, *William Greenleaf Eliot*, 17; Green, "Conservative Voices," 347.

44. On the German Americans' point of view, see Efford, *German Immigrants*, 108–10.

45. W. G. Eliot, *Story of Archer Alexander*, 96–97.

46. W. G. Eliot, journal 4, March 28, 1853, WGE Papers.

47. Abigail Cranch Eliot quoted in Holt, *William Greenleaf Eliot*, appendix C, 182; W. G. Eliot, "Free Labor" and "Slavery in Missouri," *St. Louis Missouri Republican*, October 18, 1848, pasted into W. G. Eliot, journal 1:180, WGE Papers.

48. Trollope, *North America*, 93; W. G. Eliot, April 6, 1852, journal 2:131, WGE Papers.

49. Minerva Blow to Susan Blow, February 12, 1864, Blow Family Papers.

50. C. A. Gordon, *Fire, Pestilence, and Death*, 167; Schweninger, *Black Property Owners*, 73–85.

51. C. Johnson, *Hampden County*, 346–47, 359; Pardon to Hannah, May 19, 1852, PDT Collection.

## *Chapter 3. Redefining Citizenship*

1. On the importance of the year of the Dred Scott decision, see Stampp, *America in 1857*.

2. As quoted by Kellner, "German Element," 240–41.

3. W. G. Eliot, journal 4, ca. September 1856, WGE Papers.

4. Abraham Lincoln, "A House Divided Speech," June 16, 1858, in Johnson, *Abraham Lincoln*, 68, original emphasis.

5. Abraham Lincoln, "Address at Cooper Institute," February 27, 1860, in Johnson, *Abraham Lincoln*, 90.

6. Oberholzer, "Legal Aspects of Slavery," 148; Vandervelde, *Mrs. Dred Scot*, 188–90.

7. Twitty, *Before Dred Scott*, 12.

8. Finkleman, *Dred Scott v. Sandford*, 25; Keckley, *Behind the Scenes*, 19–20.

9. Roswell Field to Montgomery Blair, January 7, 1855, TS, Dred Scott Papers, Missouri Historical Society, St. Louis, original emphasis.

10. Roswell Field to Montgomery Blair, January 7, 1855, TS, Dred Scott Papers, Missouri Historical Society, St. Louis.

11. "Justice Benjamin Robbins Curtis, Dissenting Opinion," March 6, 1857, in Finkleman, *Dred Scott v. Sandford*, 114–15.

12. Finkleman, *Dred Scott v. Sandford*, 61.

13. Taylor's drinking, bankruptcy, and turn to the Catholic Church are described in Henry Blow to Minerva Blow, March 17, 1858, Henry Blow to Susan Blow, May 11, 1861, and Nelly Blow to Minerva Blow, April 14, 1862, all in Blow Family Papers.

14. Strom, *Political Woman*, 33.

15. "Visit to Dred Scott."

16. Pardon to Hannah, April 2, 1858, PDT Papers.

17. Holt, *William Greenleaf Eliot*, 43.

18. Holt, *William Greenleaf Eliot*, 86, original emphasis.

19. See the groundbreaking assessment of this relationship by Missouri historian Stevens, "Lincoln and Missouri," 63–66.

20. See the quintessential work of Foner, *Free Labor, Free Soil, Free Men.*

21. M[ontgomery]. Blair and F. P. Blair Jr., "Address to the Democracy of Missouri," ca. 1850, pamphlet, Rare Book Room, Library of Congress.

22. For a more in-depth discussion see K. L. Anderson, "Evolving toward Abolition."

23. Blair, "Acquisition of Territory."

24. This railroad was never completed, but its promoters, Ephraim G. Squier and Amory Edwards, made large profits by selling its bonds. See Strom, "If Success Depends upon Enterprise."

25. M. P. Johnson, *Abraham Lincoln*, 58.

26. Strom, "Labor, Race, and Colonization," 261.

27. F. B. Blair, Speech at Cooper Union Institute, 7, 8. Also see F. B. Blair's January 14, 1858, speech to the House of Representatives "Speech . . . on the Acquisition of Territory," and January 26, 1859, speech "The Destiny of the Races of This Continent."

28. Lincoln biographer David Herbert Donald claims that Lincoln "had genuine respect for all the members of the Blair family." Donald, *Lincoln*, 534.

29. Keckley, *Behind the Scenes*, 28.

30. Julia Davis, "Moses Dickson, Man of Vision," centennial address to the Knights and Daughters of Tabor, August 17, 1972, folder 46, SO201, Black History Project Collection. State Historical Society of Missouri, St. Louis.

31. W. G. Eliot, journal, November 12, 1860, WGE Papers; Pardon Dexter Tiffany to Hannah Kerr Tiffany, February 10, 1861, PDT Papers.

32. Henry Taylor Blow to "My dear Children," November 23, 1860, and Minerva Blow to Susie Blow, December 18, 1860, Blow Family Papers, original emphasis.

33. Minerva Blow to Susie Blow, March 8, 1861, Blow Family Papers; Herr and Spence, *Letters of Jessie Benton Fremont*, 320.

34. Holt, *William Greenleaf Eliot*, 89–95. For an important assessment of Eliot's civic contributions and position on emancipation, see Arenson, *Great Heart of the Republic*, 53–55, 146.

35. W. Johnson, *Broken Heart of America*, 111.

36. Arenson, *Great Heart of the Republic*, 115. Many of these bonds are preserved in the Pardon Dexter Tiffany papers at the Missouri Historical Society.

37. Manning, *Troubled Refuge*, 46–52, 122–32; Romeo, *Gender and the Jubilee*, 32–33.

38. Abraham Lincoln to Orville H. Browning, September 22, 1861, in M. P. Johnson, *Abraham Lincoln*, 185.

39. This exchange is summarized and analyzed by Blight, *Frederick Douglass*, 376–77.

40. M. Blair, "Comments on the Policy."

41. "Knox v. Blair," container 20, Blair Family Papers. Blair resigned from his army command a month after the Thirty-Eighth Congress convened, but the Committee on Elections ruled that he had been too late in doing so, and Knox took his place in Washington. House of Representatives, 38th Congress, Report No. 110, June 13, 1864, 4, National Archives and Records Administration. Lincoln's letter to Montgomery Blair of November 2, 1863, indicates that the president preferred that Blair not return to the House.

42. M. P. Johnson, *Abraham Lincoln*, 201.

43. M. P. Johnson, *Abraham Lincoln*, 258.

44. For Keckley's description of Willie's death, see Keckley, *Behind the Scenes*, 41–45. Of Lincoln's reaction she describes, "I never saw a man so bowed down with grief." 43. For a thoughtful and imaginative re-creation of this time, see George Saunders, *Lincoln in the Bardo* (New York: Random House, 2017).

45. M. P. Johnson, *Abraham Lincoln*, 219.

46. Norton, "Nationalism, Political Activism," 175–76.

## *Chapter 4. Civil War in the Valley of the Mississippi*

1. Keckley, *Behind the Scenes*, 48.

2. Romeo, *Gender and the Jubilee*, 34–36.

3. Downs, *Sick from Freedom*.

4. On the WSC, see Gerteis, *Civil War St. Louis*, 205–8.

5. The Yeatman manumissions are listed in Emancipations, 24:318 and 25:210, St. Louis Circuit Court Historical Records Project, St. Louis Arch Museum; G. Anderson, *Story of a Border City*, 289.

6. Gerteis, *Civil War St. Louis*, 277.

7. Hodges, *Western Sanitary Commission*, 10. On attitudes of Union Army commanders, see Teters, *Practical Liberators*.

8. Yeatman, *Report on the Condition*, 4.

9. As quoted by Gerteis, *From Contraband to Freedman*, 121. On Maria Mann, see Faulkner, *Women's Radical Reconstruction*, 13, 15.

10. Gerteis, *From Contraband to Freedman*, 119–20.

11. Yeatman, *Report on the Condition*, 4–5.

12. William Greenleaf Eliot, journal 6:120, August 22, 1862, WGE Papers.

13. William Greenleaf Eliot, journal 6:126, August 26, 1862, WGE Papers.

14. M. P. Johnson, *Abraham Lincoln*, 286, 257.

15. Gerteis, *From Contraband to Freedman*, 124.

16. Kremer, *James Milton Turner*, 16.

17. Bruce, *New Man*; Astor, *Rebels on the Border*, 126; Sixty-Second and Sixty-

Fifth Regiments, US Infantry, cofounders of Lincoln Institute, Archival Collections, Lincoln University, Jefferson City, Missouri.

18. The new flurry of correspondence unleashed by literacy and freedom is discussed in Rita Roberts, *"I Can't Wait to Call You My Wife": African American Letters of Love and Family in the Civil War Era* (San Francisco: Chronicle Books, 2022). For several powerful examples in Missouri, see Gerteis, *Civil War St. Louis*, 289–90.

19. General Orders No. 35, Head Quarters 62nd Regt. US Colored Infantry, October 29, 1864, Archival Collections, Lincoln University, Jefferson City, Missouri.

20. Coalier, "Beyond Sympathy."

21. Clippings, W. G. Eliot, journal 7:57, August 20, 1861, 67, WGE Papers, original emphasis in the newspaper article.

22. Primm, *Lion of the Valley*, 267–70; Hodges, *Western Sanitary Commission*.

23. Parsons and Parsons, *Memoir*, 83, original emphasis.

24. Parsons and Parsons, *Memoir*, 62.

25. Manning, *Troubled Refuge*, 123.

26. Parsons and Parsons, *Memoir*, 81, 136.

27. Parsons and Parsons, *Memoir*, 136, 141.

28. Minerva Blow to Henry Blow, February 24, 1864, Blow Family Papers, Manuscripts, Missouri Historical Society, St. Louis. Minerva Blow and her sister-in-law Martha Blow were both on the Executive Committee of Ladies that organized the fair. Thomas Scharf, *History of St. Louis County*, 553.

29. Anderson, *Story of a Border City*, 313; Bender, "This Noble and Philanthropic Enterprise." Anderson's figures are the same as those reported by Scharf, *History of Saint Louis City*, 555.

30. W. Johnson, *Broken Heart of America*, 145.

31. Stansell, *City of Women*.

32. Schwalm, "Between Slavery and Freedom," 148–49.

33. G. Anderson, *Story of a Border City*, 266.

34. W. G. Eliot, journal, February 14, 1861, and April 1, 1861, WGE Papers; W. G. Eliot, *Story of Archer Alexander*, 54.

35. Burke, *On Slavery's Border*, 201, 218. On Campbell, see Ehlmann, *Crossroads*, 42, 44.

36. Keeven-Franke, "Captain Campbell's House"; Ehlmann, *Crossroads*, 116.

37. Smith and Johnson, "St. Louis," 4.

38. C. N. Roberts, "History of the Structural Brick Industry."

39. W. G. Eliot to Thomas Eliot, November 30, 1863, WGE Papers.

40. National Park Service, "Expedition."

41. Maguerite Beeby, "A Free Man of Color: Griffin Brander, 1804–1888," 1988, folder 17, Griffin Brander Papers, State Historical Society of Missouri, Columbia and St. Louis, undergraduate paper, supervised by Louis Gerteis.

42. Astor, *Rebels on the Border*, 134.

*Chapter 5. What Rights Should All Citizens Have?*

1. Bates also said that on technical procedural grounds the Dred Scott case was invalid. McClure, Johnsen, Norman, and Vanderlan, "Circumventing the Dred Scott Decision," 279.

2. Beale, *Diary of Edward Bates*, 405–8.

3. Donald, *Lincoln*, 423.

4. Merkel, *Antislavery Controversy*, 28–29; B G. Brown, *Congressional Globe*, 985.

5. M. Blair, "Comments on the Policy."

6. M. Blair, "Speech," 19.

7. F. P. Blair, "Jacobins of Missouri and Maryland."

8. For a small sample of the printed matter that appeared in 1868 justifying the subjugation of African Americans, see Edward A. Pollard, *The Lost Cause Regained* (New York: Carleton, 1868); Hinton Rowan Helper, *The Negroes in Negroland: The Negroes in America: And Negroes Generally* (New York: G. W. Carleton, 1868): John Van Evrie, *White Supremacy and Negro Subordination, or Negroes a Subordinate Race, and (So-Called) Slavery Its Normal Condition* (New York: Van Evrie, Horton, 1868).

9. Primm, *Lion of the Valley*, 329.

10. Henry Blow to Minerva Blow, ca. December 1861, Blow Family Papers.

11. This debate was recorded in Edward Bates's diary and is discussed in Cain, *Lincoln's Attorney General*, 219–22.

12. Executive Committee of the Missouri Delegation to President Lincoln, October 3, 1863, Charles Daniel Drake Papers.

13. Edward Bates to Edmund Clarence Stedman, July 19, 1863, Edward Bates Family Papers.

14. Henry T. Blow to Abraham Lincoln, draft letter, August 12, 1862, Blow Family Papers.

15. "Reconstruction: Speech of Hon. Henry T. Blow of Missouri, in the House of Representatives," February 20, 1865, Cong. Globe, 38th Cong., 2nd Sess., at 73–75, appendix (1865).

16. "Reconstruction: Speech of Hon. Henry T. Blow."

17. "Reconstruction: Speech of Hon. Henry T. Blow."

18. Howe, *Refugees from Slavery*.

19. Gould, *Mismeasure of Man*; Gilman, *Disease and Representation*; Torchia, "Tuberculosis among Negroes"; Kendi, *Stamped from the Beginning*, 228–29.

20. "Reconstruction: Speech of Hon. Henry T. Blow."

21. Edward Bates to Edmund Clarence Stedman, July 19, 1863, Edward Bates Family Papers.

22. "Reconstruction: Speech of Hon. Henry T. Blow."

23. Scharf, *History of St. Louis County*, 548–9.

24. Zornow, "Missouri Radicals and the Election of 1864"; Laughlin, "Struggle for Emancipation," 272; Primm, *Lion of the Valley*, 334–45.

25. Efford, *German Immigrants*, 93, 108, 113.

26. On the importance of the Fourteenth Amendment, see Foner, *Second Founding*, 55–93.

27. Quoted in Sacco, "Black Political Activism," 3.

28. Langston, *Speech*, original emphasis.

29. Langston, *Speech*, original emphasis.

30. W. G. Eliot to Missouri Woman Suffrage Association, W. G. Eliot journal, April 20, 1874, 93, and W. G. Eliot to Mrs. G. D. Hall, W. G. Eliot journal, April, 1875, 128, both in WGE Papers.

31. Strom, *Women's Rights*, 101–2; Gilliam, "Professional Pioneer."

32. Whites, "Tale of Two Minors," 101–118; Hoff, *Law, Gender, and Injustice*, 170–74.

33. A.M.E. Church, "To a Generous Public," July 1, 1868, found with the census record of George Kilpatrick in Latter Day Saints Family Records, Salt Lake City, Utah.

34. Julia Davis, "Moses Dickson, Man of Vision," centennial address to the Knights and Daughters of Tabor, August 17, 1972, TS, folder 46, Black History Project Collection, State Historical Society of Missouri, St. Louis; Scharf, *History of St. Louis County and City*, 1791.

35. Samuel Knox to William H. Bliss, September 8, 1876, E. Cave Barrow Collection, Missouri Historical Society; Whiskey Ring Pardon Papers, July and August 1876, Missouri Historical Society; Guese, "St. Louis and the Great Whisky Ring." Also see Strom, *Political Woman*, 45, 286n3.

36. Scharf, *History of St. Louis*, 1022–23. The terms in italics and the census figure totals are those of Scharf and the newspaper article reference as quoted by him.

37. Schweninger, *From Tennessee Slave*, 178.

38. "Blacks in St. Louis History," *St. Louis Globe Democrat*, February 20, 1979, 3D; Romeo, *Gender and the Jubilee*, 119–20.

39. Herman T. Dreer, "Highlights of Negro History," *St. Louis Argus*, July 9, 1965, newspaper clippings, Charlton H. Tandy Papers. See, in particular, "Negroes Are Weary of Empty Promises: Republicans Ride In on Their Votes and Cling to All the Spoils," undated newspaper clipping, Charlton H. Tandy Papers.

## *Chapter 6. "Nothing of the Horrors of Slavery"*

1. Blight, *Race and Reunion*.

2. Beale, *Diary of Edward Bates*, 488.

3. March, "Campaign for the Ratification," 229.

4. The Edmonia Lewis busts of the Thomases are at the St. Louis Museum of Art, along with a version of Hosmer's Zenobia in Chains. On the political implications of Hosmer's statue, see Culkin, *Harriet Hosmer*. On the controversy over the Emancipation monument, see Savage, *Standing Soldiers, Kneeling Slaves*, 117–19.

5. W. G. Eliot to James Yeatman, November 8, 1869, WGE Papers; *St. Louis Daily Democrat*, July 4, 1873, clipping in W. G. Eliot journal 8:83, WGE Papers.

6. For an astute analysis of this speech, see Blight, *Frederick Douglass*, 1–7.

7. R. Morris, *Fraud of the Century*, 108.

8. Unidentified clipping, ca. December 12, 1875, W. G. Eliot journal 9:61, WGE Papers.

9. W. G. Eliot to Thomas Eliot, September 4, 1876, W. G. Eliot journal 9:166, WGE Papers.

10. W. G. E. Eliot, journal 10:18–21, WGE Papers, original emphasis. It is reprinted verbatim in his daughter-in-law's memoir, C. C. Eliot, *William Greenleaf Eliot*, 286–89.

11. C. C. Eliot, *William Greenleaf Eliot*, 289.

12. "Negroes Are Weary of Empty Promises," unidentified newspaper clipping, ca. spring 1877, Charlton H. Tandy, State Historical Society of Missouri, Columbia and St. Louis, and Kremer, *James Milton Turner*, 104–5.

13. Du Bois, *Black Reconstruction*, 470.

14. Du Bois, *Black Reconstruction*, 483.

15. Blight, *Race and Reunion*, 135–37.

16. *St. Louis Globe Democrat*, March 18, 1879.

17. On Douglass's tortured assessment of this migration, see McFeeley, *Frederick Douglass*, 299–303.

18. Kremer, *James Milton Turner*, 105–16; Painter, *Exodusters*; Strom and Weaver, *Confederates in the Tropics*, 117–19.

19. "The Southern Exodus, a Letter from Dr. W. G. Eliot," unidentified newspaper clipping, April 22, 1879, W. G. Eliot journal, 10 (1879), WGE Papers, original emphasis.

20. W. G. Eliot to Thomas Eliot, November 4, 1876, WGE Papers.

21. W. G. Eliot to Abigail Eliot, September 17, 1872, WGE Papers.

22. W. G. Eliot, *Story of Archer Alexander*, 87.

23. W. G. Eliot, *Story of Archer Alexander*, 5, 61.

24. Thomas, "Post-Abolitionist's Narrative," 466.

25. Brown published *My Southern Home* in 1880 after a tour through the south in 1877 and 1878. Literary critic John Ernest suggests that Brown, about thirty years beyond his popular 1847 narrative, was aiming this book at a wide audience that now enjoyed humorous and derogatory depictions of rural Blacks and was promoting his now most important cause, temperance. Brown's fractured consciousness about slavery in Kentucky and Missouri is self-evident in chapter 8, where he begins, "Cruelty to negroes was not practiced in our section," and then goes on to describe the use of bloodhounds to track down escaping slaves. Ernest, introduction, 65.

26. Everett, *James*, 22–23.

27. W. G. Eliot, *Story of Archer Alexander*, 84, 88.

28. W. G. Eliot, *Story of Archer Alexander*, 90.

29. W. G. Eliot, *Story of Archer Alexander*, 41–42.
30. Arenson, "Dred Scott vs. the *Dred Scott Case*," 32; "Dred Scott Eulogized."
31. Gilbert, *Whose Fair*, 60–61.
32. Mary Louise Dalton to Frederick Trevor Hill, March 13, 1907, and "Notes Taken in a Conversation with Mrs. William T. Blow," February 18, 1907, both in Dred Scott Papers, Missouri Historical Society.
33. Foner, foreword, xi.
34. Trexler, *Slavery in Missouri*, 42; W. G. Eliot, *Story of Archer Alexander*, 100.
35. Engerman and Fogel, *Time on the Cross*; Trexler, *Slavery in Missouri*, 56.
36. Trexler, *Slavey in Missouri*, 84n9.
37. W. G. Eliot, *Story of Archer Alexander*, 39; Trexler, *Slavery in Missouri*, 95.
38. Trexler, *Slavery in Missouri*, 98n31.

## *Chapter 7. "A Race without a History Is Soon Forgotten"*

1. For helpful exploration of this idea, see Susan Hay, ed., *From Paris to Providence: Fashion, Art, and the Tirocchi Dressmakers' Shop, 1915–1947* (Providence: Rhode Island School of Design, 2000).
2. Keckley, *Behind the* Scenes, 103–8.
3. Goggin, *Carter G. Woodson*, 21–25.
4. Woodson, "Fifty Years of Negro Citizenship," 53.
5. Primm, *Lion of the Valley*, 324.
6. "A Complaint with Illustrations to the Board of Education of St. Louis, June 11, 1907, from the Colored Citizens of St. Louis Concerning Sumner High School," Julia Davis Collection, St. Louis Public Library. Someone, presumably Davis, wrote across the front page, "A Treasured Race Document." On the evolution of Sumner High School, see Primm, *Lion of the Valley*, 335.
7. Advertisement illustrations, Wright, *African Americans*, 59; "The History and Origin of the Order of Eastern Star of Missouri and Jurisdiction in St. Louis, Missouri," Black History Project.
8. Dickson, *International 777*, 73.
9. Ervin, *Gateway to Equality*, 12.
10. Mather, *Who's Who*, 127.
11. *Proud* (March–April, 1975), 5.
12. Julia Davis, "An Historical Review of the Prudence Crandall Club of St. Louis, Missouri, 1915–1975," Julia Davis Collection, St. Louis Public Library.
13. Primm, *Lion of the Valley*, 314–15; Scharf, *History of St. Louis*, 1133, 1218; Cronon, *Nature's Metropolis*, 296–99.
14. Julia Webster Blow to Julia Dalton, March 19, 1907, Dred Scott Collection, Missouri Historical Society; Scharf, *History of St. Louis*, 1,697.
15. "History of Central Baptist Church," 32, Black History Project.
16. "History of Central Baptist Church," 37, Black History Project.
17. Dreer, "Rev. George E. Stevens."

18. "History of Central Baptist Church," 36, Black History Project. Stevens' family believed they had a distinguished African American legacy because his father George E. Stevens Jr., his father, George E. Stevens Sr., served in the US Colored Troops Fifty-Fourth Massachusetts Regiment. A number of George Stevens served in various USCT during the Civil War, but pension and census records suggest that the USCT Third Infantry Regiment, heavy artillery, is the site of George Stevens's father's army service. Further confusion arises with the service of the more-famous Black Philadelphian George Stephens, another African Baptist Church member, who did serve in the Massachusetts Fifty-Fourth and filed numerous articles from the front to the *Anglo American Weekly*. Both Stevens's possible regiment and Stephens's regiment were at the notorious Fort Wagner Battle of 1863, so this misunderstanding by the Stevens descendants is understandable. The US Census of 1860 delineates the William Stevens family, among them George Stevens, age twenty-eight and a cabinetmaker, indicating either that this George Stevens changed his last name to Stephens or that it was changed for him when he enlisted in Philadelphia in 1863.

19. Weistein, "1903 Juvenile Courts Act," 26–30. On Baldwin in St. Louis, see Primm, *Lion of the Valley*, 424–27.

20. Quoted in Kelleher, "History of the St. Louis NAACP," 5.

21. Quoted in C. Gordon, *Mapping Decline*, 70.

22. See Primm, *Lion of the Valley*, 436–38.

23. Quoted in Primm, *Lion of the Valley*, 440.

24. Moon, "Dr. Julia Davis."

25. Jennifer Schuessler, "Helping Black Culture Rise upon a Mountain of Books," *New York Times*, July 5, 2014, C, 1, 8. Black women librarians also took up Woodson's call that "a race without a history is soon forgotten." In New York they grew the Arthur Schomberg African American History archival and printed-works collection at the New York Public Library and the same materials at Howard University, led by librarian Dorothy Porter and her colleague at the Schomberg, Catherine Latimer.

26. St. Louis Public Library, *Julia Davis Collection*, original emphasis. The catalog was sent to a number of libraries and archives, including the Huntington Library in San Marino, California, where this author found a copy. It is also online at the Library of Congress, https://www.loc.gov/resource/gdcmassbookdig.juliadaviscollec00stlo/?st=gallery.

27. Ervin, *Gateway to Equality*, 147. Colin Gordon begins his description of the decline of the 'Ville and other neighborhoods in St. Louis with a house at 4635 North Market Street, a few blocks west of Julia Davis's home. He describes zoning in "Greater St. Louis" as an "America Apartheid." *Mapping Decline*, 1, 145.

28. W. Johnson, *Broken Heart of America*, 309.

# Bibliography


Anderson, Galusha. *The Story of a Border City during the Civil War*. Boston: Little, Brown, 1908.

Anderson, Kristen Layne. "Evolving toward Abolition: German Attitudes toward the Fugitive Slave and Kansas-Nebraska Act." In *Fighting for a Free Missouri: German Immigrants, African Americans, and the Issue of Slavery*, edited by Sydney J. Norton, 231–54. Columbia: University of Missouri Press, 2023.

Archival Collections. Lincoln University, Jefferson City, Missouri.

Arenson, Adam. "Dred Scott vs. the Dred Scott Case: History and Memory of a Signal Moment in American Slavery, 1857–2007." *Selected Works of Adam Arenson. bepress*, 2010. https://works.bepress.com/adam_arenson/5/. Originally published in *The Dred Scott Case: Historical and Contemporary Perspectives on Race and Law*, edited by David Thomas Konig, Paul Finkelman, and Christopher Alan Bracey, 25–46. Athens: Ohio University Press, 2010.

Arenson, Adam. *The Great Heart of the Republic: St. Louis and the Cultural Civil War*. Columbia: University of Missouri Press, 2011.

Aron, Stephen. *American Confluence: The Missouri Frontier from Borderland to Border State*. Bloomington: Indiana University Press, 2006.

Astor, Aaron. *Rebels on the Border: Civil War, Emancipation, and the Reconstruction of Kentucky and Missouri*. Baton Rouge: Louisiana State University Press, 2012.

Bacon, Henry D., Papers. Manuscripts, Huntington Library, San Marino, California.

Bancroft, Frederic. *Slave Trading in the Old South*. 1931. Columbia: University of South Carolina Press, 1996.

Bates, Edward Family. Papers. Manuscripts, Missouri Historical Society, St. Louis.

Beale, Howard K., ed. *The Diary of Edward Bates, 1859–1866*. Washington, DC: US Government Printing Office, 1933.

Beito, David. *From Mutual Aid to the Welfare State: Fraternal Societies and Social Services, 1890–1967*. Chapel Hill: University of North Carolina Press, 2000.

*Bench and Bar of St. Louis, Kansas City, Jefferson City, and Other Missouri Cities, The*. St. Louis: American Biographical, 1884.

Bender, Robert Patrick. "This Noble and Philanthropic Enterprise: The Mississippi Valley Sanitary Fair of 1864 and the Practice of Civil War Philanthropy." *Missouri Historical Review* 95, no. 2 (2001): 117–39.

Black History Project. Collection. State Historical Society of Missouri, St. Louis.

Blair, Frank B. "The Destiny of the Races of This Continent." Lecture, Mercantile Library Association of Boston on January 26, 1859. Washington, DC: Buell and Blanchard, 1858.

Blair, Frank B. "The Jacobins of Missouri and Maryland." Speech, F. P. Blair of Missouri Delivered in the House of Representatives, February 27, 1864, printed pamphlet, Rare Book Room, Library of Congress.

Blair, Frank B. Papers. Library of Congress.

Blair, Frank B. Speech at Cooper Union Institute of New York, January 25, 1860. Washington, DC: Buell and Blanchard, 1860.

Blair, Frank B. "Speech in the House of Representatives, January 14, 1858." Washington, DC: Buell and Blanchard, 1858.

Blair, Frank B. "Speech of Hon. Frank P. Blair, Jr., of Missouri, on the Acquisition of Territory in Central America in Central and South America, Colonized with Free Blacks, and Held as a Dependency of the United States." Washington, DC: Buell and Blanchard, 1858. Pdf. https://www.loc.gov/item/10033467/.

Blair, M.[Montgomery], and F.[rank] P. Blair Jr. "Address to the Democracy of Missouri." Ca. 1850. Rare Book Room, Library of Congress.

Blair, Montgomery. "Comments on the Policy Inaugurated by the President in a Letter and Two Speeches." New York: Hall, Clayton, and Medole, 1863. Available at the Library of Congress.

Blair, Montgomery. *Speech of the Hon. Montgomery Blair (Postmaster General) on the Revolutionary Schemes of the Ultra Abolitionists and in Defence of the Pollicy of the President: Delivered at the Unconditional Union Meeting, Held at Rockville, Maryland, October 3, 1863*. Baltimore: Sherwood and Col, 1864.

Blight, David W. *Frederick Douglass: Prophet of Freedom*. New York: Simon and Schuster, 2018.

Blight, David W. *Race and Reunion: The Civil War in American Memory*. Cambridge, MA: Harvard University Press, 2001.

Blow Family Papers. Manuscripts, Missouri Historical Society, St. Louis.

Boman, Dennis K. "The Dred Scott Case Reconsidered: The Legal and Political Context in Missouri." *American Journal of Legal History* 44 (October 2000): 405–28.

Brander, Griffin. Papers. State Historical Society of Missouri, Columbia and St. Louis.

Brown, Benjamin Gratz. *Congressional Globe*, 38th Congress, Sess. 1, 985.

Brown, William Wells. *My Southern Home or, the South and Its People.* Edited and with an introduction by John Ernest. Chapel Hill: University of North Carolina Press, 2011. Originally published by A. G. Brown, Boston, 1880.

Browne, Cynthia. "Voices against Slavery: The Editors of Hermann's Newspapers." In *Fighting for a Free Missouri: German Immigrants, African Americans, and the Issue of Slavery*, edited by Sydney J. Norton, 93–122. Columbia: University of Missouri Press, 2023.

Bruce, Henry Clay. *The New Man: Twenty-Nine Years a Slave Twenty-Nine Years a Free Man.* York, PA: Anstadt, 1895. google.com/books.

Buchanan, Thomas. *Black Life on the Mississippi: Slaves, Free Blacks, and the Western Steamboat World.* Chapel Hill: University of North Carolina Press, 2004.

Bullock, Steven. *Revolutionary Brotherhood: Freemasonry and the Transformation of the American Social Order.* Chapel Hill: University of North Carolina Press, 1996.

Burke, Diane Mutti. *On Slavery's Border: Missouri's Small-Slaveholding Households, 1815–1865.* Athens: University of Georgia Press, 2010.

Cain, Marvin R. *Lincoln's Attorney General Edward Bates of Missouri.* Columbia: University of Missouri Press, 1965.

Cleary, Patricia. "The Destruction of the Big Mound: Defining Native American Places in Early St. Louis." *Missouri Historical Review* 113 (October 2018): 1–21.

Coalier, Paula. "Beyond Sympathy: The St. Louis Ladies' Union Aid Society and the Civil War." *Gateway Heritage Magazine* (Summer 1990): 38–51.

Coburn, Carol K., and Martha Smith. "City Sisters: The Sisters of St. Joseph in Missouri, 1836–1920." In *Women in Missouri History: In Search of Power and Influence*, edited by LeeAnn Whites, Mary C. Neth, and Gary R. Kremer, 82–100. Columbia: University of Missouri Press, 2004.

Cronon, William. *Nature's Metropolis: Chicago and the Great West.* New York: Norton, 1991.

Culkin, Kate. *Harriet Hosmer: A Cultural Biography.* Amherst: University of Massachusetts Press, 2010.

Curry, Leonard P. *The Free Black in Urban America, 1800–1850.* Chicago: University of Chicago Press, 1981.

Curtis, Samuel G. Papers. Manuscripts, Huntington Library, San Marino, California.

Dagbovie, Pero Gaglo. *The Early Black History Movement, Carter G. Woodson, and Lorenzo Johnston Greene.* Urbana: University of Illinois Press, 2007.

Davis, Julia. Collection. St. Louis Public Library, St. Louis.

Day, Judy, and M. James Kedro. "Free Blacks in St. Louis: Antebellum Conditions, Emancipation, and the Postwar Era." *Bulletin of the Missouri Historical Society* 30 (January 1974): 117–35.

Delaney, Lucy A. *From the Darkness Cometh the Light or Struggles for Freedom.* St. Louis: J. T. Smith, 1890.

Dickson, Moses. *International 777—Order of Twelve: 333 of Knights and Daughters of Tabor*. St. Louis: A. R. Fleming, 1894.

Donald, David Herbert. *Lincoln*. New York: Touchstone, 1996.

Downs, Jim. *Sick from Freedom: African-American Illness and Suffering during the Civil War and Reconstruction*. New York: Oxford University Press, 2012.

Drake, Charles Daniel. Papers. Manuscripts, State Historical Society of Missouri, Columbia.

Drake, Charles Daniel. Papers. Missouri Historical Society, St. Louis.

"Dred Scott Eulogized by James Milton Turner: A Historical Observance of the Turner Centenary, 1840–1940." *Journal of Negro History* 39 (October 1934): 1–11.

Dreer, Herman. "Rev. George E. Stevens, Pioneer Champion of Integration." *Negro History Bulletin* 19, no. 5 (1956): 99–101.

Du Bois, W. E. B. *Black Reconstruction in America*. 1934. New York: Free Press, 1992.

Duden, Gottfried. *Report on a Journey to the Western States of North America: And a Stay of Several Years along the Missouri (during the Years 1824, '25, '26, and 1827)*. James W. Goodrich, gen. ed. Columbia: State Historical Society of Missouri and University of Missouri Press, 1980.

Efford, Alice Clark. *German Immigrants, Race, and Citizenship in the Civil War Era*. New York: Oxford University Press, 2018.

Ehlmann, Steve. *Crossroads: A History of St. Charles County, Missouri*. Marceline, MO: Walsworth, 2004.

Eliot, Charlotte C. *William Greenleaf Eliot: Minister, Educator, Philanthropist*. Boston: Houghton, Mifflin, 1904.

Eliot, William Greenleaf. *The Story of Archer Alexander from Slavery to Freedom*. Boston: Cupples, Upham, 1885.

Eliot, William Greenleaf, Family. Papers and Journals. Olin Library, Washington University, St. Louis.

Ellinwood, DeWitt, Jr. "Protestantism Enters St. Louis: The Presbyterians" *Bulletin of the Missouri Historical Society* 12 (April 1956): 254–73.

Emancipations. St. Louis Circuit Court Historical Records Project, St. Louis Arch Museum, St. Louis, Missouri.

Engerman, Stanley, and Robert Fogel. *Time on the Cross: The Economics of Negro Slavery*. Boston: Little, Brown, 1974.

Ernest, John. Introduction to *My Southern Home or, the South and Its People*, by William Wells Brown. Edited by John Ernest. Chapel Hill: University of North Carolina Press, 2011. Originally published by A. G. Brown, Boston, 1880.

Ervin, Keona K. *Gateway to Equality: Black Women and the Struggle for Economic Justice in St. Louis*. Lexington: University of Kentucky Press, 2017.

Everett, Percival. *James*. New York: Doubleday, 2024.

Faulkner, Carol. *Women's Radical Reconstruction: The Freedmen's Aid Movement*. Philadelphia: University of Pennsylvania Press, 2004.

Finkleman, Paul. *Dred Scott v. Sandford: A Brief History with Documents*. Boston: Bedford, 1987.

Foley, William E. "Slave Freedom Suits before Dred Scott: The Case of MarieJean Scypion's Descendants." *Missouri Historical Review* 79 (October 1984): 1–23.
Foley, William E., and C. David Rice. *The First Chouteaus: River Barons of Early St. Louis*. Lexington: University of Kentucky Press, 1983.
Foner, Eric. Foreword to *The Dunning School: Historians, Race, and the Meaning of Reconstruction*, edited by John David Smith and J. Vincent Lowery, ix–xii. Lexington: University of Kentucky Press, 2013.
Foner, Eric. *Free Soil, Free Labor, Free Men: The Ideology of the Republican Party before the Civil War*. New York, Oxford University Press, 1995.
Foner, Eric. *Reconstruction: America's Unfinished Revolution, 1863–1877*. Rev. ed. New York: Harper Perennial, 2014.
Foner, Eric. *The Second Founding: How the Civil War and Reconstruction Remade the Constitution*. New York: Norton, 2019.
Frederickson, Mary E. *Race, Gender, and the Transformation of Labor from Reconstruction to Globalization*. Tallahassee: University of Florida Press, 2011.
Gerteis, Louis. *From Contraband to Freedman: Federal Policy toward Southern Blacks, 1861–1865*. Westport, CT: Greenwood, 1973.
Gerteis, Louis. *Civil War St. Louis*. Lawrence: University of Kansas Press, 2001.
Gilbert, James. *Whose Fair? Experience, Memory, and the History of the Great St. Louis Exposition*. Chicago: University of Chicago Press, 2009.
Gilliam, Nancy T. "A Professional Pioneer: Myra Bradwell's Fight to Practice Law." *Law and History Review* 5 (Spring 1987): 105–33.
Gilman, Sander L. *Disease and Representation: Images of Illness from Madness to Aids*. Ithaca, NY: Cornell University Press, 1988.
Goggin, Jaqueline. *Carter G. Woodson: A Life in Black History*. Baton Rouge: Louisiana State University Press, 1993.
Goodwin, Doris Kearn. *Team of Rivals: The Political Genius of Abraham Lincoln*. New York: Simon and Schuster, 2005.
Gordon, Christopher Alan. *Fire, Pestilence, and Death: St. Louis, 1849*. St. Louis: Missouri Historical Society Press, 2018.
Gordon, Colin. *Mapping Decline: St. Louis and the Fall of the American City*. Philadelphia: University of Pennsylvania Press, 2008.
Gould, Stephen J. *The Mismeasure of Man*. New York: Norton, 1996.
Green, Judith Kent. "Conservative Voices in the 'Western Messenger': William Greenleaf Eliot and Harm Jan Huidekoper." *Harvard Theological Review* 77 (July–October, 1984): 331–52.
Guese, Lucius E. "St. Louis and the Great Whisky Ring." *Missouri Historical Review* 36 (January 1942): 160–83.
Herr, Pamela, and Marly Lee Spence. *The Letters of Jessie Benton Fremont*. Urbana: University of Illinois Press, 1993.
Hill, Timothy. *Historical Outlines of the Presbyterian Church in Missouri*. Kansas City, MO: VanHorn and Abeel, 1871.
Hodges, William R. *The Western Sanitary Commission*. Military Order of the

Loyal Legion of the United States. N.p., 1906. Rare Books, Huntington Library, San Marino, California.

Hoff, Joan. *Law, Gender, and Injustice: A Legal History of U.S. Women.* New York: New York University Press, 1991.

Hoffert, Sylvia. "The Emancipation of Elizabeth Hobbs Keckley." *Missouri Historical Review* 112 (July 2018): 243–59.

Hoig, Stan. *The Chouteaus: First Family of the Fur Trade.* Albuquerque: University of New Mexico Press, 2008.

Holt, Earl K., III. *William Greenleaf Eliot: Conservative Radical.* 2nd ed. Bellville, IL: Village, 2011.

Howard, Victor B. *Religion and the Radical Republican Movement, 1860–1870.* Lexington: University of Kentucky Press, 2014.

Howe, Samuel Gridley. *The Refugees from Slavery in Canada West.* Boston: Wright and Potter, 1864.

Hunter, Lloyd A. "Slavery in Missouri, 1804–1860." *Bulletin of the Missouri Historical Society* 30 (July 1974): 233–65.

Jackson, Luther Porter. *Free Negro Labor and Property Holding in Virginia, 1830–1850.* New York: D. Appleton–Century, 1942.

Jacobs, Robert P., ed. *Religions in St. Louis.* St. Louis: Interfaith Clergy Council, 1976.

Janin, Charles. Papers. Manuscripts, Huntington Library, San Marino, California.

Johnson, Clifton. *Hampden County, 1636–1936, Vol. 1.* New York: New York Historical Society, 1936.

Johnson, Michael P., ed. *Abraham Lincoln, Slavery, and the Civil War: Selected Writings and Speeches.* Boston: Bedford, 2001.

Johnson, Walter. *The Broken Heart of America: St. Louis and the Violent History of the United States.* New York: Basic Books, 2020.

Kaufman, Kenneth C. *Dred Scott's Advocate: A Biography of Roswell M. Field.* Columbia: University of Missouri Press, 1996.

Keckley, Elizabeth. *Behind the Scenes: Or, Thirty Years a Slave and Four Years in the White House.* Edited by Dolen Perkins-Valdez. Repr., Hillsborough, NC: Eno, 2016. Originally published New York: Carleton, 1868. Citations are to the Eno version.

Keeven-Franke, Dorris. "Captain Campbell's House." *St. Charles County History*, June 2, 2021. https://stcharlescountyhistory.org/2021/06/02/captain-campbells-house/.

Kelleher, Daniel T. "The History of the St. Louis NAACP, 1914–1955." Master's thesis, Southern Illinois University Edwardsville, 1969. https://spark.siue.edu/etd/62. St. Louis Black History Project Collection, State Historical Society of Missouri, St. Louis.

Kellner, George. *The German Element in the Urban Frontier: St. Louis, 1830–1860.* PhD diss., University of Missouri, Columbia, 1973.

Kendi, Ibram S. *Stamped from the Beginning: The Definitive History of Racist Ideas in America.* New York: Nation Books, 2016.

Kennington, Kelley M. *In the Shadow of Dred Scott: St. Louis Freedom Suits and the Legal Culture of Slavery in Antebellum America*. Athens: University of Geogia, 2017.

Kremer, Gary R. Foreword, "German Immigrants, Slavery, and Race: Reflections on the Missouri Experience," to *Fighting for a Free Missouri: German Immigrants, African Americans, and the Issue of Slavery*, edited by Sydney J. Norton, xvi–xvii. Columbia: University of Missouri, 2023.

Kremer, Gary R. *James Milton Turner and the Promise of America: The Public Life of Post-Civil War Leader*. Columbia: University of Missouri Press, 1991.

Langston, J. Mercer. *A Speech on "Equality under the Law" delivered by J. Mercer Langston in the Hall of Representatives, in the Capitol of Missouri, on the evening of the 9th day of January, 1866*. St. Louis: Democrat Book, 1866. PDF. https://www.loc.gov/item/91899132/.

Latter Day Saints Family Records, Salt Lake City, Utah.

Laughlin, Sceva Bright. "Missouri Politics during the Civil War: Chapter 4, The Struggle for Emancipation." *Missouri Historical Review* 24, no. 2 (1930): 261–84.

Manning, Chandra. *Troubled Refuge: Struggling for Freedom in the Civil War*. New York: Vintage, 2017.

March, David D. "The Campaign for the Ratification of the Constitution of 1865." *Missouri Historical Review* 47, no. 3 (1953): 223–32.

Mather, Frank Lincoln, ed. *Who's Who of the Colored Race*. Chicago: 1915.

McClure, James P., Leigh Johnsen, Kathleen Norman, and Michael Vanderlan, eds. "Circumventing the Dred Scott Decision: Edward Bates, Salmon Chase, and the Citizenship of African Americans." *Civil War History* 43 (December 1997): 279–309.

McFeeley, William S. *Frederick Douglass*. New York: Simon Schuster Touchstone, 1991.

McLear, Patrick E. "The St. Louis Cholera Epidemic of 1849." *Missouri Historical Review* 63, no. 2 (1969): 171–81.

Meachum, John B. *An Address to All the Colored Citizens of the United States*. Philadelphia: Self published, King and Baird, Andeslte Press, 1846.

Melish, Joanne Pope. *Disowning Slavery: Gradual Emancipation and "Race" in New England, 1780–1860*. Ithaca, NY: Cornell University Press, 2000.

Merkel, Benjamin. *The Antislavery Controversy in Missouri, 1819–1865*. PhD diss., Washington University, St. Louis, 1942.

Miles, Tiya. *All That She Carried: The Journey of Ashley's Sack, a Black Family Keepsake*. New York: Random, 2022.

Moon, Katie J. "Dr. Julia Davis: She Dedicated Her Life to Teaching African American History." mohistory.org, February 26, 2013.

Morris, Ann N. "The History of the St. Louis Protestant Orphan Asylum." *Bulletin of the Missouri Historical Society* 36 (January 1980): 80–91.

Morris, Roy, Jr. *Fraud of the Century: Rutherford B. Hayes, Samuel Tilden, and the Stolen Election of 1876*. New York: Simon and Shuster, 2003.

National Park Service. "Expedition from Brazos Santiago, Palmito Ranch." Civil War Search, AC reference TX005.

Norton, Sydney J. "Nationalism, Political Activism, and Abolitionism in Missouri Turner Societies." In *Fighting for a Free Missouri: German Immigrants, African Americans, and the Issue of Slavery*, edited by Sydney J. Norton, 169–94. Columbia: University of Missouri, 2023.

Oberholzer, Emil. "The Legal Aspects of Slavery in Missouri." *Bulletin of the Missouri Historical Society* 6 (January 1950): 139–61.

Olsen, Greg. *Indigenous Missourians, Ancient Societies to the Present.* Columbia: University of Missouri Press, 2023.

Painter, Nell Irvin. *Exodusters.* New York: Norton, 1976.

Parsons, Theophilus, ed., and Emily Elizabeth Parsons. *Memoir of Emily Elizabeth Parsons.* Boston: Little, Brown, 1880.

Peck, J. M. "Historical Sketch of the Baptist Denomination in Missouri." *Baptist Memorial and Monthly Chronicle*, July 15, 1842, 207–10. Reprinted at Baptisthistoryhomepage.com.

Post, A. *Truman Marcellus Post: A Biography.* Boston: Congregational Sunday-School and Publishing Society, 1891.

Primm, James Neal. *Lion of the Valley: St. Louis, Missouri.* Boulder, CO: Pruett, 1981.

*Proud*, March–April, 1975, 5.

Roberts, Anna K. "Crossing Jordan: The Mississippi River in the Black Experience in Greater St. Louis, 1815–1860." *Missouri Historical Review* 113, no. 1 (2018): 22–40.

Roberts, Clarence N. "History of the Structural Brick Industry in Missouri." *Missouri Historical Review* 37, no. 4 (1953): 318–28.

Romeo, Sharon. *Gender and the Jubilee: Black Freedom and the Reconstruction of Citizenship in Civil War Missouri.* Athens: University of Georgia Press, 2018.

Rowan, Steven. "Henry Boernstein and the Abolition of Slavery: A Wild Ride." In *Fighting for a Free Missouri: German Immigrants, African Americans, and the Issue of Slavery*, edited by Sydney J. Norton, 145–68. Columbia: University of Missouri, 2023.

Rushforth, Brett. *Bonds of Alliance: Indigenous and Atlantic Slaveries in New France.* Chapel Hill: University of North Carolina Press, 2012.

Sacco, Nick. "Black Political Activism and the Fight for Voting Rights in Missouri." *Journal of the Civil War Era.org*, 2020.

St. Louis Public Library. *The Julia Davis Collection: Negro and African Literature and Culture, a Bibliography.* St. Louis: St. Louis Public Library, 1961.

"St. Louis Real Estate in Review." Glimpses of the Past. *Bulletin of the Missouri Historical Society* 4 (October–December 1927): 119.

Savage, Kirk. *Standing Soldiers, Kneeling Slaves: Race, War, and Monument in Nineteenth Century America.* Princeton, NJ: Princeton University Press, 1997.

Scharf, J. Thomas. *The History of Saint Louis City and County, from the Earliest Periods to the Present Day.* 2 vols. Philadelphia: Louis H. Everts, 1883.

Schmidt, Kelly L. "Slavery and the Shaping of Missouri." *Missouri Historical Review* 116 (April 2022): 173–202.

Schwalm, Leslie A. "Between Slavery and Freedom: African American Women and Occupation in the Slave South." In *Occupied Women: Gender, Military Occupation, and the Civil War*, edited by Ann Whites and Alicia P. Long, 137–54. Baton Rouge: Louisiana State University Press, 2009.

Schweninger, Loren. *Black Property Owners in the South 1790–1915.* Urbana: University of Illinois Press, 1990.

Schweninger, Loren, ed. *From Tennessee Slave to St. Louis Entrepreneur: The Autobiography of James Thomas.* Columbia: University of Missouri Press, 1984.

Scott, Dred. Papers. Manuscripts, Missouri Historical Society, St. Louis.

Skocpol, Theda, Ariane Liazos, and Marshall Ganz. *What a Mighty Power We Can Be: African American Fraternal Groups and the Struggle for Racial Equality.* Princeton, NJ: Princeton University Press, 2006.

Smith, John David, and J. Vincent Lowery. *The Dunning School: Historians, Race, and the Meaning of Reconstruction.* Lexington: University of Kentucky Press, 2013.

Smith, T. K., and Izaiah Johnson. "St. Louis: Navigating the Brick City." Text by Smith; photographs by Johnson. *Art Papers*, Fall 2018/2019. www.artpapers.org/st.louis-navigating-the-brick-city.

Stampp, Kenneth. *America in 1857: A Nation on the Brink.* New York: Oxford University Press, 1990.

Stansell, Christine. *City of Women: Sex and Class in New York, 1789–1860.* Urbana: University of Illinois Press, 1987.

Stevens, Walter B. "Lincoln and Missouri." *Missouri Historical Review* 10, no. 2 (1916): 63–119.

Stewart, A. D. J., ed. *The History of the Bench and Bar of Missouri.* St. Louis: Legal, 1898.

Strom, Sharon Hartman. "'If Success Depends upon Enterprise'. Central America, U.S. Foreign Policy, and Race in the Travel Narratives of E. G. Squier." *Diplomatic History* 35, no. 3 (2011): 403–43.

Strom, Sharon Hartman. "Labor, Race, and Colonization: Imagining a Post-Slavery World in the Americas." In *The Problem of Evil: Slavery, Freedom, and the Ambiguities of American Reform*, edited by Steven Mintz and John Stauffer, 260–75. Amherst: University of Massachusetts Press, 2007.

Strom, Sharon Hartman. *Political Woman: Florence Luscomb and the Legacy of Radical Reform.* Philadelphia: Temple University Press, 2001.

Strom, Sharon Hartman. *Women's Rights.* Westport, CT: Greenwood, 2003.

Strom, Sharon Hartman, and Frederick S. Weaver. *Confederates in the Tropics: Charles Swett's Travelogue of 1868.* Jackson: University of Mississippi Press, 2011.

Tandy, Charlton H. Papers. Manuscripts, Black History Project, State Historical Society of Missouri, St. Louis.

Teters, Kristopher A. *Practical Liberators: Union Officers in the Western Theater during the Civil War*. Chapel Hill: University of North Carolina Press, 2021.

Thelen, David P. *Paths of Resistance: Tradition and Democracy in Industrializing America*. New York: Oxford University Press, 1986.

Thomas, Joseph M. "The Post-Abolitionist's Narrative: William Greenleaf Eliot's *The Story of Archer Alexander*." *New England Quarterly* 73 (September 2000): 463–81.

Tiffany, Pardon Dexter. Papers. Manuscripts and Documents, Missouri Historical Society, St. Louis.

Torchia, Marion M. "Tuberculosis among Negroes: Medical Research on a Racial Disease, 1830–1930." *Journal of the History of Medicine and Allied Sciences* 32 (July 1977): 252–70.

Trexler, Harrison Anthony. *Slavery in Missouri, 1804–1865*. Series 32, no. 2, Johns Hopkins University Studies in Historical and Political Science, 191–441. Baltimore: Johns Hopkins, 1914. Reprint, Leopold Classic Library.

Troen, Selwyn K., and Glen E. Holt, eds. *St. Louis*. New York: Franklin Watts, 1977.

Trollope, Anthony. *North America*. Philadelphia: Lippincott, 1862.

Tucker, Frank C. "The Methodists." In *Religions in St. Louis*, edited by Robert P. Jacobs, 89–100. St. Louis: Interfaith Clergy Council, 1976.

Turner, Charles W. "Reuben Knox Letters, 1849–1851." Part 2. *North Carolina Historical Review* 37 (April 1960): 243–70.

Twitty, Anne. *Before Dred Scott: Slavery and Legal Culture in the American Confluence, 1787–1857*. New York: Cambridge University Press, 2016.

VanderVelde, Lea. *Mrs. Dred Scott: A Life on Slavery's Frontier*. New York: Oxford University Press, 2009.

VanderVelde, Lea. *Redemption Songs: Suing for Freedom before Dred Scott*. New York: Oxford University Press, 2014.

VanderVelde, Lea, and Sandhya Subramanian. "Mrs. Dred Scott." *Yale Law Journal* 106 (January 1997): 1042–85.

Van Ravenswaay, Charles. "Years of Turmoil, Years of Growth: St. Louis in the 1850s." *Bulletin of the Missouri Historical Society* 23 (July 1957): 304–24.

Volkman, Lucas P. *Houses Divided: Evangelical Schisms and the Crisis of the Union in Missouri*. New York: Oxford University Press, 2018.

Weistein, Noah. "1903 Juvenile Courts Act." *Washington University Law Quarterly* (1903): 26–30.

Whites, LeeAnn. "The Tale of Two Minors." In *Women in Missouri History*, edited by LeeAnn Whites, Mary C. Neth, and Gary R. Kramer, 101–18. Columbia: University of Missouri Press, 2004.

Whites, LeeAnn, and Alicia P. Long, eds. *Occupied Women: Gender, Military Occupation, and the Civil War*. Baton Rouge: Louisiana State University Press, 2009.

Whites, LeeAnn, Mary C. Neth, and Gary R. Kremer, eds. *Women in Missouri History: In Search of Power and Influence.* Columbia: University of Missouri Press, 2004.

Williams, Helen DeVault. "Factors in the Growth of St. Louis from 1840 to 1860." Master's thesis, St. Louis University, June 1954.

Winch, Julie. *The Clamorgans: One Family's History of Race in America.* New York: Hill and Wang, 2011.

Woodson, Carter G. "Fifty Years of Negro Citizenship as Qualified by the United States Supreme Court." *Journal of Negro History* 6 (January 1921): 1–53.

Woodson, Carter Godwin. *Free Negro Heads of Families in the United States in 1830, Together with a Brief Treatment of the Free Negro.* Washington, DC: Association for the Study of Negro Life and History, 1925.

Wright, John A., Sr. *African Americans in Downtown St. Louis.* Chicago: Arcadia, 2003.

Yeatman, James V. *A Report on the Condition of the Freedmen of the Mississippi, Presented to the Western Sanitary Commission, December 17th, 1863.* St. Louis: Western Sanitary Commission, 1864.

Zornow, William Frank. "The Missouri Radicals and the Election of 1864." *Missouri Historical Review* 45 (July 1951): 354–70.

# Index

Note: Page references in *italics* refer to illustrations.

**SHARON HARTMAN STROM** is an emerita professor in the History and Women's and Gender Studies Department at The University of Rhode Island. Her books include *Fortune, Fame, and Desire: Promoting the Self in the Long Nineteenth Century.*

The University of Illinois Press
is a founding member of the
Association of University Presses.

---

Composed in 10.5/13 Minion Pro
by Jim Proefrock
at the University of Illinois Press

University of Illinois Press
1325 South Oak Street
Champaign, IL 61820-6903
www.press.uillinois.edu